Counselling
for Post-
Traumatic
Stress
Disorder

Counselling in Practice

Series editor: Windy Dryden
Associate editor: E. Thomas Dowd

Counselling in Practice is a series of books developed especially for counsellors and students of counselling which provides practical, accessible guidelines for dealing with clients with specific, but very common, problems.

Counselling Survivors of Childhood Sexual Abuse
Claire Burke Draucker

Counselling with Dreams and Nightmares
Delia Cushway and Robyn Sewell

Counselling for Depression
Paul Gilbert

Counselling for Anxiety Problems
Richard Hallam

Career Counselling
Robert Nathan and Linda Hill

Counselling for Post-traumatic Stress Disorder
Michael J. Scott and Stephen G. Stradling

Counselling for Alcohol Problems
Richard Velleman

Counselling for Post-Traumatic Stress Disorder

Michael J. Scott &
Stephen G. Stradling

SAGE Publications
London • Newbury Park • New Delhi

First published 1992
Reprinted 1993

SAGE Publications Ltd
6 Bonhill Street
London EC2A 4PU

SAGE Publications Inc
2455 Teller Road
Newbury Park, California 91320

SAGE Publications India Pvt Ltd
32, M-Block Market
Greater Kailash – I
New Delhi 110 048

British Library Cataloguing in Publication Data

Scott, Michael J.
 Counselling for Post-traumatic Stress
 Disorder. – (Counselling in Practice
 Series)
 I. Title II. Stradling, Stephen G.
 III. Series
 616.85

 ISBN 0–8039–8408–1
 ISBN 0–8039–8409–X (pbk)

Library of Congress catalog card number 92–056709

Typeset by Mayhew Typesetting, Rhayader, Powys
Printed and bound in Great Britain by
Biddles Ltd, Guildford and King's Lynn

Contents

List of Boxes   ix
List of Figures   xi
Preface   xiii

1 **Post-Traumatic Stress Disorder – Definition,**
   Presentation and Assessment   1
   Criteria for PTSD   1
   The components of PTSD   5
   Rating scales   8
   Presentation of PTSD   9
   The assessment process   13
   Paul – PTSD following a disaster   13

2 **A Cognitive-Behavioural Conceptualization of Post-**
   Traumatic Stress Disorder   18
   The cognitive-behavioural perspective   18
   Who is most at risk?   22
       Amount of stress or level of exposure   22
       Pre-existing personality or psychological disorder   23
       Family history   24
       Coping style   24
       Support   25
   A case example   27
       Degree of exposure to the trauma   27
       Pre-existing personality or emotional disturbance   27
       Family history of psychiatric disorder   28
       Coping responses and support   28

3 **An Overview of Cognitive-Behavioural Counselling for**
   PTSD   30
   General features of cognitive-behavioural counselling   31
   Outcome of cognitive-behavioural counselling   33
   The structure of a cognitive-behavioural counselling
       session   34

Cognitive-behavioural techniques for PTSD   36
  Intrusive imagery/thoughts   36
  Avoidance reactions   41

4 Counselling for Acute PTSD – Illustrative Cases   47
  Making contact   48
  Pat – acute PTSD following a disaster   50
  George – acute PTSD following an assault   53
  Maureen – acute PTSD following an assault   56
  Susan – acute PTSD following indecent assault   59
  Greta – acute PTSD following the 'bombing' of a coach 60

5 Counselling for Chronic PTSD – Illustrative Cases   65
  Paul – chronic PTSD following a disaster   65
  Jane and Sean – chronic PTSD following an assault 71
  Marina – chronic PTSD following sexual assault   78
  *Gillian – chronic PTSD from witnessing an armed
    robbery*   81

**6 Counselling for PTSD from Prolonged Duress (PDSD) –
  Illustrative Cases**   86
  Disa – PDSD from prolonged duress in the workplace 87
  Jamie – PDSD from prolonged duress in the workplace 94
  *Charles – PDSD from prolonged duress in the
    workplace*   98
  Margaret – PDSD from prolonged duress in the home 103
  Penny – PDSD from prolonged childhood sexual abuse 106

7 Counselling for Concurrent Anxiety and Depression   110
  Features of anxiety and depression   110
  PTSD and anxiety   113
    Generalized anxiety disorder   113
    Panic disorder   113
    Agoraphobia   114
  Loretta – PTSD with concurrent anxiety   114
  PTSD and concurrent depression   120
    Assessing for suicidal risk   121
  Paul – PTSD with concurrent depression   122
  *John – PTSD with concurrent depression and suicidal
    behaviour*   129

8 Counselling for Concurrent Irritability   133
  Simon – the 'out of control' policeman   136
  Diane – the 'short fuse' general practitioner   138

Rose – a battered spouse   143
Irfon – a personality-disordered mercenary   145

9 Counselling for PTSD – Service Delivery   152
Service provision   152
Duration of provision   153
Relapse prevention   153
  Relapse prevention: substance abuse and PTSD   155
Kuma – PTSD from childhood sexual abuse, with adult
  alcohol abuse   156
Group counselling   160
PTSD and children: symptoms and assessment   161
PTSD and children: childhood trauma and adult
  disorder   164
When counselling fails   168
Counsellor survival   170

References   172

Appendix A   Horowitz's Impact of Event Scale   177

Appendix B   Hammarberg's PENN Inventory   178

Appendix C   Trauma Belief Inventory   183

Appendix D   Guidelines for crisis counselling   185

Index   188

List of Boxes

Box 1.1 *DSM-III-R* criteria for PTSD   2
Box 1.2 Five ways in which trauma event may be re-
        experienced (criterion B)   3
Box 1.3 Seven indicators of avoidance or numbing
        (criterion C)   3
Box 1.4 Five examples of increased arousal (criterion D)   4
Box 1.5 The five axes of *DSM-III-R*   4
Box 1.6 *DSM-III-R* examples of stressors leading to
        PTSD   5
Box 1.7 Areas of inquiry for case assessment   10
Box 2.1 Three vulnerability and two prophylactic features
        in the development of PTSD   22
Box 2.2 Epstein's four questions   23
Box 2.3 Thoughts characteristic of Antisocial Personality
        Disorder   23
Box 2.4 Dysfunctional attitudes characteristic of
        depression   24
Box 2.5 Dysfunctional trauma beliefs   25
Box 2.6 Trauma beliefs salient to support   26
Box 3.1 Outline of a cognitive-behavioural counselling
        session   35
Box 3.2 Cognitive biases in environmental appraisal   43
Box 3.3 Problem-solving procedures   45
Box 4.1 Greta's coping self-statements   62
Box 4.2 Practice summary – acute PTSD   63
Box 5.1 Case summary of Paul   66
Box 5.2 Case summary of Jane   72
Box 5.3 Marina's relaxation tape   79
Box 5.4 Gillian's coping statements   84
Box 5.5 Practice summary – chronic PTSD   85
Box 6.1 Ravin and Boal's example of PTSD from
        prolonged duress   87
Box 6.2 Practice summary – PTSD from prolonged
        duress (PDSD)   109

Box 7.1   Thought content of anxiety and depression in
relation to Beck's cognitive triad of self, world
and future   110
Box 7.2   Typical feelings, behaviours and reactions
associated with anxiety and depression   111
Box 7.3   Indicators of anxiety and depression from Snaith
and Zigmond's HAD Scale   112
Box 7.4   Homework task for Loretta   117
Box 7.5   *DSM-III-R* criteria for major depressive disorder   120
Box 7.6   Homework task for Paul: monitoring shifts in
mood   128
Box 7.7   Practice summary – concurrent anxiety and
depression   132
Box 8.1   Personality disorders as defined in *DSM-III-R*
cluster B   134
Box 8.2   Communication guidelines   142
Box 8.3   Example from Diane's 'How I Felt' diary   143
Box 8.4   Negative and positive communication habits   150
Box 8.5   Practice summary – concurrent irritability   151
Box 9.1   Janis and Mann's conditions for stable decision
making   158
Box 9.2   Prochaska and Di Clemente's five stages of
addiction quitting   158
Box 9.3   Summary of Jehu's ten-session Assertion Training
Programme   162
Box 9.4   Young's early maladaptive schemas   166

List of Figures

Figure 1.1 McFarlane's model of the interaction of PTSD components 6

Figure 1.2 Extended model of the interaction of PTSD components incorporating pre-existing major depressive disorder 7

Figure 1.3 A model of the maintenance of PTSD symptoms 7

Figure 2.1 Cognitive-contextual model of individual functioning 19

Figure 7.1 Paul's trap 124

Figure 8.1 Formulation of Irfon's case: Anti-social and Narcissistic Personality Disorder 147

Figure 9.1 Childhood post-traumatic stress disorder, early maladaptive schemas and personality disorders 165

Preface

This book outlines and illustrates a range of predominantly cognitive-behavioural techniques for dealing with the three main symptoms of post-traumatic stress disorder (PTSD) – intrusive thoughts or images, avoidance behaviour, and disordered arousal, especially irritability. Chapter 1 sets out the criteria that need to be met for a client to be considered as suffering PTSD, describes a simple model of the typical relationship between the three main symptoms, and discusses the presentation and assessment of PTSD cases, exemplified by a case example (all of the twenty one cases presented in this book are disguised composites of real cases that have been counselled by the first author). Chapters 2 and 3 introduce the reader to the cognitive-behavioural approach, derived from the work of Beck (e.g. Beck et al., 1985; Beck and Freeman, 1990), Meichenbaum (e.g. Meichenbaum, 1977, 1985) and others. Chapter 2 concentrates on looking at PTSD from the cognitive-behavioural perspective, while chapter 3 describes the cognitive-behavioural approach to counselling and outlines a number of common techniques used in cognitive-behavioural counselling which may be applied to the treatment of PTSD.

Chapters 4 and 5 then give a number of case examples of these techniques being applied to acute cases (chapter 4) and chronic cases (chapter 5). Acute cases are those presenting with symptoms of between one and three months' duration, while chronic cases, which can be more difficult to treat, are those presenting with symptoms of greater than three months' duration. Chapter 6 looks at a number of interesting cases where clients have suffered all the indicative symptoms of PTSD without having experienced a single, overwhelming trauma. We believe that such cases, which we call Prolonged Duress Stress Disorder, may be more common than previously suspected and, indeed, may be more common than those triggered by a single, dramatic event. Both types of case rarely present as 'pure' examples of PTSD, however, typically showing co-morbidity with some other emotional disorder. The treatment of clients suffering concurrent anxiety and/or depression is discussed in chapter 7, while chapter 8 looks at the counselling complications presented by clients with PTSD and concurrent irritability.

Finally chapter 9 discusses questions of service provision, and also looks at relapse prevention, particularly in relation to coexisting substance abuse, at the efficacy of group counselling, at childhood PTSD and the relation between childhood abuse and adult PTSD, and at the trials and tribulations of the counsellor in this area.

Mike Scott
Personal Service Society,
Liverpool
Steve Stradling
Psychology Department,
University of Manchester

Post-Traumatic Stress Disorder – Definition, Presentation and Assessment

The incidence of post-traumatic stress disorder (PTSD) in the general population is approximately the same as that of schizophrenia, affecting about 1 per cent of the population at any one time (Helzer et al., 1987). For approximately half those suffering from PTSD the disorder is not transient and they go on to develop a chronic form of the disorder. Thus PTSD is a serious mental health problem, but one which was only given official recognition as a general diagnostic category in 1980 when the American Psychiatric Association included the disorder in the third edition of its *Diagnostic and Statistical Manual of Mental Disorders* (APA, 1980). This chapter begins with an examination of the current criteria which need to be met for an individual to be said to be suffering PTSD, and a number of commonly used PTSD rating scales are described which can help the counsellor monitor the severity of stress reactions and thereby gauge the progress of clients in counselling.

One of the reasons for the delay in defining PTSD was that symptoms are usually presented in conjunction with some other problem such as depression or substance abuse. The various guises of PTSD and the diagnostic problems caused by co-morbidity form the second focus of this chapter. There then follow some guidelines for assessment which, while not strictly diagnostic, carry implications for the counselling of PTSD sufferers, and these are illustrated with a case example.

Criteria for PTSD

The notion that extreme situations produce extreme reactions is an ancient one. In Homer's Odyssey, warriors' diaries revealed gruelling accounts of intense panic and disturbance both during and following battlefield encounters (Trimble, 1985). Shakespeare too showed his understanding of stress reactions. In *Henry IV part II* he has Hotspur's wife describing her husband as having what

---

Box 1.1   *DSM-III-R criteria for PTSD*

A   The client must have witnessed or experienced a serious threat to their life or physical well-being.

B   The client must re-experience the event in some way.

C   The client must persistently avoid stimuli associated with the trauma or experience a numbing of general responsiveness.

D   The client must experience persistent symptoms of increased arousal.

E   Symptoms must have lasted at least a month.

---

would nowadays be regarded as fairly typical post-traumatic stress reactions. The two world wars introduced a variety of synonyms for traumatic stress such as shell shock, war neurosis, combat exhaustion and flight fatigue. However studies on non-combat populations such as survivors of fire (Cobb and Lindemann, 1943), explosion (Leopold and Dillon, 1963), flood (Titchener and Kapp, 1976) and concentration camps (Trautman, 1964) showed them also to be experiencing very similar symptoms. This has led to the suggestion that there is a single post-traumatic syndrome, a final common pathway which may be reached through exposure to a wide variety of relatively severe stressors. In 1980 the American Psychiatric Association endorsed this notion by defining a disorder called post-traumatic stress disorder. A revised third edition of the *Diagnostic and Statistical Manual (DSM-III-R)* (APA, 1987) has since been published and this sets five criteria to be met for a diagnosis of PTSD. These are given in Box 1.1.

Each of these criteria may be met in a number of ways. Under criterion A it may be seen that it is not necessary that the client themselves be a victim; witnessing a tragedy may be enough to trigger subsequent PTSD. This broad definition of who may suffer serves to highlight the need to consider more than the physically injured or threatened. Criterion B for diagnosis of PTSD is a re-experiencing of the trauma event. *DSM-III-R* specifies five ways in which the trauma may be re-experienced, at least one of which must be present for a diagnosis of PTSD. The five are shown in Box 1.2.

The third criterion, C, persistent avoidance of stimuli associated with the trauma or numbing of general responsiveness, has to be represented by at least two of the seven indicators shown at Box 1.3. Note that it is important that symptoms C4 to C7 must not have been present before the trauma.

Box 1.2 *Five ways in which trauma event may be re-experienced (criterion B)*

B1 Recurrent and intrusive recollections of the event. In young children repetitive play may occur in which themes or aspects of the trauma are expressed.

B2 Recurrent dreams of the event.

B3 Acting or feeling as if the traumatic event were recurring (this includes a sense of reliving the experience, illusions, hallucinations and dissociative (flashback) episodes including those that occur upon awakening or when intoxicated). In young children trauma-specific re-enactment may occur.

B4 Intense psychological distress at exposure to internal or external cues that symbolize or resemble an aspect of the traumatic event, including anniversary of the trauma.

B5 Psychological reactivity upon exposure to internal or external cues that symbolize or resemble an aspect of the traumatic event. (For example a woman who was raped in a lift breaks out in a sweat when entering a lift.)

Box 1.3 *Seven indicators of avoidance or numbing (criterion C)*

C1 Efforts to avoid thoughts or feelings associated with the trauma

C2 Efforts to avoid activities, situations or play that arouse recollections of the trauma

C3 Inability to recall an important aspect of the trauma (psychogenic amnesia)

C4 Markedly diminished interest in significant activities (in young children, loss of recently acquired developmental skills such as toilet training or language skills)

C5 Feeling of detachment or estrangement from others

C6 Restricted range of affect, for example unable to have loving feelings

C7 Sense of a foreshortened future, for example does not expect to have a career, marriage or children, or a normal life span

---

Box 1.4 *Five examples of increased arousal (criterion D)*
D1 Difficulty falling or staying asleep
D2 Irritability or outbursts of anger
D3 Difficulty concentrating
D4 Hypervigilance
D5 Exaggerated startle responses

The fourth criterion, D, persistent symptoms of increased arousal, is met if at least two of the five symptoms shown in Box 1.4 are present. Again these should not have been present before the trauma. The final criterion in Box 1.1 (E) stipulates that symptoms should have lasted for at least a month for a diagnosis of PTSD to be made. *DSM-III-R* distinguishes acute, chronic and delayed PTSD on the basis of both onset and duration of symptoms. For the cases described in this book we shall distinguish between acute sufferers who have experienced symptoms for more than one but less than three months (some cases are described in chapter 4), chronic sufferers who have endured PTSD symptoms for more than three months (chapter 5), and delayed sufferers who do not develop symptoms until at least three months post-trauma.

Box 1.5 *The five axes of DSM-III-R*

Axis 1 Clinical psychiatric syndromes such as anxiety, depression and post-traumatic stress disorder
Axis 2 Personality disorders such as paranoid (cluster A), antisocial (cluster B) and obsessive compulsive (cluster C) personality disorders
Axis 3 Physical disorders
Axis 4 Severity of psychosocial stressors, with stressors divided into acute events such as death of a spouse and enduring circumstances such as being held hostage
Axis 5 Highest level of adaptive functioning during the past year

---

DSM-III-R is a multi-axis classification system with five axes. The axes are given in Box 1.5. It is a classification of disorders, not of individuals, and each disorder 'is conceptualized as a clinically significant psychological syndrome that is typically associated with either a painful symptom (distress) or impairment in one or more important areas of functioning' (Duckworth, 1987: 176). A particular individual's problems may be located on more than one of the five axes. Thus not all clients with an Axis 1 disorder such as PTSD will be regarded for treatment purposes in exactly the same way. Some PTSD sufferers may have in addition an Axis 2 personality disorder that the counsellor will need to address. Indeed there is evidence that a pre-trauma Axis 2 disorder may make an individual more prone to PTSD in the event of a major trauma – evidence which is reviewed in chapter 2 (pp. 23–4). Axis 4 with its distinction between acute and enduring stressors is of particular significance given the current definition of PTSD. *DSM-III-R* requires for PTSD that the individual has experienced an event outside the range of usual human experience which would 'be markedly distressing to anyone' and cites as example the four dramatic acute stressors listed in Box 1.6. We argue here that PTSD symptoms also arise as a result of prolonged duress under enduring circumstances which are not necessarily dramatic, for example persistent maltreatment by an employer (and examples are given in chapter 6).

Box 1.6   *DSM-III-R examples of stressors leading to PTSD*

- An event posing a serious threat to one's life or physical integrity
- An event which presents the possibility of serious threat or harm to one's loved ones
- Sudden destruction of one's environment
- Seeing another person injured or killed as the result of accident or physical violence

---

The components of PTSD

McFarlane (1991) has proposed a model to describe the interaction of the different components of PTSD, and the relationships he posits are shown diagrammatically in Figure 1.1. The traumatic event leads to intrusive imagery (criterion B) which in turn leads to avoidance of situations (criterion C) that might serve as cues for the intrusive imagery. Thus a woman who has been raped may be troubled by intrusive flashbacks of the assault. In an effort to reduce flashbacks she may avoid close contact with men. The avoidance behaviour may indeed serve to reduce the intrusive imagery. However, if she is unexpectedly in close contact with a male then the intrusive imagery is likely to be heightened. There is

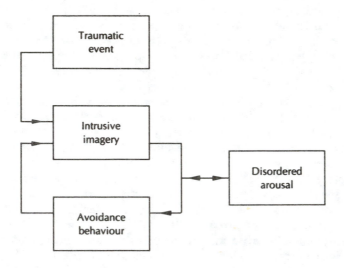

Figure 1.1   *McFarlane's model of the interaction of PTSD components*

a reciprocal interaction between intrusive imagery and avoidance behaviour. This can lead to disordered arousal (criterion D). The disordered arousal can in turn enhance the intrusive imagery.

In McFarlane's study of firefighters tackling a bushfire (McFarlane, 1988) he found that the best predictors of who would progress from intrusive imagery to disordered arousal were the firefighters' neuroticism scores and whether they had a family history of emotional disorder. That is, the major predictors (which accounted for 65 per cent of the variance in the results) were pre-trauma characteristics. However Best's (1991) studies of rape victims found that pre-trauma characteristics did not predict who would suffer from PTSD in the event of rape. Consequently caution has to be exercised in generalizing McFarlane's predictors to other groups of sufferers.

McFarlane further suggests that if the PTSD sufferer is also suffering from a major depressive disorder then this serves to heighten the PTSD, via a reciprocal interaction between disordered arousal and the major depressive disorder. This extension of the basic model to incorporate a pre-existing morbidity is shown in Figure 1.2.

McFarlane's formulation characterized in Figure 1.1 is a model of the onset of PTSD. Whether the disorder is maintained will probably depend on the efficacy of the individual's coping

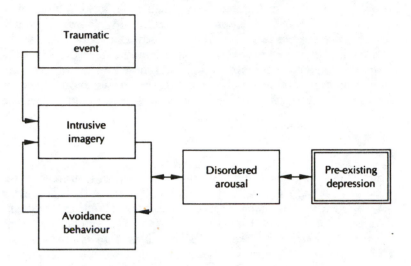

Figure 1.2 *Extended model of the interaction of PTSD components incorporating pre-existing major depressive disorder*

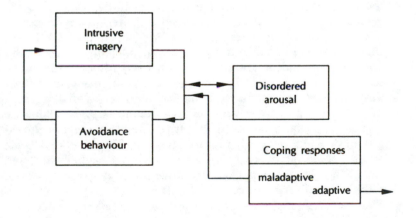

Figure 1.3 *A model of the maintenance of PTSD symptoms*

responses. If, for example, the coping strategy is to turn to drink the symptoms will persist even if the experience of them is anaesthetized, whereas if the coping stategy is to continue to engage in pre-trauma activities there is a better chance that the condition will be ameliorated. A mechanism for the maintenance or mastery of PTSD symptoms is suggested in Figure 1.3, where maladaptive coping responses fuel the feedback loop whilst adaptive coping responses may break the cycle and enable exit from the loop. In chapter 2 a cognitive-contextual model of individual functioning is presented in which the coping responses and behaviours adopted are seen as shaped by pre-existing, pre-trauma schemata and beliefs.

Rating scales

Scales for rating the severity of the victim's post-traumatic stress reactions are very useful to the counsellor because they provide a way of measuring a client's progress in counselling and of highlighting those areas still needing attention. The Impact of Event Scale (IES: Horowitz et al., 1979) provides data on two crucial PTSD symptoms – re-experiencing (criterion B) and numbing or avoidance phenomena (criterion C) – both regarded as hallmarks of the disorder in the *DSM-III-R* formulation. Sample items include, for intrusion, 'Pictures about it popped into my mind' and, for avoidance, 'I stayed away from reminders of it.' This scale has been validated on a wide range of traumatized civilian populations, and is reproduced here as Appendix A.

Saunders et al. (1990) have produced a 28-item scale for crime-related post-traumatic stress disorder in women (the CR-PTSD Scale). Each item is a description of a psychological symptom and is rated by respondents on a 5-point scale according to how much discomfort (from none to extreme discomfort) it has caused them during the past week. Sample items include 'Repeated unpleasant thoughts that won't leave your mind', 'Feeling hopeless about the future', 'Sleep that is restless or disturbed' and 'Shouting or throwing things'. Saunders et al. found that use of the CR-PTSD Scale identified three quarters of the women who had actually suffered from PTSD. The scale is likely to prove a useful screening device for this particular group of PTSD sufferers.

Hammarberg (1992) has produced a 26-item self-report measure for PTSD, the PENN Inventory, which is reproduced here as Appendix B. When the PENN was administered to sixteen survivors of the Piper Alpha oil rig disaster who had been diagnosed as suffering from PTSD, the mean score was 48.8 (standard deviation 7.6) on a range from 0 to 78. For three Piper Alpha survivors not suffering from PTSD, their mean score was 23.3 (SD 2.1). Hammarberg found that general psychiatric patients (n = 18) averaged 28.2 (SD 14.2) on the PENN while PTSD patients admitted to hospital (n = 15) yielded a mean of 55.2 (SD 9.4). He suggests using a score of 35 as a likely cutoff between cases of PTSD and non-cases.

Presentation of PTSD

The context in which PTSD is presented can greatly affect the accurate identification of the problem. A counsellor to whom a client has been referred some weeks after their involvement in a major natural disaster such as a flood is likely to be alert for symptoms of PTSD. However the counsellor referred a couple for marital therapy may fail to appreciate the significance of, for example, the wife's over-reaction and withdrawal in response to conflicts at home with her husband. It may be that the minor hassles with her husband serve to lower her mood, that she then has greater access to recollections of what was to her a serious assault some time ago, and she becomes bedevilled by intrusive images and thoughts. To take another example, a client may be referred for depression yet there seems to be an absence of provoking events; it transpires that many years ago he had to deal with a road traffic accident in which a child was killed and the memory has continued to haunt him and finally comes to impede his functioning, manifesting as depression. The presentation of a PTSD case may be further complicated if the client is referred with a substance abuse problem when in fact this is actually his coping response to experiencing PTSD symptoms and a related depression. Family descriptions of the client as having 'always been an awkward customer' may mislead the counsellor, who may think that perhaps the client is simply attention-seeking or perhaps manufacturing symptoms to seek some financial compensation. On the other hand there is some evidence that those with an anti-social personality disorder pre-dating the trauma are more likely to suffer PTSD after a trauma.

A study by Davidson et al. (1985) of thirty-six consecutive admissions for treatment to a PTSD ward found alcohol abuse in 41 per cent, unipolar depression in 25 per cent, anxiety disorder in 19 per cent, substance abuse in 16 per cent and schizophrenia in 6 per cent. For combat veterans with PTSD who seek treatment, between 40 and 60 per cent are also suffering from a personality disorder (Friedman, 1990). Clients who suffer from PTSD also have some tendency towards deleterious personality change. Because of the high levels of co-morbidity involved with PTSD, much of this text is devoted to providing the counsellor with a framework for dealing with the associated probems (in particular chapter 7 deals with concurrent anxiety and depression and chapter 8 with concurrent irritability).

Box 1.7 *Areas of inquiry for case assessment*

1 *Motivation*

Do you see yourself as having any particular problems since the trauma?

Do you have recurring memories that interfere with your joining in with or your enjoyment of life?

Do you feel you need help for any problems that may have arisen?

Do you feel you have been pushed by others into seeking counselling help?

How do you feel about being offered counselling help?

Do you have any previous experience of or views about counselling?

2 *The Trauma Event(s)*

When did it happen?

What (if any) are the sort of memories that sap your enjoyment of or engagement in life?

What happened to you exactly?

Did you think you were going to die?

Did anyone close to you die?

Were you injured?

How do you feel you coped at the time?

Sometimes people feel they let themselves or others down; did you feel anything like that?

What got to you most about the whole thing?

3 *Coping Since*

How do you feel you have coped since the trauma?

How do you feel you have coped with unpleasant memories?

Are some situations now difficult to handle in a way they were not before the trauma?

Have you felt so distressed that you cannot carry on with the usual things you did before the trauma?

4 *Avoidance*

Are there any situations you now avoid?

Do you try and avoid certain thoughts or pictures related to the trauma? (If *yes*, how?)

Do you try and avoid certain memories?

5   Intrusions

Do you have nightmares about certain types of incidents in your life?

Do you have nightmares about the trauma? (Probe how often in the past week.)

What happens in the nightmares?

Do you wake at a certain point?

When you are awake are your thoughts and pictures of the trauma: (a) so bad that you cannot think of anything else? (b) always at the back of your mind but you can usually get on with things? (c) there occasionally, but they do not really bother you?

6   Reactivation of Earlier Trauma

Has the trauma reawakened any earlier painful memories?

Do your painful memories trigger other painful memories?

7   Irritability

Do you find you are more irritable than before the trauma?

Do you fly off the handle more?

Do you get more irritated than before the trauma when others make mistakes?

Do you link your irritability (if any) to extremely negative enduring circumstances?

8   Neurotic Symptoms

Do you often have headaches?

Is your appetite poor?

Do you sleep badly?

Are you easily frightened?

Do your hands shake?

Do you feel nervous, tense or worried?

Is your digestion poor?

Do you have trouble thinking clearly?

Do you feel unhappy?

Do you cry more than usual?

Do you find it difficult to enjoy your daily activities?

Do you find it difficult to make decisions?

Is your daily work suffering?

Are you unable to play a useful part in life?

Have you lost interest in things?

Do you feel that you are a worthless person?

Has the thought of ending your life been in your mind?

Do you feel tired all the time?

Do you have uncomfortable feelings in your stomach?
Are you easily tired?
Note: Positive responses to 8 or more items indicates probable neurotic disorder.

9 Substance Abuse
Do you use alcohol or drugs to help you cope with your distress?
Do you feel alcohol or drug use is a problem to you?
Do others who are important to you say your alcohol or drug taking is a problem to them?

10 Looking at the overall circumstances of your life do you think that most people would regard it as having been (a) not stressful; (b) mildly (c) moderately (d) severely (e) extremely or (f) catastrophically stressful? (If d, e or f probe why.)

11 Life before the Trauma
How satisfied were you with life in the 12 months before the trauma?
Has the trauma made worse any difficulties you were experiencing previously?
Did you get into trouble more than most as a child or as a teenager?
Have you had previous trouble with your nerves? If so, what? When?

12 Suicidal Tendencies
Have you felt that life is not worth living?
Have you had thoughts of committing suicide?
Have you thought of a specific plan for committing suicide?
Have you started to do things according to that plan?
Have you actually made an attempt on your life?

13 Support
Do you have anyone that you feel you can talk to about what you have been through?
How have your friends and your family responded to you since the trauma?

The assessment process

Whether a client is suffering from PTSD, as defined by *DSM-III-R*, can be gauged by using the structured clinical interview (SCID) for *DSM-III-R* (Spitzer and Williams, 1985). The SCID is a comprehensive examination for a spectrum of major psychiatric disorders. As PTSD often presents in conjunction with another disorder (co-morbidity), casting a wide net at assessment is very important. Thus a general interview format rather than a focused interview for PTSD is to be preferred. Though focused interview formats have been developed for combat-related PTSD (Keane et al., 1985), there is as yet no equivalent for other groups of trauma victims (for example rape survivors).

Most counsellors will not be concerned to conduct the full diagnostic interview required for research purposes. Rather, their concern will be to assess those aspects of the client's functioning that may have counselling implications. Accordingly the guidelines in Box 1.7 are offered. It is important that the questions are not posed in an inquisitorial way, but emerge naturally from the interview format. With this in mind the counsellor should move freely about the domains of inquiry and not struggle to maintain the numeric order. If any domain of inquiry seems important for a particular client the assessment can usually be supplemented by having them complete a standardized self-report measure. Appropriate measures are indicated at various points in the chapters that follow. A number of general PTSD rating scales were described earlier in this chapter and the Impact of Event Scale and the PENN Inventory are given at Appendices A and B. Assessment should not be confined to the initial assessment interview but should be an integral part of counselling.

The case example that follows illustrates how to use the area of inquiry domains to assess a client.

Paul – PTSD following a disaster

'Paul' (like all the cases in this book, a composite) was involved in the Hillsborough football stadium disaster in April 1989 when ninety-five persons died. He was referred to a counsellor by the occupational health service of his employer, which was concerned about his agitated state and his five-month absence from work since the event. The counsellor's first concern was to put Paul at his ease; the session began with the counsellor introducing himself and making small talk.

Counsellor: Did you have much trouble finding the building?
Paul: Well, I went into your other building down the street first, but they showed me the way.
Counsellor: Yes, people often do that.
Paul: It's stupid really I have been in town for an hour and I end up ten minutes late.
Counsellor: How come you were so early into town?
Paul: I just have to get things over with, I didn't sleep last night thinking about coming.
Counsellor: Have you always been that way?
Paul: Only since Hillsborough.
Counsellor: Has Hillsborough brought many changes for you?

The counsellor gave Paul space to introduce the trauma into the discussions in his own time. But having a problem is not the same as wanting to do something about it. The counsellor went on to examine Paul's motivation.

Counsellor: What has Hillsborough stopped you doing?
Paul: I can't face any crowds. I can't even get in the lift at work and I can't sit in the cab of the bus I drive.
Counsellor: How did you feel about your employer sending you to me?
Paul: Well, something has got to be done, I can't go on the way I have been.

Here the counsellor checked that Paul was not attending under duress from his employer and that he appreciated the necessity for change. Avoidance is a major feature of PTSD and the counsellor goes on to clarify just what it is Paul now avoids.

Counsellor: You were mentioning you now avoid crowds. How big do they have to be for you to avoid them?
Paul: Well, I can't go into a football crowd at all. Even when I am watching a game on the TV I am looking at the crowd not the match. If I go to a pub I have to sit by the door. I wouldn't go through a crowd to the bar. I cannot go back to work because as a bus driver I would be closed in. At home I have the front door open all the time even when it is cold and there could be burglars.
Counsellor: Is it a fear of being trapped?
Paul: Yes, that's right but I know it's stupid.

The counsellor is helping Paul to be specific about what he is avoiding in order to ascertain the sort of accomplishments that would constitute an improvement. In passing, Paul mentions one of the classic symptoms of PTSD, hypervigilance. The counsellor next seeks to clarify Paul's conflict.

Counsellor: Your head says there is no danger in the everyday situations you're in but your guts say something else. Is that right?
Paul: Yes, I am just stupid. I should just get on with it, others do. My

cousin who was with me has just got on with his life, and look at me.
Counsellor: Do you get pretty fed up with yourself?
Paul: I am just a pain to everyone. I can't be bothered with anyone or anything. I pick the paper up and just read the headlines.

Paul is experiencing considerable self-blame. He also mentions impaired concentration and says that life is losing its flavour. All of these are symptomatic of depression. Given that depression is probably present the possibility of suicidal intent or behaviour has to be examined.

Counsellor: What sort of solutions have you come up with for dealing with it at all?
Paul: If I just stay in the house then I am safe but then I complain because I am bored. There's no pleasing me, sometimes I think I would be better off out of it. My mother wouldn't have to worry about me then.
Counsellor: Have you attempted suicide?
Paul: No, I just wake up of a morning thinking another bloody day! But I wouldn't do anything because of my mother.

The counsellor has established that Paul is not actively suicidal, but nevertheless there is a strong sense of hopelessness. The origins of the hopelessness require elaboration.

Counsellor: What gets to you most about Hillsborough?
Paul: Just seeing the little boy I had just tried to revive taken off on a stretcher with a handkerchief over his face. [*At this point Paul began to weep.*]
Counsellor: How often is that picture in your mind?
Paul: It is always at the back of my mind. Sometimes the pictures just take over and I spend hours going through it all from arrival at the ground to leaving the hospital a few days later.

Here Paul is describing a key feature of PTSD, intrusive imagery, and his inability to control it. The counsellor is also interested in the client's functioning before the trauma as this may also be influencing his emotional state.

Counsellor: How were things before Hillsborough?
Paul: I was just beginning to get along nicely after a terrible year and Hillsborough put me back even further than square one.
Counsellor: What had happened to you?
Paul: My marriage broke up after I found out she had been having an affair with a rep. at work. After months of hassle she went to live with him and took the two kids.
Counsellor: That must have been pretty awful.
Paul: It was. There's worst to come. When I had access to the kids I found she had poisoned their mind against me. They were only babies, four and six, I couldn't stand it, I wanted to do away with

myself. But my mother and cousin kept me going. I don't know how I managed to keep on working but I did. Then things began to settle down a bit, I just put them out of my life.

In this extract Paul informs the counsellor that he has a support network that has carried him through a previous major life event. This is a hopeful sign as the network may be harnessed again to help him cope with the trauma of the disaster. However, the counsellor has to consider the possibility that the negative emotional state arising from the trauma may increase access to painful memories of the marriage, thus compounding Paul's overall level of distress. Paul's dominant coping strategy in response to the marriage break-up was to distract himself. The counsellor helps Paul look at coping strategies.

> *Counsellor:* What do you see yourself doing in the long run?
> *Paul:* I am not fit for anything now.

The counsellor changes tack at this point, as Paul is preoccupied by the feelings of the present.

> *Counsellor:* What did you want to do with your life years ago?
> *Paul:* Well I know it sounds daft but I used to enjoy maths at school. But I messed around at school, didn't take it seriously. I wouldn't mind doing some more maths. But my concentration is just hopeless now.
> *Counsellor:* What about physical things?
> *Paul:* I used to cycle a lot, I enjoyed that. I suppose I could do that but I just keep putting things off.

Clearly there are distraction possibilities, but symptoms of depression, impaired concentration and procrastination impede their execution. At the beginning of the interview Paul had also mentioned a great deal of apprehensiveness about coming to the session. The counsellor thought this might be a hint of an anxiety problem, and investigated further.

> *Counsellor:* Do you often feel tense or wound up or is it just the thought of seeing me?
> *Paul:* I am that way all the time, I just can't seem to relax.
> *Counsellor:* Do you get panicky, light-headed or dizzy?
> *Paul:* No I am just like a tightly coiled spring, the least little thing and I bite somebody's head off.

Paul has some anxiety difficulty but it is not an overriding concern compared to the outward irritability. The counsellor investigates the effects of the irritability on Paul's relationships.

> *Counsellor:* How are getting on with people around you?
> *Paul:* My Mum and cousin are OK, they understand me, but some

friends have stopped calling me up to go for a drink.

Counsellor: Why do you think they stopped calling?

Paul: I think they think I just use Hillsborough as an excuse now because it's six months since it happened and I wasn't the only one affected. I don't know whether I do make excuses to myself, I don't know anything any more. I am just confused.

Paul has become more isolated and alienated since the trauma. This has been unwittingly compounded by his friends, who have generated an expectation that he should be over his troubles by now. The counselling implication is that repair work may have to be done on relationships. At this stage in the session Paul has reached emotional exhaustion. The counsellor finishes the interview and goes on to suggest an agenda for the next meeting.

Counsellor: You must be pretty shattered bringing all this up?

Paul: I am, yes, but it is good to get it off my chest.

Counsellor: Maybe next time we can talk about (1) what you take the whole thing to mean about you as a person, (2) what you now make of the world, (3) what you now make of other people. Is that OK?

Paul: Yes, fine.

Counsellor: Is there anything else you would like to put on the agenda for next time?

Paul: No, what you said is fine.

Counsellor: Could you just complete these questionnaires and bring them with you next time just to make sure I have got the complete picture.

[*The counsellor hands Paul the Impact of Event Scale, PENN Inventory, Hospital Anxiety and Depression Scale (a measure discussed in chapter 7) and the Trauma Belief Inventory (a measure reproduced as Appendix C and discussed in chapter 2).*]

Paul: I will do that.

The scene has been set for a second assessment interview to inquire into the meaning Paul gives to the various aspects of his trauma experience. We meet Paul again at the end of chapter 2, where a cognitive-behavioural formulation of his difficulties is presented.

2

A Cognitive-Behavioural Conceptualization of Post-Traumatic Stress Disorder

Depression was the first emotional disorder to be conceptualized in cognitive-behavioural terms. This led to the development of an extremely fruitful counselling intervention – cognitive behaviour therapy (CBT or cognitive therapy). Cognitive therapy has been shown in a substantial number of studies to produce lasting results amongst depressed clients after a relatively brief period of help, and to prevent relapse (see Scott, 1989a). A wide range of other client difficulties including anxiety, marital problems and substance abuse have now also been conceptualized in cognitive-behavioural terms. Whilst as yet too few studies of the efficacy of the interventions that have been derived from this framework have been conducted to allow definitive conclusions to be drawn, the results to date show promise (see Scott, 1989a). It is therefore appropriate to now conceptualize PTSD in CBT terms, though the final judgement on the utility of the model must rest on the demonstrated efficacy of the counselling interventions derived from it.

This chapter begins with a brief overview of the cognitive-behavioural perspective. A central tenet of this approach is the individuality of people's responses to environmental stressors. Research studies are cited which show that even when confronted by major trauma there is considerable variability in people's response. Further, a significant minority of those traumatized continue to suffer from chronic or long-lasting PTSD, highlighting the need for an effective counselling response. The important question of why some people succumb to PTSD and others do not is then addressed. Finally, the factors that affect recovery from PTSD are discussed.

The cognitive-behavioural perspective

The cognitive-behavioural approach to counselling represents a systematic application of the ancient notion that 'people are disturbed not so much by events as by the views which they take

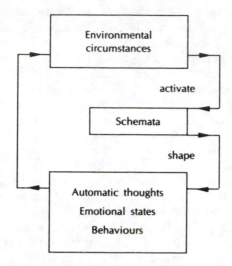

Figure 2.1   *Cognitive-contextual model of individual functioning*

of them' (Epictetus, first century AD). Different people react to objectively similar situations differently. For example one person may react to a divorce with disappointment and sadness whilst another becomes suicidal. It is as if different individuals take snapshots of the same situation from different angles: some snapshots may be more accurate representations of the situation than others. Within the cognitive-behavioural perspective the counsellor's task is to help the client consider the accuracy of their representations and to evolve adaptive coping strategies to deal with their situation and symptoms.

The view or snapshot a client takes depends partly on what is available in their environment and what advice and encouragement they get from others on where to 'focus the camera'. Thus the individual's functioning cannot be divorced from their environmental context. Further, the sort of snapshot taken will also be influenced by their background beliefs as to what constitutes an appropriate picture. These considerations are depicted in the cognitive-contextual model of individual functioning shown in Figure 2.1.

Environmental circumstances in the context we are considering here include major traumas, enduring circumstances and interpersonal feedback from others. These features of the external world are seen as activating an individual's schemata, which are the long-standing and relatively stable basic assumptions that he or she holds about the way the world works, his or her place in it, and their programmes for relating to others and the world. Once triggered, these schemata shape the content of the individual's stream of consciousness, which is comprised of automatic thoughts. The occurrence of automatic thoughts is often outside a person's conscious control (that is they appear as if by reflex and seem to have a life of their own). For example, Jane's colleagues were perplexed that she always came to work carrying numerous bags. They discussed with her the likelihood of her flat being burgled whilst she was at work and Jane agreed there was little chance. Nevertheless, Jane continued to experience the automatic thought 'I have got to take what is important to me with me' and continued to bring her bags in. It transpired that she had been regularly abused at boarding school (environmental influence) and this had led to a persuasive belief that she was vulnerable (schemata) which in turn generated automatic thoughts such as 'Take everything with you, leave nothing unguarded.'

Her automatic thoughts followed a theme of threat and consequently the associated emotional state was anxiety. She became very agitated if there was a hint of criticism at work and tried to over-justify her decisions. Driven by her perceived vulnerability, her behavioural response was avoidance of colleagues. This led to a further negative environmental circumstance: lack of affirmative feedback from colleagues. This in turn served to underline her self-schema that she was worthless. The cognitive-contextual model of Figure 2.1 suggests that a major trauma, for example, will initiate a cyclic process, involving both intrapsychic and interpersonal variables. While Jane's behaviours – her current coping responses – will serve to manipulate the environment to either perpetuate or alleviate her distress, the counselling task is to minimize the former and maximize the latter.

The schemata characteristic of PTSD sufferers are typified by the beliefs contained in the Scott Trauma Belief Inventory (Appendix C). A consequence of holding such trauma beliefs is that the person's threshold of responsiveness to signs of danger is lowered. It is as if, compared to normal functioning, the PTSD sufferer has their alarm set much more sensitively to the point where they register many false alarms.

In the cognitive-behavioural perspective, each emotional disorder or problem in living is held to have its own characteristic set of negative automatic thoughts and typical schemata. A central prediction of the cognitive-contextual model illustrated in Figure

2.1 is that in the wake of an environmental event such as a major trauma there will be variability in individual response (that is in automatic thoughts, emotional states and behaviours) because of variablity in schemata. Probably the most reliable finding in studies of the development of PTSD is the variability of people's responses to trauma. A number of the key studies in this area are now briefly reviewed.

A study by Parker (1977) of people evacuated after a cyclone in Darwin, Australia, showed that one week after the evacuation 58 per cent could be classified as psychiatric 'cases'. Twelve weeks later this proportion had dropped to 41 per cent. A later study of cyclone victims by Patrick and Patrick (1981) in Sri Lanka found 70 per cent of the disaster population psychologically disturbed. Four weeks later the proportion had dropped to 46 per cent. Thus a significant proportion of people do not get better in the three months after the trauma, that is they have a chronic form of disorder. There is also an as yet unquantified group who do not show any symptoms in the first three months post-trauma, but exhibit trauma symptoms after that period, suffering a delayed trauma. McFarlane (1988) conducted detailed interviews with 300 victims of the Australian bushfire disaster. The range of immediate reactions was considerable, with a number seeing the experience as a personal challenge for survival which they found stimulating. So an external threat of considerable magnitude is not necessarily distressing, and the individual's response is determined to a significant degree by the personal meaning of the event.

A study by Sorenson and Golding (1990) of victims of crime found that overall 15 per cent became clinically depressed and 6 per cent entertained suicidal ideas or had made suicide attempts. The proportions varied with the type of crime, with approximately one-third of those sexually assaulted or mugged becoming depressed and 10 per cent suicidal, whereas for burglary the corresponding figures were 15 and 5 per cent. For rape victims the proportions are even higher. Kilpatrick et al. (1989) found that 57 per cent developed PTSD at some time after their assault and 16 per cent still showed PTSD symptoms when assessed an average of seventeen years later.

There is also some evidence for the cumulative nature of traumas. Sorenson and Golding (1990) found that of those who had two or more criminal victimizations in the previous six months, almost 30 per cent became clinically depressed, whereas the corresponding proportion for single victimization in that period was 13 per cent. In short, there is no inevitability about a major trauma causing chronic PTSD but it does do so in a significant minority of cases. In the next section the factors that increase the likelihood of an individual succumbing to PTSD are discussed.

Who is most at risk?

From a review of the literature, whether a person remains distressed after a major trauma seems to depend on the five factors depicted in Box 2.1. High levels of stress or of exposure to a major stressor, a pre-existing personality or emotional disorder, and a family history of psychiatric disorder all seem to contribute to the establishment of PTSD. Contrarily an adaptive coping style and effective support network tend to serve to attenuate PTSD. The evidence concerning each of these predictors of response is now considered.

Box 2.1 *Three vulnerability and two prophylactic features in the development of PTSD*

Vulnerability
1 High levels of stress or exposure
2 Pre-existing personality or emotional disorder
3 Family history of psychiatric disorder

Protection
4 Adaptive coping style
5 Effective support

Amount of stress or level of exposure
As the intensity of exposure to a disaster such as the Mount St Helen's eruption increases, the number of victims who develop PTSD increases progressively (Shore et al., 1986). However the correlation between the amount of stress in a traumatic event and the resultant psychopathology is usually low (for example, Pearlin et al., 1981). Nevertheless, it seems likely that a trauma has to be of a sufficient intensity to force individuals to put on their agenda fundamental questions about their self and about their relationship to the world.

Epstein (1990) suggests that when people experience a traumatic event four questions may be forced upon them. These are shown in Box 2.2. Such questions may arise following not only an acute trauma, such as the Hillsborough football stadium disaster, but also as a result of extreme or catastrophic enduring circumstances, such as being held as a hostage or repeatedly abused. The answers

> **Box 2.2   Epstein's four questions**
>
> Is the world benevolent or malevolent?
> Is the world meaningful or meaningless?
> Am I worthy or unworthy?
> Are other people trustworthy or untrustworthy?

an individual gives to these fundamental questions depend in part on the remaining four factors.

Pre-existing personality or psychological disorder
In a community study of the incidence of PTSD in the USA, Helzer et al. (1987) found that behavioural problems before age fifteen predicted PTSD in the event of a trauma. The behavioural problems assessed were stealing, lying, truancy, vandalism, running away from home, fighting, misbehaving at school, early sexual experience, substance abuse, school expulsion or suspension, academic underachievement and delinquency. Having four or more of these symptoms predicted PTSD. It seems likely that some of those with behavioural problems would in fact have qualified for a diagnosis of a personality disorder in *DSM-III-R*, such as Antisocial Personality Disorder or Paranoid Personality Disorder. Beck and Freeman (1990) have described the characteristic thought content (schemata) of the different personality disorders, for example the individual suffering the Antisocial disorder tends to have thoughts such as those shown in Box 2.3.

> **Box 2.3   Thoughts characteristic of Antisocial Personality Disorder**
>
> - I should do whatever I can get away with.
> - It is not important to keep promises or honour debts.
> - I have been unfairly cheated and am entitled to get my fair share by whatever means I can.
> - If I don't push other people, I will get pushed around.
> - If people don't take care of themselves that's their problem.

It may be that specific clusters of attitudes (schemata in Figure 2.1) make an individual more vulnerable to PTSD. Beck has also described the dysfunctional attitudes that make individuals vulnerable to depression, and the examples in Box 2.4 are taken

---

Box 2.4   *Dysfunctional attitudes characteristic of depression*
- I am nothing if a person I love doesn't love me.
- If you cannot do something well, there is little point in doing it at all.
- If I don't set the highest standards for myself, I am likely to end up a second-rate person.
- It is awful to be disapproved of by people important to you.

---

from his Dysfunctional Attitude Scale (reproduced in full in Scott, 1989a). With regard to anxiety, Beck et al. (1985) see the disorder as arising from an exaggerated appraisal of the degree of threat. As PTSD most commonly occurs in conjunction with other disorders such as depression and anxiety, it seems likely that the associated dysfunctional attitudes will also, to some degree, be vulnerability factors for PTSD.

Family history
Two studies indicate that over half of those suffering from PTSD have a family history of psychiatric disorder. The first, by Davidson et al. (1985), found that 66 per cent of combat veterans suffering PTSD had such a history. In a second study, by McFarlane (1988), 55 per cent of traumatized emergency service workers were found to have a family history of psychiatric disorder.

It is within a family context that an individual's basic attitudes to life are distilled. In the cognitive-contextual model interpersonal feedback constitutes an important environmental influence on thoughts, feelings and behaviour. Where there is a family history of disorder there is more likelihood of a set of maladaptive attitudes being adopted by the offspring. Thus the findings on family history are consistent with the cognitive-contextual model of distress.

Coping style
Perhaps the most promising predictor of trauma response so far is coping style. Lazarus (1966) distinguished between two basic forms of coping: active versus palliative, that is direct confrontation of the stress versus managing one's emotional reaction by, for example, taking alcohol or a holiday.

There is empirical support for the value of active coping. Gleser et al. (1981) reported that the best predictor of level of psychopathology following the Buffalo Creek flood was whether people were able to clean and repair their homes and give personal help to others. In similar vein McFarlane (1988) reports that fire-fighters from the Australian bushfires who scored high on avoidance of thinking about problems were more prone to both acute and chronic distress.

Avoidance can, of course, in the short term reduce stress, increase hope, and allow for short assimilative episodes of grief and distress. It is thus a seductive course. However, the most adaptive long-term response to a trauma is likely to be a subtle interweaving of problem-focused and emotion-focused coping which will match the changing internal and external cues the client experiences.

Coping responses are an expression of the programmes for relating to others and the world which are embedded in the schemata in Figure 2.1. Such programmes may, however, themselves be derived from dysfunctional trauma beliefs engraved in the schemata. A set of dysfunctional trauma beliefs is contained in the Scott Trauma Belief Inventory (TBI) (Appendix C). Some example items from this measure are given in Box 2.5. The TBI draws on belief items from two other questionnaires, the Trauma Constellation Identification Scale (Dansky et al., 1990) and Jehu's Belief Inventory (Jehu, 1989). These two scales had sexual abuse as a main focus, but the items have been selected to have applicability to other extreme stressors. Whilst the TBI awaits validation, it offers the counsellor at least a provisional framework of pertinent dysfunctional beliefs.

Box 2.5 *Dysfunctional trauma beliefs*

- I believe that I over-reacted to what happened to me.
- Nothing in the world is any good.
- I will never be able to lead a normal life, the damage is permanent.
- It doesn't matter what happens to me in my life.

Support

It has been found that how recovered depressives fare after discharge from hospital very much depends on the level of emotion expressed by their family. If the family is over-involved or critical then relapse is much more likely (Hooley et al., 1986). As noted earlier, depression is often a major problem in the wake of trauma and often overlaps with PTSD. So it is reasonable to anticipate that the nature, degree and quality of the support or interaction with significant others that a sufferer receives may either buffer or exacerbate PTSD. Exacerbation is possible because trauma often leads to increased irritability, which in turn can sour interpersonal relationships, the perceived deterioration of which may also usher in depression. A steady relationship may reduce the risk of depression. Brown and Harris (1978) found that approximately 40 per cent of women without a steady relationship became depressed following a serious event in contrast to 10 per cent of women who were enjoying a steady relationship. Interpersonal feedback features as an important environmental influence on the development and maintenance of an emotional disorder.

It seems likely that an individual without support is both more vulnerable to the effects of a trauma and more at risk that the distress will be maintained. The important point, however, is that it is the person's perception of support that seems to buffer the effects of a stressor. 'Support' is not something that can simply be provided for a client: the client's trauma beliefs may greatly influence whether they perceive elements of their social network as sources of support. A number of beliefs from the TBI may be particularly salient here, for example those shown in Box 2.6. A client operating on these beliefs is unlikely to avail him or herself of support and will be relatively impervious to the offer of it. The client who continues to avoid all situations that in any way resemble the trauma is likely to perpetuate symptoms. Similarly the client with no opportunity to share feelings is unfortunately more likely to continue to be distressed.

Box 2.6 *Trauma beliefs salient to support*

- It is dangerous to get close to anyone because they always exploit or hurt you.
- Only bad, worthless people would be interested in me.
- Other people can never understand how I feel.

Finding an adaptive coping response depends both on having a wide range of skills and on judging their appropriateness. But technique is as naught without motivation. Not only do coping responses and support influence PTSD, the reverse is also the case. When PTSD becomes established the client is less likely to be problem orientated and will not be searching for the best coping response or for supportive friends or family but is likely to sit immobile. In this way a vicious circle is set up of disorder, insufficient coping responses, inadequate support and perpetuated or amplified disorder.

A case example

To illustrate how a client's PTSD is conceptualized in cognitive-behavioural terms, we return to Paul who was introduced in chapter 1. Paul, you will recall, was involved in the Hillsborough football stadium disaster, together with his cousin and nephew. Six months after the trauma he was referred to a counsellor, manifesting PTSD symptoms.

To formulate Paul's case it is useful to organize the information under the headings of the five predictors of PTSD described earlier. There are significant cognitive and behavioural components to each of the five predictors which the counsellor may use in remediating PTSD.

Degree of exposure to the trauma
Paul witnessed many horrors at Hillsborough – he had found himself standing on bodies with their eyes bulging out, gasping for breath and fainting in the crush; he had not been able to revive a child; he had seen a youngster desperately trying to climb a perimeter fence to escape, defecating in the process and being pushed back into the crowd by a policeman unaware of the true nature of the event. In hospital he spent time trying to console a father whose son had died in the tragedy. Paul was clearly at the epicentre of the trauma. It is in just such circumstances, Epstein (1990) has suggested, that an individual is confronted with pressing questions about him or herself, about other people and about the world. For Paul, core beliefs he held about the trustworthiness of people (for example the police) and the meaningfulness of life ('How could it happen on a beautiful spring day, with everyone looking forward to an exciting game') were called into question.

Pre-existing personality or emotional disturbance
Paul had suffered from depression when his marriage broke up. Given the way in which the marital breakdown occurred – precipitated by his wife's unfaithfulness – themes of the untrustworthiness of people (his wife as an exemplar) and of the capriciousness of life (losing contact with his children because of his wife's actions) were dominant. The marital experiences were readily and vividly available in memory. These memories had become latent in the months immediately before Hillsborough and he had been functioning free of depression. The disaster activated themes that arose during his depression. Paul then saw confirmation of these themes in the disaster experience.

Family history of psychiatric disorder
In Paul's case there was no such history.

Coping responses and support
Coping responses can be viewed as an attempt to terminate an aversive emotional state. Paul's main coping strategy since the tragedy was to withdraw from life. He had, as he put it 'placed myself on the sideline of life's games'. Over time, however, it had become abundantly clear that this strategy was not working – he was still plagued by intrusive memories of the trauma, he was unable to work, which in turn was creating financial problems, and he was having frequent rows with friends and relatives over what he saw as his need for solitude. The fact that his coping strategy was not working heightened his distress, particularly as there seemed no viable alternative. Nevertheless there were two sources of support for Paul: his mother and a friend of hers. The importance of his mother in his life was highlighted during the disaster when he was thinking not so much that he was likely to die himself but how she would berate him if he did not not effectively protect his nephew. Looking after his mother and her physically incapacitated friend provided Paul with an important reason for living and they were appreciative of his efforts for them.

Paul's coping responses and use of support were behavioural expressions of the following beliefs identified from the Trauma Belief Inventory he completed:

'Other people can never understand how I feel';
'I see this world as a bad place to live in';
'I feel like there isn't anything I can do to manage what happens to me'.

His distress was maintained by other trauma beliefs which included the following:

'I will never be able to lead a normal life, the damage is permanent';
'I believe that I over-reacted to what happened to me';
'There is something wrong with me';
'I don't like myself'.

In summary, for a comprehensive description of a client's response to a trauma, attention has to be paid to the intensity of the trauma; to pre-existing beliefs associated with personality and/or psychological disturbance; to the availability of models of anxiety or other morbidity in the family of origin; to the adaptivity of coping responses and their associated trauma beliefs; to the use of support and its associated trauma beliefs; and finally to the client's trauma beliefs about their own distress.

To illustrate how these factors are differential predictors of outcome we can return to Paul, his cousin and nephew at the Hillsborough disaster. All three were in tears when they finally met up outside the football ground. Each reported feeling numbed in the days that followed. However, Tom, Paul's cousin, soon came almost to relish the opportunity to talk about the tragedy (much to Paul's chagrin). Tom had led a very settled life, had a happy marriage, young children he adored, and ran a successful taxi business. Hillsborough had no lasting effect on Tom. Paul's nephew Colin, however, was affected. Colin was just eighteen when the tragedy occurred. He had been a very placid, easygoing person. Neither he nor his immediate family had any history of emotional or behavioural problems. Since the tragedy, however, he has refused to talk to anybody about it and has become very irritable, though otherwise he is functioning normally.

3

An Overview of Cognitive-Behavioural Counselling for PTSD

Cognitive-behavioural counselling (CBC) is based on the notion that cognitions can have a crucial influence on emotions. To rephrase Epictetus, 'People suffering a major trauma are, it seems, disturbed, in the long term, not so much by the trauma as by the consequent view which they take of themselves and their world' ('long-term' referring here to a period greater than three months beyond the trauma). This is the basic principle underlying the counselling approach outlined in this chapter.

It is not simply that thinking influences feeling. The reverse is also the case, such that there is a reciprocal relationship between the two. Once a person becomes low they have better recall of negative memories (Blaney, 1986), and these negative thoughts can serve to further lower their mood, setting up a vicious circle. Cognitive-behavioural counselling seeks to break the circle by targeting unrealistic negative thoughts for change. It should be noted that the task of the CB counsellor is not to help the client 'think positive'. Positive thinking is as much a distortion as negative thinking. The CB approach focuses on realistic thinking.

This chapter begins with a description of the main features of CBC. The strongest justification for using a particular counselling approach is that 'it works', and as yet studies on the efficacy of CBC or indeed any therapeutic approach with PTSD are scarce. However, the literature on CBC with other disorders such as depression and anxiety (with which PTSD has much in common) suggests it as an appropriate and effective approach there, encouraging its application to PTSD. In the second section of this chapter some of the outcome findings on CBC are summarized. This is followed in the third section by a description of the structure of a CBC session. CBC incorporates basic counselling skills as well as behavioural and cognitive strategies, so the final sections of this chapter are devoted to basic counselling skills married with specific cognitive-behavioural techniques.

General features of cognitive-behavioural counselling

Cognitive-behavioural counselling arose out of dissatisfaction with behavioural and psychodynamic models of human behaviour. The behavioural model asserted that an individual's behaviour should be viewed solely as a result of environmental contingencies, that is rewards and punishments. Counsellors could, using this model, help clients overcome their difficulties by arranging rewards for the behaviours desired and aversive consequences for unwanted behaviours. The therapeutic focus was on discrete, observable behaviour or on changes which were visible on some physiological measuring instrument. Bandura (1977) elaborated the behavioural model further, suggesting that environmental manipulation may not be the sole determinant of behaviour. He hypothesized that behaviour could also be learned simply by observing the behaviour of others and its consequences.

Yet it is difficult to think of an evaluation of a counselling modality being comprehensive without the client being asked for a report of their thoughts and feelings. Indeed behaviour therapists typically included client self-reports in their assessment of the effectiveness of help given. But thoughts and feelings are private events, not observable behaviours, and are therefore outside the domain of the behavioural perspective. This highlights the difficulty of describing a client's symptomatology without recourse to the concepts of thoughts and feelings. It was these sorts of consideration that led behaviourists such as Meichenbaum (1977) to embrace cognitive-behavioural approaches.

Psychodynamic counselling, in contrast to behaviour therapy, takes an historical view of human behaviour. Various childhood events may be so traumatic as to precipitate adult disorders. For example, in the case of a housebound agoraphobic client a psychodynamic counsellor may conceptualize the difficulties as arising from an anxiety-ridden relationship between client and parent in childhood. The counsellor would mirror the parent/child relationship in their relationship with the client. As the client came to understand the influence of childhood factors on their current behaviour, difficulties such as the fear of going out alone would resolve themselves. However, it is problematic whether it is possible to create in a counselling session an accurate microcosm of childhood experiences. Even if it were possible, it is not clear how this would necessarily lead to a change in current difficulties.

Reservations such as these led Aaron Beck away from psychodynamic considerations to become a prime mover in the establishment of a cognitive-behavioural perspective (see, for example, Beck et al., 1985). The CB counsellor takes something from both the behavioural and the psychodynamic perspectives. There is the behavioural insistence on measuring the outcome of interventions, structured counselling sessions with an agenda, and homework assignments. But in the CB perspective it is also acknowledged that the dysfunctional beliefs that make a person vulnerable to emotional disorders often have their historical roots in childhood experiences. The cognitive-behavioural perspective on PTSD goes beyond the psychodynamic view of disorder (which highlights the role of childhood traumas in causing adult disturbance) though, to suggest that major traumas in adult life can also be of such intensity as to produce disturbance.

Cognitive-behavioural counselling retains many of the features of behavioural counselling. It is problem oriented, active and directive. The counselling strategy is one of a careful listing and defining of the nature of the client's difficulties. Problems are defined in a highly specific manner; for example a client experiencing dissatisfaction with their partner's 'attitude these days' would be encouraged to crystallize it further into problems that admit of a solution, for instance 'I don't like it when he goes for a drink straight from work.' In CBC the counsellor is active and directive in helping the client by posing questions to evaluate critically the thinking that is leading to distress. The counsellor encourages the client to adopt this critical stance independently, by prescribing homework assignments that involve the self-monitoring and self-modification of distress. The setting of homework assignments is a collaborative venture between CB counsellor and client, and the review of homework is an integral part of each session.

Openness between counsellor and client is a prerequisite for the setting and evaluation of homework assignments, and is an important general feature of CB counselling. One of the core distinguishing features of CB counselling is the setting up of 'experimental tests' to confirm or deny irrational beliefs. Typically the client may have what the counsellor sees to be an irrational belief. Rather than impose a view, the counsellor suggests the client conduct an experiment to test out the truth of the matter. Thus a CB counsellor might say to an agoraphobic client 'I know that you have not been out by yourself, but I think just maybe you could manage to walk to the garden gate each day. Neither of us really knows until you try. Would that be a reasonable homework task this week?' The emphasis is on the counsellor encouraging the client to view negative beliefs as hypotheses to be tested, rather than as facts to be submitted to. In this way the client is cast in the role of a scientist with regard to his or her own experiences.

The counsellor's main method of helping the client is by posing questions about the veracity of the latter's negative beliefs. It is not only that the client is encouraged to be a scientist, but that the whole CB counselling endeavour is located in an empirical framework.

In keeping with this emphasis in CBC on testing out beliefs there is a concern to evaluate the effectiveness of CBC itself. Thus CBC is often compared with standard treatments. For example a number of studies have compared cognitive behaviour therapy with anti-depressants in the treatment of depression. Within a CB perspective the question of therapeutic effectiveness and efficiency is addressed by asking 'What client groups does CB counselling work with, in what circumstances, delivered by which counsellors?' A comprehensive answer to this question is not yet available, but there are sufficient grounds for believing that CB counselling can make a significant contribution to relieving client distress. This evidence will now be briefly reviewed.

Outcome of cognitive-behavioural counselling

It is currently quite difficult to find a disorder or problem in living that the CBC approach has not been applied to. But the most systematic evaluations of all have been in the sphere of depression. Blackburn and Davidson (1989) provide a thorough review of the studies and conclude that clients undergoing CB counselling have a relapse rate of only half that of those on antidepressant medication alone. This suggests that once clients learn CB skills, then provided they continue to practise them many of them will be protected against relapse. Considerably fewer large-scale studies have been conducted of the efficacy of CB counselling with anxiety disorders, though the findings to date are, as Blackburn and Davidson conclude, very hopeful. PTSD is classified in *DSM-III-R* with the anxiety disorders and there are then, on the basis of this commonality, reasonable grounds for hope that CBC will be effective with PTSD. However, as noted earlier, pure PTSD is a rarity as it is often complicated by other disorders such as substance abuse or depression. It may be that PTSD can only be addressed when the complicating disorder such as the substance abuse has first been resolved. A recent review of brief cognitive-behavioural coping strategies for alcohol problems (Heather, 1989) provides reasonable support for their effectiveness in this domain.

Few controlled studies have been published on the treatment of PTSD. In one study, (Keane et al., 1989), Vietnam veterans received counselling which included relaxation and deliberate imagining of their traumas (imaginal exposure) or were assigned to a waiting list control condition. Those receiving counselling showed decreased re-experiencing of the trauma and a decrease in startle reactions, memory and concentration problems, impulsivity and irritability. Avoidance behaviour, however, did not improve. From the design of this study it is not clear whether the changes that occurred in the counselling group were a consequence of the strategies taught, or simply the result of the clients receiving attention. In a second study (Foa et al., 1991) forty-five rape victims with PTSD were randomly assigned to one of four conditions: stress inoculation training (SIT); prolonged exposure (PE); supportive counselling (SC); or waiting list control (WL). Post-treatment the four groups differed in the percentage of patients who had clinically significantly improved (defined in this study as those who had moved more than two standard deviations below their pre-treatment mean). Of the SIT group 70 per cent (10 patients) had improved, as had 40 per cent (4) of the PE group, against 18 per cent (2) of the SC group and 20 per cent (2) of the WL group. Follow-up conducted at around three and a half months after treatment found 67 per cent of the SIT group, 56 per cent of the PE group and 33 per cent of the SC group improved. This study showed a superiority of SIT and PE treatments over SC and WL. Supportive counselling (SC) involved encouraging the clients to focus on current daily problems rather than discussing the assault, with the counsellor playing an indirect though unconditionally supportive role. Thus both SIT and PE appeared to make important contributions to the remediation of PTSD. Nevertheless, it remains to be demonstrated which are the 'active ingredients' in the SIT package and how much imaginal exposure is actually necessary to achieve change. The most parsimonious solution, and the one elaborated in this text, is to recommend a cognitive-behavioural package that incorporates imaginal exposure. Care has to be taken in generalizing from the Foa et al. study in that the mean pre-counselling scores of clients in her PE group were just within the mild depression region on the Beck Depression Inventory. Mildly depressed, as opposed to severely depressed, clients may be more likely to agree to and endure imaginal exposure.

The structure of a cognitive-behavioural counselling session

The framework of a cognitive-behavioural counselling session is summarized in Box 3.1. It is natural to begin a session by asking the client how they have been since the last session. Typically the

> **Box 3.1** *Outline of a cognitive-behavioural counselling session*
>
> - Inquiry into client's emotional state, hassles and uplifts since last session
> - Setting a collaborative agenda for the session
> - Review of previous session's homework assignment(s)
> - Focusing on the agenda items
> - Setting of homework
> - Session feedback

client will relate their emotional state and specific difficulties. The counsellor then has to locate the information furnished by the client in the cognitive-behavioural framework described in chapter 2. To do this successfully, the counsellor may have to interrupt the client's descriptions to summarize and rephrase what is being said in CB terms. It is important that the counsellor avoids becoming a 'sponge' simply soaking up the client's negativity. The counsellor has to be listening to what the client says whilst at the same time distilling the implications for coping responses. The client may wish to put some of these difficulties since the last session on the agenda for discussion. Usually the counsellor would put a review of the previous week's homework assignments as the first item on the agenda. However, clearly if the client were suicidal the agenda would be suspended and the session would be spent clarifying the nature of the suicidal wishes and countering the sense of hopelessness. The homework assignments emphasize the importance given in cognitive-behaviour therapy to practice outside the counselling session.

The counsellor is not going to solve the client's difficulties any more than a driving instructor solves the problems of a learner driver. The practice and refinement of coping responses by the client is at a premium in CBC, with the counsellor simply as a guide. It is important that the guide or counsellor is very specific as to what the client should practise, that is the counsellor should help clarify what thoughts and behaviours would be most appropriate for what situations. In the setting of the homework assignments the counsellor has to clarify the answers to two questions: first outcome expectations – 'Does the client believe that the task I am suggesting be attempted would make a worthwhile difference if successful?'; and second efficacy expectations – 'Does the client believe they have the ability to perform the task I am suggesting?' A homework assignment is unlikely to be complied with if the client does not have both a positive outcome expectation and a belief in their capacity to perform the task. Some client's have a standard response towards authority figures of deference, and it is not sufficient to take the polite nods from the client as evidence of understanding or agreement. The counsellor has to seek feedback from the client throughout the session and in summary form about the whole session at the end. The counsellor's prompts for feedback should be sufficiently open ended to allow for a negative reply by the client. To secure realistic feedback it is necessary that the counsellor display basic counselling skills involving the use of empathy, warmth and genuineness. But though these basic skills are essential ingredients for counselling, they have been shown to be insufficient alone to bring about significant improvements in anxiety disorders and depression (Covi et al., 1974; Klerman et al., 1974). It is unlikely that the possession of these 'human' qualities by a counsellor, important though they are, will be sufficient to address the problems posed by PTSD. The counsellor must also possess the technical skills we now outline below.

Cognitive-behavioural techniques for PTSD

The two characteristics that most uniquely describe PTSD are intrusive imagery or thoughts, and avoidance reactions. Strategies for dealing with each of these are now described in turn.

Intrusive imagery/thoughts

Intrusive imagery/thoughts are the hallmark of PTSD. These symptoms are a threat to the client's sense of control, the images or thoughts arising unbidden and often at inappropriate times. In extreme and rare cases the client becomes cut off or dissociated from normal functioning, perhaps moving to another town and taking on another identity and name, without any recall of the past – psychogenic amnesia. More commonly the PTSD client feels 'not himself/herself' any longer; there is an aspect of their mental life that seems largely independent of them – the intrusive imagery or thoughts. The extent to which these dominate a client's life will vary considerably, both from case to case and from time to time. In the immediate aftermath of a major trauma they may be present most of the time, perhaps preventing the onset of sleep, and when sleep does occur resulting in nightmares related to the trauma. As the client begins to improve, the intrusive imagery or thoughts may be present only as they try to get off to sleep and in the daytime they may be in the background of their mind provided they distract themselves with activity. There are four strategies which are of use in enabling the client to cope with intrusion: containment, desensitization, cognitive restructuring and 'balancing out'. The strategies may be used in combination and are now described in turn.

Containment Typically clients simply want to be rid of their intrusive imagery or thoughts, yet the harder they try not to recall the trauma the worse they tend to feel. It can be explained to clients that this approach is rather like being told not to think of pink elephants. The harder one tries not to think of pink elephants, the more one thinks of them. The counselling goal is not to seek to obliterate the intrusive imagery or thoughts but to contain them. The client can be instructed to place an elastic band on their wrist and each time the intrusion comes to mind to pull it and let it go. At the same time they tell themselves that they will watch a 'mental video' of the trauma, for twenty minutes at a certain time of the day. This is a more realistic scenario than attempting to cut out the memories of the trauma. An alternative strategy is for the client to be taught to shout *Stop!* when the intrusions occur and again make a mental note to watch the 'video' of the trauma at a prearranged time. This strategy leaves more of the client's day 'free' for themselves, and almost invariably when the 'video-time' comes around playing the video seems pointless. In turn this generates a sense of the client controlling the imagery or thoughts rather than the other way around. On occasion, however, this strategy is unsuccessful and desensitization may be called for.

Desensitization to the trauma When intrusion persists despite all efforts at containment it may be useful to employ a desensitization procedure, but this strategy should not be used unless there is a sound therapeutic alliance. PTSD clients tend to be more difficult to engage in counselling than those with disorders such as depression and anxiety. Because of this, great care has to be taken not to prematurely introduce a procedure that initially is likely to amplify the client's distress before reducing it. It is probably best used when other strategies such as containment and cognitive restructuring have proved inadequate.

The desensitization procedure involves encouraging the client to make a 10–15-minute audio tape of the original trauma, describing the events that occurred and the associated thoughts, feelings and behaviours. Then they should play the tape at least once a day, but not switch the tape off until they have become more relaxed. Unless there is habituation to the trauma (a decrease in distress) during a listening session there will be no decrease in distress from session to session. It is therefore very important that the tape is not switched off until the client is more relaxed. The particular aspects of the tape that create maximum distress will often vary from day to day, as the client, rather like a photographer, is taking sightings of the trauma from new angles to try to make sense of it. In this way the imaginal desensitization procedure is not a passive process; rather the whole trauma is being reconstructed and worked through. The intention is that the client be exposed to an intermediate level of fear (Foa and Kozak, 1986), not so great that they are prevented from processing the trauma material, nor so slight that they are not engaging with the trauma material. If a relaxation procedure is used in conjunction with the imaginal desensitization it should be only to maintain fearfulness at an intermediate level, not to reduce it to zero. To help a client attain and maintain an appropriate intermediate level of fear whilst listening to the tape, they may be instructed to use a simple breathing procedure, for example to place the hand on the stomach and breathe in smoothly for a count of four then out smoothly for a count of six, checking carefully that the stomach moves out on inhaling and in on exhaling. Some clients find it useful initially to attach themselves to a biofeedback device whilst listening to their audio tape. Such a device consists of Velcro electrodes attached to a sound emitter. The electrodes are attached to two fingers of one hand and the device measures skin conductance. As the client becomes more distressed the skin conducts electricity more easily and this is reflected in a high-pitched note from the sound emitter. As the client relaxes, the pitch of the note changes. The device then gives the client feedback on which aspects of the audio tape or trauma affect them most and on their success in relieving the distress. Such devices are cheap and readily available.

There are certain cautions that must be observed with this procedure. First, clients rarely like the idea of recording their trauma and listening to it. Typically they have spent months trying to avoid thinking about it! One useful analogy is to suggest that it is like having back trouble and going into hospital for traction – there is worse pain soon after admission but that is a necessary prelude to long-term health: essentially trading short-term pain for long-term gain. The counsellor can also ease matters by offering to construct the tape with the client. If the client is prepared to listen to the tape at home they should initially have a supportive friend or family member listen with them. In some instances the tape may be so distressing that initially the client will agree to listen to it only in the counsellor's office.

Positive results with this procedure usually occur within two to three weeks. There are not too many problems with this procedure when the trauma is a single unique event such as a disaster or an assault. However where a client recalls a series of traumas – for example childhood sexual abuse and adulthood sexual assault – there is often greater resistance to recording a trauma tape. Additionally, if the client's traumatic event was of their own making – for example in committing an atrocity, as is sometimes the case with a combat veteran – then the making of a tape can evoke intense distress and it is recommended that for the client's safety this desensitization procedure should be conducted only on an in-patient basis.

Writing about the trauma Having the client write about the trauma for half an hour a day for four consecutive days can help the client to engage with the material of the trauma. The familiarity with the details of the trauma over a few days can serve to diminish the intensity of the response. This strategy has elements of both containment and desensitization. Alternatively, the client can be asked to construct a collage of the trauma.

Cognitive restructuring – accurately perceiving the trauma In constructing a trauma tape with a client the counsellor will probably find that the client emphasizes some details and minimizes others. Indeed this highlights the cognitive-behavioural perspective that a trauma does not simply exist in objective reality but that the client responds to their construction of it. For example, a traffic policeman may recount graphically the horror of seeing an accident victim's thumb rolling across the road whilst passing over the fact that he prevented more cars being involved in a pile-up by courageously diverting the high speed traffic. The counselling strategy is to encourage the client to represent the whole picture and not use a mental filter on the positive aspects. Thus the traffic policeman might be instructed to use an image of the thumb as a cue to recall the faces of the people whose lives he probably saved. The purpose of cognitive restructuring is to describe a trauma as it was, not seeking to minimize the negative aspects nor negating the positive aspects but balancing negative and positive memories. The client can be helped to perceive the trauma more accurately using Meichenbaum's (1985) Self-Instruction Training. This involves identifying the specific thoughts or self-verbalizations related to the trauma that generate distress. The counsellor then assists the client in modifying the negative self-verbalizations and replacing them with positive self-statements.

Balancing out By their very nature major traumas tend to be extremely graphic and vivid in the client's memory. Yet the client may readily acknowledge that there have been more good times than bad in their life. The problem in PTSD is that the positive memories are less available and vivid. The consequence is that trauma memories assume an overwhelming importance in terms of emotional state. It is useful to explain to clients that emotional health depends on a balance between positive and negative memories, rather like a see-saw. If there are too many negative memories relative to positive memories the see-saw becomes unbalanced. The counselling task is to help the client access positive memories and utilize these memories to counterbalance negative memories. The following dialogue illustrates this.

> *Client:* This Gulf War has unlocked a box, it reminds me of when I was in the Army in Cyprus in 1957.
> *Counsellor:* What happened then?
> *Client:* It was terrible.
> [*Pause*]
> *Client:* I remember the first person I saw shot. He was a Greek Cypriot shot through the back on a hillside. Just an ordinary bloke looking after his sheep. His guts had come out the front and blood was pouring down the hillside. What for?
> *Counsellor:* Sounds horrific.
> *Client:* I haven't thought about it for years but there was a family. They had a grenade thrown into their house. I was involved in gathering together the limbs of the children and mother.
> *Counsellor:* They must be incredibly painful memories to carry.
> *Client:* Yes, but I have had more good times than bad.
> *Counsellor:* What good times were there?
> *Client:* I remember being on duty as a policeman on Christmas Day, about twenty-five years ago and there was a little girl just skipping on waste ground.
> *Counsellor:* What else do you remember about her?
> *Client:* Well she had new red plastic shoes on her and she was from a very poor area of the city and she had a new skipping rope. She was beaming from ear to ear. She showed you didn't need expensive things to be happy, just the simple things.
> *Counsellor:* Maybe you could make a list of such positive events and describe each in great detail. Then when a horrible memory comes back reply to it with an equally detached positive memory from your menu. Try and generate two positive memories for each negative one.
> *Client:* OK, I'll try that. I have got to do something. Sometimes my wife speaks to me and I am not really listening, I am just getting all these flashbacks. Then she gets angry with me for not listening. But it's not fair to burden her with these horrors.

The success of this strategy depends not only on the number of positive memories that can be listed by the client but on their depth and vividness. The difficulty is that with regard to positive memories clients tend to remember generality rather than specifics and it is this which the counsellor seeks to reverse.

Avoidance reactions

Avoidance reactions may take two forms. The first may involve an avoidance of situations that in some way are seen to stimulate recollection of the major trauma and the second an escape from situations perceived as similar to the trauma. As well as behavioural avoidance there is also cognitive avoidance, that is avoidance of thinking about the trauma or aspects of it. It is as if the PTSD client continually inspects current surroundings (often in a state of hypervigilance) for any similarities between it and the major trauma. If the client concludes there is similarity, this generates thoughts of threat, which in turn lead to avoidance reactions. This is not to suggest that the matching of current situation to past trauma is necessarily a fully conscious process. From the client's point of view it often seems to happen automatically.

Three strategies are particularly useful in overcoming avoidance behaviour: desensitization to avoided situations; cognitive restructuring – reassessing the degree of threat; and task orientation – a problem-solving approach. With PTSD the avoidance behaviour has usually generalized well beyond the original context of the trauma. Because of this the client's life becomes increasingly circumscribed and mood becomes lower as opportunities for a sense of achievement or pleasure became reduced.

Desensitization to avoided situations In the wake of a major trauma, situations that seem to approximate in some way to it are avoided and if unexpectedly encountered are escaped from as quickly as possible. Desensitization is appropriate when avoidance is based on threat. It is also possible that following a major trauma some situations are avoided more because the client has lost interest in them and is too preoccupied. In this case, counselling for depression would be appropriate (as discussed in chapter 7).

The starting point for the desensitization procedure is to ascertain those situations which now pose a threat to the client. However, for the client to begin to learn to tolerate the discomfort involved in a threat situation, that situation must be important to them. Those situations which are important to the client and are currently being avoided are ranked by the client in terms of the amount of discomfort they would be expected to evoke. Subjective units of discomfort (SUDS) are assigned. A SUDS ladder should be constructed with the most difficult task at the top rung of the ladder and the least difficult at the bottom rung, with other tasks arranged in order of anticipated difficulty on the rungs between. It is explained that the client's homework assignments will involve attempting to 'climb the ladder'.

The client may be armoured against possible failure experiences by suggesting in advance that the size of the steps on the ladder is adjustable. It is possible that a client may find movement from one rung to the next too large a step. Demoralization can be prevented by suggesting in advance that it is always possible to introduce an intermediate step. Climbing the ladder is portrayed as conducting a series of mini-experiments: in advance it is not possible to know with certainty whether a particular step is possible. Depending on the result of one 'experiment', the next step is determined. The success of the desensitization procedure depends at least as much on the client embracing this experimental orientation as on their progressively exposing themselves to avoided situations.

Cognitive-restructuring – reassessing the degree of threat A major trauma raises forcibly for the client questions about the dangerousness of the world. The answers to these questions have an important influence on a client's emotional state and behaviour. The counselling task is to help the client focus on the current environment and assess realistically the degree of threat posed by it. Clients' appraisal of their environment can be subject to a range of biases of the kinds instanced in Box 3.2. Correcting a client's cognitive biases is a major target of the cognitive-behavioural approach in general, and no less so in the case of CB counselling for PTSD. The biases are manifested as the client recounts the major trauma and difficulties in adjusting to it.

Biases may be corrected by the counsellor using the style of TV detective Columbo (actor Peter Falk). The counselling proceeds by the counsellor juxtaposing questions, for example: 'How come you spend a lot of time dwelling on the physical state of the lady who died in the fire, but not about the sort of life the little boy you revived is now able to have?' In this way the counsellor draws the client's attention to their thought processes, and this can serve as a prelude to helping the client label them. The client then has a shorthand way of modifying their thinking. For example the client above might instruct himself to pause each time he thinks of the trauma and check out whether he was using a mental filter – ignoring the positive aspects (the little boy saved) and zooming in on the negative aspects (the lady lost).

Helping the client to sift the evidence for the beliefs indicated in the Trauma Belief Inventory (TBI: Appendix C) is a useful starting

---

Box 3.2   *Cognitive biases in environmental appraisal*

- *All or nothing thinking.* Everything is seen in black and white terms, for example 'I am either in control of what's happening to me or I am not.'
- *Over-generalization.* Expecting a uniform response from a category of people because of the misdeeds of a member, for example 'All men are potential rapists.'
- *Mental filter.* Seizing on a negative fragment of a situation and dwelling on it, for example 'I could have been killed in that encounter.'
- *Automatic discounting.* Brushing aside the positive aspects of what was achieved in a trauma, for example 'I was only doing my duty in saving the child.'
- *Jumping to conclusions.* Assuming that it is known what others think, for example 'They all think I should be over it by now, it was six weeks ago after all.'
- *Magnification and minimization.* Magnification of short-comings and minimization of strengths, for example 'Since the trauma I am so irritable with the family and just about manage to keep going to work.'
- *Emotional reasoning.* Focusing on emotional state to draw conclusions about oneself, for example 'Since it happened, I am frightened of my own shadow, I guess I am just a wimp.'
- *'Should' statements.* Inappropriate use of moral imperatives – 'shoulds', 'musts', 'haves', and 'oughts' – for example 'Its ridiculous that since the attack I now have to take my daughter with me shopping. I should be able to go by myself.'
- *Labelling and mislabelling.* For example 'I used to think of myself as a strong person. I could handle anything, but since it happened I am just weak.'
- *Personalization.* Assuming that because something went wrong it must be your fault. 'I keep going over my handling of the situation. I must have made a mistake somewhere for the child to have died.'

---

point. It should be remembered, however, that this is not intended as an exhaustive list of dysfunctional trauma beliefs. Such beliefs can be challenged at two levels: inference and evaluation. Inferential questions seek to ascertain whether something is actually true. Thus a client who believed item 4 of the TBI, 'It is dangerous to get close to anyone because they always hurt or exploit you' might be asked 'Are you absolutely sure that everyone you have been close to has exploited you?' The concern here is to help the client view matters realistically. The other line of questioning is evaluative. Thus a client who believed item 19 'I believe that I over-reacted to what happened to me' might be asked 'So what if you did?' The evaluative questioning can be used in the 'downward arrow' technique to elucidate the client's bottom-line belief. For example:

> *Counsellor:* So what if you did over-react to what happened to you? What does that mean to you?
> *Client:* I made a fool of myself.
> *Counsellor:* Does it matter that you may have made a fool of yourself?
> *Client:* I couldn't stand them thinking I'm stupid.
> *Counsellor:* Would they all think that way about you? [*Here the counsellor has posed an inferential question aimed at countering the client's tendency to over-generalize.*]
> *Client:* Well no, but some would.
> *Counsellor:* Well, what would be awful about that? [*A return to the evaluative question.*]
> *Client:* I just couldn't stand it.
> *Counsellor:* It sounds almost as if you believed you had to have everybody's approval all the time.

Having elicited the client's bottom line using the downward arrow, the counsellor could, in this case, go on to challenge the utility of the belief, asking whether the belief helps the client to achieve what they want.

Task orientation – a problem-solving approach   Not only do clients with PTSD tend to avoid threatening situations but they also tend to disengage from any purposeful activity. Disengagement from an activity is entirely appropriate when faced with a major trauma because it is often, by its nature, overwhelming. However, continued disengagement from routine activities is unlikely to be an appropriate response to a changed environment. For example, a client may have suffered the trauma of a flood and the flood has subsided by the time he sees a counsellor. Whilst the counsellor would commiserate with the client – about losses, damage to furniture, etc. – it would not be appropriate to continue simply to facilitate such emotion-focused coping. It is unhelpful to the client and wearing on the counsellor to continually have a catalogue of woes deposited in the counselling session. The CB counsellor would point this out to the client. A poignant way of doing this is role reversal. Using gentle humour the counsellor takes on the role of

Box 3.3 *Problem solving procedures*

1 *Problem definition*. What is the problem exactly? Define the problem in specific terms, no 'fuzzies'.
2 *Brainstorm*. Generate as many solutions as possible. At this stage go for quantity rather than quality.
3 *Weigh up the advantages and disadvantages of each of the solutions*. Look at advantages and disadvantages, both short- and long-term.
4 *Choose a solution*. Plan its implementation in specific terms, one step at a time.
5 *Review coping efforts*. If the chosen solution is not successful or is incomplete go back to stage 2, *Brainstorm*, and continue cycling through the problem-solving procedure until reasonably content.

the client, and begins to re-enact what has become the typical expression of negative sentiments. Clearly care has to be taken with this procedure that the client is not humiliated, and their response should be carefully checked. In addition, such role reversals would be inappropriate if there were genuinely no options open to the client for resolving difficulties.

Task orientation is a very useful strategy for engaging the client because it deals with tangible concerns in their environment. A major concern in task orientation is to teach the client to switch from self-evaluative concerns, such as 'How well am I doing as a human being compared to before the trauma', to problem-solving ones. Essentially the client is taught to focus on their hassles one by one and go through the problem solving procedures shown in Box 3.3.

Let us return to the example of the client who had been flooded, to illustrate the procedure. The client would typically present with an interwoven bundle of concerns: anger at the Council for not building better sea defences, sadness at the loss of some memorabilia in the flood, worry about insufficient insurance cover, and so on. The counsellor would help the client separate out each of the worries and encourage him/her to put each through the problem-solving procedure one at a time. Thus if the focus was on the client's financial worries, stage 1 of the problem-solving procedure involves problem definition. It would therefore be necessary to help the client specify exactly by how much the money falls short of what is required. Problem definition tends to be the most difficult aspect of the whole problem-solving procedure.

Often problems are posed in such vague terms ('fuzzies') that they do not easily admit of solution. In the second stage brainstorming, the client might come up with a range of solutions such as a bank loan, a loan from a relative, sell the property and move down-market, go and live with a daughter, sell the property and move into sheltered accommodation and so on. The next step involves sifting through the solutions followed by choosing a solution. In this case the client might have chosen, say, to sell the property and move into sheltered accommodation. The client may decide to implement this solution in stages: first check the availability of sheltered accommodation, second check whether it is possible to have a trial run in the new accommodation before actually selling the house, and third to sell the property. The final stage of problem solving would be to review how the client fared in the sheltered housing after some fixed period. If the move was unsatisfactory, the client would return to stage 2 and try one of the other solutions by, for example, moving to a daughter's home.

This problem-solving procedure is also perfectly applicable to clients who, whilst not suffering from full PTSD, nevertheless have problems in living following a major trauma.

4

Counselling for Acute PTSD – Illustrative Cases

Part of the reason for the delay in PTSD being recognized as an emotional disorder was a belief that negative responses to major trauma were usually transient. This is at best a partial truth; whilst approximately half of those initially affected by PTSD are recovered from the disorder three months later, this also means that half are still affected. The changing nature of PTSD symptoms in the months following a major trauma led to the recommendation embodied in *DSM-III-R* that PTSD should not be diagnosed until symptoms have persisted for at least a month.

Counsellors encountering clients in the first few weeks after a trauma might most profitably use a crisis counselling model (see Appendix D) rather than see themselves as treating PTSD-like symptoms. In this early stage clients are often too disoriented to work systematically through a counselling programme. Nor have they had the space to test out the efficacy of their own coping mechanisms. It is only when PTSD symptoms persist for more than a month that clients can be considered as suffering from acute PTSD, and that the strategies recommended in this chapter apply.

The thesis outlined in chapter 2 was that the variability in response to major trauma may be accounted for largely by cognitive variables. Specifically, both the negative schemas underlying any pre-trauma personality or psychological disorder and post-trauma beliefs will influence the symptoms experienced by the client. In the immediate aftermath of a major trauma a person may conclude that it was a one-off, an atypical event, and therefore of little relevance to the rest of their life. As a consequence they may not suffer from PTSD at all, experiencing little but shock in the days afterwards. Alternatively, a person may conclude that they are much more vulnerable to the vagaries of life than they ever thought, and within weeks of the trauma may be manifesting PTSD-like symptoms. However, with the help of friends and family they may engage in their usual activities. Again their experiences may serve to disconfirm the belief that they are extraordinarily vulnerable. As a consequence their PTSD symptoms become much reduced. Those who suffer PTSD symptoms initially but retreat into their shell deprive themselves of opportunities to disconfirm their trauma beliefs, and symptoms are more likely to be maintained. A lack of perceived support would increase the likelihood of this outcome.

The first step for a counsellor meeting a client after a major trauma is to ascertain the presence of PTSD symptoms using the assessment guidelines. This assessment should be repeated between one and three months later because of the variable course of the disorder and the possibility of delayed onset. The counsellor cannot assume that there will necessarily be any particular progression in the client's difficulties. For example, where a victim of a major trauma has suffered the death of a relative the stage model of Kubler-Ross (Oberfield, 1984) is often invoked. This model suggests that the client moves through stages of denial, anger, bargaining, depression and acceptance. But these stages have been found to be neither universal nor necessarily progressive (Worden, 1983). All that can be said with any certainty is that some responses, when they occur, are likely to predominate early in the course of the condition – for example denial – and some are more likely to appear later – for example depression and acceptance. There is no substitute for the counsellor looking at the meaning of the major trauma to the client. In this chapter the counselling approach to clients showing early symptoms of PTSD is illustrated by a number of cases. Chapter 5 illustrates the approach with chronic cases.

Making contact

The context within which the counsellor first meets the trauma victim will affect the nature of the help proffered. The counselling needs of a victim in the immediate aftermath of a trauma are likely to be different from their needs four weeks or four months later. In the immediate aftermath of a trauma much of the counsellor's concerns will inevitably focus on practical matters. For example, following a major disaster victims will be concerned to find out what has happened to relatives and friends, and relatives of the deceased may need support in the identification of bodies. At this stage the pain of victims is raw indeed, and a counsellor can easily feel overwhelmed by it all. Counsellors themselves need opportunities for debriefing. The chance to meet periodically with other counsellors and recount the pain they have been exposed to, their feelings about it and more general matters about how help is being organized is particularly useful. Often trauma counsellors are drafted in from their usual tasks as counsellors, psychologists or social workers. The counsellors themselves very easily feel set apart from colleagues back at the office who have not been exposed to the traumatized victims, and this can make for problems of adjustment when they return to their normal work. However, the necessary concentration on practical matters immediately after the trauma should not obscure the requirements for the deployment of the basic counselling skills of empathy, warmth, genuineness and positive regard. Without these 'human' aspects to the relationship, any help given is unlikely to be perceived by the victim as help.

The initial reactions of victims to major trauma may include numbness, anger and sadness. The counsellor needs to be prepared for each of these emotional states, and for the possible rapid oscillation between anger and sadness.

The counselling strategy in the immediate aftermath of a trauma is essentially one of making contact. This allows the victims to define themselves as not having an ongoing problem or, alternatively, to debate and contemplate whether there is a problem. If a counsellor insists that a client 'must' have a problem because of having experienced some objectively major trauma, the client is likely to default from contact with the counsellor. Where a client is experiencing some distress about post-trauma symptoms and is concerned about their normality, that is they are in a contemplative stage, then it is clearly worthwhile offering opportunities for further contact. At this contemplative stage, the client is not asking for 'treatment', and the counsellor should be offering to accompany the victim on a journey to describe the terrain. At certain stages in the journey the victim may conclude 'Yes I do really have a problem' and make a decision for treatment. It is thus important for the counsellor to decide whether the client is pre-contemplative, contemplative or in a decision phase. Not to do this can result in a great deal of misunderstanding between victim and counsellor. The fact that a client might be pre-contemplative does not, of course, exclude the possibility that they may suffer from delayed post-traumatic disorder at some future point in time (delayed PTSD is usually triggered by some similarity between a new stressor and the original trauma). Even for those who are pre-contemplative, it is worthwhile for the counsellor to give the victim a contact address in case they experience difficulties in the future.

This was highlighted in the case of Pat, who was involved in the Hillsborough football stadium disaster.

Pat – acute PTSD following a disaster

Pat: I thought I would get back in touch. I was OK when we met a week after Hillsborough. I went to Anfield [the home of Liverpool Football Club] to pay my respects, and I called into the drop-in centre there to have a cup of tea and a chat. I was upset but fine.

Counsellor: How are things now?

Pat: I was fine for four weeks but this week I have just gone to pieces.

Counsellor: How do you mean?

Pat: I was in work, got the lift to the seventh floor where my office is, the lift was a bit crowded and I became frantic to get out. I was like an animal to get out. I felt embarrassed afterwards.

Counsellor: So you had coped right up to the event in the lift?

Pat: Well on the day of the disaster my friends and I were speechless when we came out the ground, we just saw lines of bodies. Somehow, for the past couple of weeks all the media publicity took my mind off it. I said to myself 'It's just another disaster, therefore it didn't happen to me.' It is only now that I remember I knew others were dying around me. I tried to reassure a guy who was screaming by shouting 'You are not dying, you are at a football match.' But I knew it was not true.

The above extract illustrates a common feature of trauma response, psychogenic amnesia. In order to continue to function the individual, usually temporarily, forgets aspects of the trauma.

The following extract shows the importance of presenting the client with a coherent rationale for his experiences.

Pat: I must be going mad. I was looking at the alphabetical list of the dead in the newspaper, and I just thought over and over again that's where I could have easily been, between the G and the L. I couldn't put the paper down. This week I have just gone over and over the events of the day in my mind. I am stupid, I just can't concentrate at work. I am shattered when I go to work because I am not sleeping.

Counsellor: If something really great had happened to you, like winning £1 million on the football pools, how do you think you would be?

Pat: I would feel great.

Counsellor: Do you think you would go over how you chose the teams on your entry and where you posted it, what the weather was like on that day?

Pat: I guess I would.

Counsellor: How do you think your concentration at work would be, and your sleep?

Pat: I think I can see what you are driving at. I would have the same reaction for anything extreme.

Counsellor: Sounds like it and I guess many others would have a similar experience.

The counsellor's strategy in the above extract is to locate the client's experience within the realms of a normal response, albeit to a statistically unlikely event (a major trauma or pools win).

Further, that the client's response is not unusual for those experiencing a major trauma. Note, however, that the counsellor should avoid implying that ongoing PTSD symptoms are a necessary and inevitable response to major trauma. Common quips such as 'It is a normal response to an abnormal situation' do not quite do justice to the variability of response. The counsellor goes on to help the client to tolerate rather than get angry at his symptoms.

Counsellor: Why do you call yourself stupid for going over and over the events of Hillsborough?

Pat: Well there's no point, it does not get me anywhere. I just feel worse.

Counsellor: I wonder whether you feel worse because you tell yourself you *should* be able to stop the thoughts? If you weren't telling yourself you should be able to stop them, you might not feel quite as bad.

Pat: But I should be able to stop them, shouldn't I?

Counsellor: Should you?

Pat: Well, I suppose so.

Counsellor: What if a person's mind is very like a railway station? You are standing on one of the station platforms. You cannot control what trains come into the station. On some days there may be, say, special trains to take people to a race meeting. The trains that come into the station depend upon what is going on in the outside world. But you can choose whether you get on a train or not, or ignore it or wave the occupants of the train goodbye.

Pat: So, I don't have much control of thoughts about Hillsborough coming into my mind?

Counsellor: That's right. In fact, it is as if you are jumping on to the railway track to try and stop the train. That's pretty painful.

Pat: What do I do then?

Counsellor: Maybe calmly greet the thoughts and then wave them goodbye. Practise keeping your cool about them.

Pat: But how long are they going to last?

Counsellor: It is difficult to say, but they will go quicker if you don't get angry with yourself about them. Just as you can't force a physical wound to heal quickly, you can't force a psychological wound either. In both cases, you have to flow with the healing process not fight it.

In the above extract the counsellor is concerned with preventing a form of secondary traumatization, stopping the client getting distressed about his trauma response. This is often a necessary prelude to teaching management of the trauma response itself. The next extract is taken from a counselling session a week later.

Pat: I have been thinking a lot less about Hillsborough this week, but I have still been edgy travelling in the lift.

Counsellor: You mean that you have actually managed to continue using the lift?

Pat: Oh, yes.

Counsellor: That's pretty good, many people would have been tempted not to bother.

Pat's 'radical apathy' stance towards the intrusive imagery seems, from the above extract, to be paying dividends. The counsellor keeps the discussion problem-focused by emphasizing Pat's achievement (going into the lift), rather than let the discussion become emotion-focused in which case his negativity could well have pervaded the exchange. Implicit in this dialogue is the cognitive-behavioural principle that overcoming problems involves increasing tolerance of discomfort. A week later Pat had progressed further.

> *Pat:* It's not been a bad week at all.
> *Counsellor:* What happened?
> *Pat:* It's more what didn't happen. I don't get uptight now about hassles. I am not screaming and shouting at the wife and kids for the least little thing.
> *Counsellor:* How did you manage that change?
> *Pat:* I just said to myself 'The hassle doesn't matter, I am here, I'm alive. That's what counts.'

This extract illustrates that though a major trauma may cause a reassessment of one's vulnerability and an examination of the meaningfulness of life, the outcome is not necessarily negative. Later in this interview, Pat reviewed the place of work in his life.

> *Pat:* Before Hillsborough, I was working lots of overtime. My wife was complaining she hardly saw me. I told her that if she wanted the lifestyle, she had to put up with it. She knew I was right but I could tell she resented it.
> *Counsellor:* So the marriage had been a bit strained before Hillsborough?
> *Pat:* Yes, we weren't so much arguing as distant. But we have started talking more this past week. I told them in work I wasn't working Sunday. They were amazed and so was the wife. I took my little boy, he is six, on the ferry instead. It was absolutely great to see him so excited. It makes you think.
> *Counsellor:* Makes you think?
> *Pat:* Yes, what the hell am I working for? OK we do have some financial difficulties, but I have got a fairly good and safe job. We are not starving and we can afford some luxuries.
> *Counsellor:* So you could be at least just reasonably content bringing in less money?
> *Pat:* Yes, the quality of life would be better.

It is simple to explain to clients why they are distressed following a disaster. It is often more difficult in instances where the major traumas are occupational hazards. The next case illustration is of George, a policeman, who was assaulted.

George – acute PTSD following an assault

George, a thirty-year-old policeman was driving his patrol car at 11 p.m. on a winter's night when he saw two men acting suspiciously near a parked car. As he stopped his car and began walking towards the two men they ran off in opposite directions. George gave chase to one of them and eventually caught up with him on waste ground. They wrestled on the ground then the man produced a knife and began slashing at George. By this time George was exhausted, his legs felt like jelly and he felt sure he was going to die. Then suddenly the man ran off. Subsequently George was off work for a week with minor bruising. Though physically recovered after a week, he felt nauseous about putting on his uniform again, and was unable to do so. Over the next few weeks his PTSD symptoms became more prominent, and he dwelt on 'what could have happened'. A month after the assault he was referred to a counsellor. In the first session George was highly critical of himself.

George: I have had lots of skirmishes before, I have just over-reacted to this one.

Counsellor: Getting slashed with a knife sounds like more than a skirmish.

George: Well, I have had a broken arm, broken jaw and cracked ribs in other fights. My injuries were worse but I just got on with the job afterwards.

Counsellor: In what situation did those injuries occur?

George: I broke my jaw and cracked my ribs when we were policing a strike.

Counsellor: So there were other policemen about?

George: Oh, yes.

Counsellor: Did you think then that your life was on the line?

George: No, I was actually trying to calm the strikers who hit me. I had actually a lot of sympathy with them because years ago I used to work for the organization.

Counsellor: What about when you broke your arm?

George: A colleague and I were called out for the third time in one evening to some teenagers who kept congregating and making a disturbance in a passageway between a coffee bar and a house. I try and talk my way through these situations, but James, my colleague, had had enough by this time. James went into the group, picked up the ringleader by the lapels and held him over the car. Some of them then attacked me and in the scuffle I broke my arm.

Counsellor: But was it life threatening?

George: No, they were only kids really. I was as annoyed with James as with them.

Counsellor: What happened to you on the waste land when you were by yourself and attacked with a knife seems in a different league to those other incidents.

> *George:* Yes, when I really think about it it is. But I don't want to give up the job, I love it and I am not qualified for anything else. I've got to get back.

George's distress is intensified by his alarm at his distress. He is over-generalizing, expecting his response to the recent assault to be no different to his responses to other assaults. The counsellor makes the point that the PTSD symptoms are a response to a qualitatively different type of event (a life-threatening one). In the next extract the counsellor helps George look at the issue of self-blame.

> *George:* I could kick myself, I should have gone back to the car and radioed for help instead of giving chase.
> *Counsellor:* But how were you to know he would have a knife?
> *George:* I should not have taken a chance.
> *Counsellor:* Have you given chase before?
> *George:* Yes.
> *Counsellor:* Has it turned out before that they have ever wielded a knife against you?
> *George:* No.
> *Counsellor:* I don't follow why on this occasion you should have known that it would be near fatal to give chase, when on all other previous occasions there had been no dire consequences. How could you have known that this occasion was different?
> *George:* I couldn't have at the time.

This extract illustrates the inappropriate use of 'shoulds' which is often characteristic of depressive mood. The counsellor uses the style of the TV detective Columbo, utilizing a bemused befuddlement to challenge George's 'shoulds'. If left unchallenged, George's exaggerated self-blame might lead to depression. A combination of PTSD and depression would be even more debilitating for George and would impede his cherished goal of a return to work. In the next extract the counsellor helps George overcome a cognitive obstacle to the return to work.

> *George:* I keep thinking that the same thing could happen again.
> *Counsellor:* It's certainly not impossible, but what are the odds?
> *George:* I don't really know.
> *Counsellor:* Are the odds as great as having a serious accident in your car?
> *George:* Less, I think.
> *Counsellor:* Does it bother you to drive around, when you know there is a risk of a serious or indeed fatal accident?
> *George:* No, the chances are so slim, I don't even think about it.
> *Counsellor:* So if the odds of a serious assault on you are about the same as having a serious traffic accident, why do you run one risk and not the other?
> *George:* I suppose because the assault has actually happened and the traffic accident hasn't.

Counsellor: If you were a betting person would you put money on either event occurring in the next ten years?

George: No.

Counsellor: Maybe you are thinking about the assault not so much because it is probable, but because it is salient. It is rather like thinking you are going to catch a rare illness because a friend of yours caught it. As a consequence you become very familiar with the illness and you could easily fall into the trap of thinking that the same fate would befall you.

George: It is just trying to remind myself what the odds are.

Here the counsellor is implicitly challenging dichotomous thinking, 'Either I am safe or I am vulnerable', by introducing the notion of probabilities. He then goes on to make the point that one can be mindful of an event for reasons quite divorced from its actual probability of occurrence. One of the common consequences of PTSD is that the client ceases to handle everyday hassles and then sees this as confirmatory evidence of their inadequacy. The following extract from the third counselling session with George illustrates this.

George: I felt a bit better after the last session and was doing OK until Friday. I was driving along with my wife in the passenger seat, and the baby was in the special seat in the back of the car. All of a sudden this guy cuts in front of me, just misses the passenger side of the car. I was furious. I caught up with him at the next set of traffic lights and the next minute the same guy does it again. I was livid. Thinking of the damage he could have done to my wife and child, I pursued him into town and forced him to pull over. When I got out I was furious. I showed him my warrant card even though I was off duty. He was actually quite apologetic, but I could feel my legs going to jelly, I could hardly get back to my car. I have been wiped out ever since.

Counsellor: What was it actually that got to you about it?

George: Oh no, I didn't think I could have died or anything like that. It was more that I didn't handle it well.

Counsellor: What would you have thought of yourself if you had not pursued him?

George: That I was a wimp.

Counsellor: So you accomplished something in not avoiding the situation.

George: That's true, but I can't get in that state every time I meet the public.

Counsellor: Maybe with practice you will get less in that sort of state. But at least you are still prepared to get stuck in.

Once again the counsellor is challenging George's dichotomous thinking, 'I either handle a situation perfectly well or disastrously', by implying that there are varying degrees of competence. Further, that this competence is not simply given but something than can be improved upon with practice. In the next extract the counsellor moves on to the specifics.

George: But how am I going to handle conflicts?

Counsellor: Perhaps you can begin by saying to yourself 'So what if I feel shaky afterwards?'

George: But I want to feel the way I used to in those situations.

Counsellor: I guess you will eventually, but the starting point might have to be a 'so what?' attitude. Then perhaps when you feel shaky you could, say, take a deep breath, inhaling very slowly, and exhaling slowly while you repeat a calming word like rela-a-ax-x-x.

George: It is not going to be easy to do that when you are talking to someone.

Counsellor: Maybe not; you could try it, though. There are other strategies you could use as well, like imagining the person you're challenging is wearing a nappy and has excrement coming out!

George: You must be joking. I would start laughing and they would think I really had flipped my lid.

Counsellor: I guess that in a conflict situation it wouldn't be that amusing, it would simply take the edge off your tension.

The above extract highlights the need to negotiate what the client perceives to be a viable homework assignment as opposed to the counsellor imposing a homework assignment. It also illustrates that it is not so much bodily symptoms *per se* which are debilitating but the meaning assigned to those symptoms.

The effects of an assault can be particularly traumatic for occupational groups such as social workers and medics whose expectations are typically very different from policemen or prison officers. The next case illustration involves a social worker, Maureen, who was assaulted.

Maureen – acute PTSD following an assault

Maureen paid a surprise visit to one of her clients, Jane, a drug addict with an eighteen-month-old baby. When she arrived the client was in a drunken stupor and her common-law husband, Matt, was lying sprawled on the settee, she guessed the worse for drugs. The baby was sitting in his playpen, staring blankly, not bothering with the few toys in it. The conditions confirmed what she had suspected for some time, though Jane had contended that neither she nor Matt were substance abusers any longer. Maureen had, over the previous six months, spent considerable time with Jane, encouraging her to attend a nursery with the baby, and generally helping her to develop an alternative lifestyle. Maureen felt exasperated by the conditions in which the baby was living and inquired of Jane what was happening. Jane hurled a torrent of abuse at Maureen, who decided it was best to leave the scene and summon help from the department to have the baby removed. As

Maureen turned to leave, Jane realized what was about to happen and assaulted her about the head and body with a hairbrush. Matt woke with the screams and pulled Jane off Maureen. Then Maureen staggered into the street and back to the office, which was fortunately only a few hundred yards away. That day the baby was taken into care. A neurological examination of Maureen revealed that the use of her right arm and leg was impeded in that she had lost the sensation of pressure in both, though she could move them voluntarily. The neurologist was unsure how quickly, if at all, the damage would be repaired. Maureen was prescribed daily physiotherapy and had to wear a support collar for the damaged neck. In addition, part of her head continued to feel numb.

Maureen was referred to the counsellor four weeks after the assault. She had constant flashbacks to the day of the assault. She was reliving the whole scene as if it were conducted in slow motion, starting with the baby's blank gaze, the sight of Matt sprawled out on the settee, and Jane picking up the hairbrush and advancing towards her. Maureen could no longer go out alone and she felt uncharacteristically angry at home and with work colleagues. In the second interview with Maureen the counsellor looked at the anger issue with her.

Maureen: I was so angry with my senior, all he could say was why didn't I do the home visit with a colleague if I suspected it might be dangerous.
Counsellor: Was that all he said?
Maureen: Well, he did make noises about taking my time to feel well again before returning to work.
Counsellor: How come you are sure that they were just noises?
Maureen: I suppose he is not so bad, just a bit of a pillock. I mean I know it is departmental policy to visit dangerous situations in twos but (a) I didn't know it was going to be that dangerous, and (b) we just haven't the staff resources to cover all the difficult situations.
Counsellor: What, you feel the department places you in a no-win situation?
Maureen: It does.
Counsellor: How is the anger at home?
Maureen: I just blow my top for no reason, well almost no reason.
Counsellor: Almost no reason?
Maureen: The family were fine for the first week after the incident, when I was still hobbling around, but then it was business as usual – 'Have you ironed this?', 'Have you made my school lunch?', 'Can you drop me off at ____?'
Counsellor: Sounds like maybe you are doing a bit of mind-reading, thinking that others should know how you feel without you telling them.
Maureen: They would know what I was feeling if they cared enough.

Counsellor: Can they know without having been through something like it?
Maureen: I guess not. My husband's been OK. I have just been asking him for lots of hugs.

In this extract, Maureen's thinking seems dominated by mind-readings, first that her boss *should* have known that she thought the situation was possibly dangerous and not probably dangerous and second that if her children cared enough for her they would understand her feelings. The counsellor also challenges Maureen's over-generalization that 'they' don't care and she finally acknowledges that her husband is at least a notable exception.

At the third counselling session Maureen began to seriously question the meaning of her career.

Maureen: When I think what happened I begin to wonder what the hell I am doing in the job.
Counsellor: You have protected a child from neglect.
Maureen: But it is like swimming in a sewer all the time.
Counsellor: Aren't there moments of satisfaction?
Maureen: It is hard to think of them. You don't often get any thanks from clients, though I have some good friends in work.
Counsellor: Would it help to work outside of child care?
Maureen: I've been at it ten years, maybe I should work with, say, the physically disabled for a while.
Counsellor: What makes you think that?
Maureen: Going to physiotherapy has made me more aware of their needs than I was previously. There was a chap who had become paralysed from the waist down as a result of diving into a swimming pool, yet he was always cheerful, cracking jokes. It made me think by comparison I have nothing to complain about.

In this extract the counsellor is helping Maureen construct a life post-trauma. It seems that the trauma served to heighten a demoralization that was already there.

However, by the fourth counselling session Maureen is depressed about her lack of physical progress and this seems to be heightening the intrusive imagery.

Maureen: I am fed up with the physiotherapy, my leg is no better. I have to deliberately tell myself to put my right leg in front of my left when I walk, but I don't get any feedback when I use it. It is a constant reminder of the assault. It makes me dwell on it even more.
Counsellor: Has the physiotherapist given you any time scale in which it should get better by?
Maureen: That's the problem, they can't say, they just say exercise increases the chances.
Counsellor: So you could worry twenty-four hours a day about how your leg is going to turn out eventually?

Maureen: That would not be much use!
Counsellor: But is it useful to dwell on it at all?
Maureen: No, but I can't seem to stop myself thinking about it and the assault.
Counsellor: Try digging your fingernail into your thumb each time you agonize about your leg and the assault. Keep digging it in until the pictures of the incident and worry over your leg stops.
Maureen: I will give that a try.

This extract illustrates how intrusive imagery may be triggered by a feature associated with the original trauma. The next case shows how this can be particularly pertinent for an adult woman who was sexually abused in childhood.

Susan – acute PTSD following indecent assault

Susan was attending a Christmas party with her husband at a neighbour's house. Her husband, a chief hospital laboratory technician, was summoned to the hospital and had to leave early. One of her neighbours had, in Susan's words, 'pestered' her for years, making suggestions. Susan had not mentioned it to her husband as she did not want to get the neighbour into trouble. The neighbour indecently assaulted her when she went up to the bedroom to retrieve her bag. Four weeks later Susan consulted a counsellor. She felt guilty that she had not taken action about this neighbour earlier. In addition she was now having flashbacks, not only of this assault but also of a period in childhood and early adolescence when she was sexually abused by her father. In this first interview she is full of self-blame.

Susan: There must be something about me that attracts men who abuse me.
Counsellor: But not all men have abused you.
Susan: No, my husband is very understanding. But for it to happen now and as a child is too much.
Counsellor: It is too much bad luck I agree, but luck does change.
Susan: Life was going along nicely until this happened. Though there was the 'pest', but I thought I could handle him with humour. My husband is so angry now. I don't know why I didn't tell him earlier and perhaps all this would not have happened.
Counsellor: When you were a child did you try confiding in anyone what was happening?
Susan: Yes, eventually, I told my mother. She wouldn't believe me and said it was wicked to make up the stories I had.
Counsellor: Maybe it's not surprising then to expect to be dismissed if you confide a tale of abuse.
Susan: I have to admit, I thought my husband Joe would either make a joke of it all, he has a great sense of humour and makes me laugh, or really go over the top.

Counsellor: Given your experiences as a child you wouldn't quite know how to play it.

Susan: I just avoid my father now when we do meet. It infuriates me that we cannot discuss what happened. It's just nonsensical pleasantries. Yet he was the only adult that showed any real interest in me as a child.

This extract illustrates how historical material can affect later response to traumas. In particular it emphasizes the often ambivalent relationship between victimizer and victim. Susan was also finding that her traumas were affecting her sexual relationship with her husband. The following is an extract from the second interview.

Susan: Sex is a waste of time now.

Counsellor: What do you mean a waste of time?

Susan: I just freeze.

Counsellor: When do you freeze?

Susan: When I am about to have an orgasm. I start thinking of my father and of this neighbour and it just stops everything.

Counsellor: How does your husband take it?

Susan: He just gets so mad at this neighbour. I am worried what he might do to him.

Counsellor: Sometimes people find it useful when they are beginning to lose control to focus in detail on some aspect of their partner's body and describe it vividly. It may be the texture of the skin, the smell, etc.

Susan: Sounds a good idea, if I could concentrate on my husband I would be a lot better.

Again, the counsellor is suggesting using a distraction technique in the event of intrusive imagery.

Greta – acute PTSD following the 'bombing' of a coach

Greta had been returning on a coach with a party of pensioners from an outing to the seaside. As they were nearing the end of the journey their coach was bombarded with missiles from a bridge over the motorway. A brick came straight through the window and hit Greta on the side of the head. A number of other passengers were similarly injured but, miraculously, there were no fatalities. Greta was referred by her general practitioner eight weeks after the 'bombing' because of persistent panic attacks. She still had some head pain but it was getting easier.

This was a rather typical case in so far as PTSD is rarely given as the reason for referral. The counsellor only became alert to the possibility of PTSD when exploring the events surrounding the date of onset of the panic attacks. Greta had no previous history of emotional disorder. She was uncharacteristically irritated by the wish of her fellow pensioners at her club to discuss the event *ad nauseam*. Previously, she had enjoyed their company but was now thinking of not attending at all. The counsellor began exploring why the 'bombing' seemed somehow different for Greta.

Counsellor: How are the others who were injured getting on?
Greta: Mostly OK. There is just one chap who is still in hospital – something hit him in the chest.
Counsellor: Apart from him the others are OK?
Greta: Yes, just a couple of bruises. But I can't even get on a bus now. When I go out to the shops I want to run back home.
Counsellor: Do you get pictures of the bombing coming into your mind?
Greta: Yes, a lot.
Counsellor: What do you see?
Greta: The brick coming through the window and hitting me on the side of the head. [*She begins to sob.*]
Counsellor: As you began to cry then what went through your mind?
Greta: That I might lose the sight of my good eye. You see I have one glass eye already.

This extract illustrates that the particular meaning of a major trauma is often inaccessible outside of the emotional arousal associated with the original trauma. The counsellor hypothesized that the 'bombing' incident might resonate with an earlier trauma.

Counsellor: How did you lose the sight of your eye?
Greta: It was at school, I was only thirteen and a friend of mine was trying to throw the javelin, and the back of it caught me in the eye. She was devastated, she could never really face me after that, even though I never blamed her.
Counsellor: That must have been a real bad time for you.
Greta: Yes, it was. Some children were really great but some can be so cruel. I threw myself back into school then work and rarely thought about my eye. Though sometimes I blame that for the one really close relationship I had with a boy that broke up. But then again I don't know whether that's making excuses.

In the client's mind head injury has been associated with all the major losses of her life. The 'bombing' had reactivated these losses. Her current interactions with fellow pensioners at the club seemed set to heighten the sense of loss. The counsellor then utilizes Meichenbaum's (1985) Self-Instruction Training to develop a coping routine for the client. The coping self-statements agreed between the client and counsellor are shown in Box 4.1. Greta put the coping self-statements on cue-cards and rehearsed them daily. To help Greta deal with her intrusive imagery the counsellor targeted her 'I could have been blinded' statement by using it as a cue for reframing the experience as follows:

'I could have been killed, *but I wasn't.*'

Box 4.1 *Greta's coping self-statements*

- *Preparing for the stressor:* 'Talking about the bombing will be a five-minute wonder at the pensioners, if I just keep my cool.'
- *Encountering the stressor:* 'I knew that when I actually saw them my temperature would rise, but it will go down again if I concentrate on conversation with Eileen and Marge.'
- *Coping with feeling overwhelmed:* 'I knew that sometimes I would be caught off guard, I knew that I could become very agitated but who says I have to have perfect control? It is no big deal if occasionally I go over the top.'
- (a) *Coping with stressor resolved:* 'I am getting better at this with practice, well done.'
  (b) *Coping with stressor unresolved:* 'You can't win them all.'

'I could have been seriously injured, *but I wasn't.*'
'I could have been blinded, *but I wasn't.*'
'It could have impaired my eyesight, *but it didn't.*'
'I have just got a bit of a hangover.'

In this way the experience is reframed as being of little more significance than a hangover. The client found the notion of having a hangover quite amusing as she was almost totally teetotal.

Greta's panic attacks were dealt with using the 'hyperventilation challenge'. Without prior explanation she was asked to breathe deeply and quickly. After forty-five seconds the counsellor asked her what she was experiencing. Greta reported the classic feelings of panic, light-headedness, dizziness and palpitations. The counsellor then asked her whether she had experienced these before and she replied with great surprise that they were exactly what she had regularly experienced since the 'bombing'.

The counsellor then asked her to repeat the 'overbreathing' (hyperventilating) and at a signal from the counsellor to begin controlled breathing. This involves the client placing a hand on the stomach and breathing in for a slow count of four and out for a slow count of six. The client practised the controlled breathing for a minute and the counsellor then asked her how she felt. Greta reported that she felt much calmer. It is much more powerful to demonstrate the effects on hyperventilation in this way than to simply explain to clients that they should use controlled breathing

Box 4.2 *Practice summary – acute PTSD*

1 Emphasize the 'normality' of PTSD symptoms following a major trauma.
2 Teach the client to seek to calmly contain intrusive imagery. Simply trying to stop the imagery tends to make it worse.
3 Focus the client's attention on what has been gradually achieved in the way of overcoming avoided situations, rather than on the discomfort involved.
4 Check whether the client's expectations of performance are inappropriate at present.
5 Assess the client's irritability and the reasonableness of their expectations of others. In particular, check whether they are expecting others to be 'mind-readers'.
6 The event that triggered the onset of PTSD may not itself be particularly traumatic, but may have served to rekindle earlier, usually childhood, traumas that had been denied for many years. Both recent and previous traumas will need addressing.
7 Often the most effective way to challenge a trauma belief is to change a behaviour.
8 Homework assignments should be carefully negotiated and reviewed in each session.

in the event of a panic. The demonstration reassured Greta that she was not 'going mad' and gave her a coping skill she knew she could apply effectively.

With the help of her two friends, Greta began travelling a few bus stops to a local shopping centre. Initially she sat away from the window with a friend next to her. Over a six-week period she managed to travel alone on the bus sitting by the window. She used a novel to distract herself on the journey, but by the end of the six weeks found that she was forcing herself to look out of the window, though still scanning her surroundings more intensely than she would have wished (hypervigilance).

The changes in PTSD symptomatology in the first three months after a major trauma suggest that in this period trauma beliefs are in the process of formation, and that they may be open to modification by the counselling strategies described in this chapter. But when PTSD symptoms persist beyond three months post-trauma, that is in cases of chronic PTSD, the trauma beliefs will have become more impermeable, repeated avoidance behaviours having served to confirm them. In addition, clients with chronic PTSD are more likely to default from counselling. The counselling task with clients suffering chronic PTSD is consequently often more difficult, and is the subject of the next chapter.

5

Counselling for Chronic PTSD – Illustrative Cases

Though the symptoms of PTSD – intrusive imagery, avoidance behaviour, disordered arousal – may be similar across trauma categories, the concerns expressed within the counselling sessions are often very different. And even within a category of major trauma – such as combat veteran, victim of sexual abuse, etc. – clients with PTSD will vary, their own particular view of their trauma will have some unique features, and the counsellor has to have the flexibility to adapt. For the first case of chronic PTSD – where symptoms had persisted for more than three months – we return to Paul whose typical PTSD symptoms were described in chapter 1 and a cognitive-behavioural formulation of whose difficulties was presented in chapter 2.

Paul – chronic PTSD following a disaster

As mentioned earlier, Paul, his cousin and nephew were in the crowd at the Hillsborough football stadium disaster in which ninety-five people died. Six months after the tragedy he was referred to a counsellor. The details that emerged from the first two interviews with Paul are summarized in Box 5.1. The headings of Box 5.1 form a useful pro forma. Paul experienced intense PTSD symptoms within days of the tragedy and these symptoms had continued unabated in the six months before the referral. Thus in Box 5.1 'Chronic PTSD' is selected. Paul's marriage had broken up a year prior to the disaster and he had suffered severe depression and become suicidal, though he had it seems recovered from the depression by the time of the trauma (heading 5). There was no family history of anxiety disorder (heading 6). Paul's scores of 19 and 16 on the Intrusion and Avoidance sub-scales of the Impact of Event Scale (IES: Appendix A) are typical of many with PTSD. With regard to the Intrusion items on the IES he indicated that he often experienced pictures about it popping into his mind and that other things (such as crowds) kept making him think about the

Box 5.1   *Case summary of Paul*

1   *Major trauma:* Hillsborough football stadium disaster
2   *Date of major trauma:* 15 April 1989
3   *Date of referral:* October 1989
4   *Acute, delayed or chronic PTSD:* Chronic
5   *Pre-trauma personality or psychological disturbance:* Depression
6   *Family history of anxiety disorder:* Yes/No
7   *Impact of Event Scale (IES):*

> Intrusion: 19
> Avoidance: 16

8   *Perceived support:*

	Friends	Family
Tangible	Poor	Not applicable
Emotional	Poor	Good

9   *Coping responses:*
  (a)   *How is client handling hassles?:* Disengagement. Rage
  (b)   *How is client handling distressing emotions?:* Anger at self
10   *Medication:*   Antidepressant   Prothiaden,   taken spasmodically
11   *Trauma beliefs from Trauma Belief Inventory held to be 'absolutely' or 'mostly' true:*

> It is dangerous to get close to anyone because they always hurt or exploit you.
> I will never be able to lead a normal life, the damage is permanent.
> I've lost a part of myself.
> I feel responsible for the bad things that happen to me.
> There is something wrong with me.
> Other people can never understand how I feel.
> I see this world as a bad place to live in.
> I don't like myself.
> I feel isolated from others.
> I believe that I over-reacted to what happened to me.

trauma. On the Avoidance sub-scale he indicated he often tried to remove it from memory, tried to stay away from reminders of it and was aware that he still had lots of feelings about it, but did not deal with them.

Though Paul had a wide circle of friends and they were in regular contact with him after the trauma, he did not perceive them as a support but as an irritation. By the time of referral he had become even more irritated with them because he now saw them as backing away from him. His main source of positive emotional support (heading 8) was his elderly mother and her disabled female friend, though they could not help him tangibly, for example with finance, now that he was off sick from work. Paul's way of dealing with life's daily hassles was to ignore them, particularly bills. If he had to confront a problem he flew into a rage. He kept telling himself to pull himself together and saw himself as coping less well than others, for example the relatives who went to the football match with him (heading 9). His general practitioner had prescribed medication, the antidepressant Prothiaden, but Paul had only been taking this occasionally 'on a bad day', because of the dry mouth the tablets gave him (heading 10). The themes running through the trauma beliefs that serve to maintain the distress were ones of hopelessness, isolation and being under threat (heading 11).

The following extract from the second interview with Paul focuses on avoidance issues, a key feature of PTSD.

Counsellor: How have things been since our last session?
Paul: Not bad.
Counsellor: What, sometimes better than others?
Paul: Yes, that's right.
Counsellor: When were the better times?
Paul: Like you said last week I have got to begin life again. So I took my mother and her friend for a drive to the Delamere Forest. They enjoyed it, chattering away. I liked seeing them happy.

Disengagement from potential sources of enjoyment is usually a problem in PTSD. At the end of Paul's first session a homework assignment had been negotiated about taking his mother and friend for a drive. Other homework possibilities were discussed, such as going to the pub with friends, but at this stage Paul was too fearful of crowds to agree to this. In the next extract it can be seen that Paul's avoidance is not confined to observable behaviours but that there is also a mental avoidance.

Counsellor: So it was worth making the effort of going to the Forest?
Paul: Yes it was.
Counsellor: What were the bad times?
[*Paul's eyes fill up and a tear trickles down his face.*]

Counsellor [*Pauses for Paul to continue.*]

Paul: Just the thought of coming here brings it all back. I wasn't too bad until yesterday, when I started thinking of why I was coming here today. I'm better off if I don't think about it.

Counsellor: Can you avoid thinking about it?

Paul: Not really, it's always there, though sometimes it's more at the back of your mind if you're busy.

Counsellor: Maybe it's a bit like having back trouble. You can get by in a fashion, for example picking things up from the floor without bending your back. Then sometimes, you turn quickly or lift something too heavy and the pain is excruciating. You can go on in this way for maybe years but your back would get steadily worse. Trouble is if you choose to go into hospital for your back and they put you on traction, to begin with you would feel worse. It is only in the long run that you are likely to feel better. Coming to see me is rather like that; for many people it brings the memory of the trauma forcibly to mind. But precisely because it causes such pain we need to re-examine the memory and ensure it is properly filed away. Again it is short-term pain for long-term gain.

Paul: I see what you mean, but will I get better?

Following the principle that you become more committed to what you verbalize, the counsellor starts the above extract by restating the gains for Paul of being active, and Paul gives his agreement. The counsellor then goes on to take seriously Paul's confusion and distress. Paul has come to the counsellor for relief from his pain, only to find that in some respects it has intensified. The counsellor has to provide the client with a convincing rationale to help him tolerate the increased discomfort. The engagement of the client in counselling depends in part on the generation of hope, and it is this which is addressed in the next extract.

Counsellor: Many people do get a lot better after counselling. But it is a marathon made up of lots of small steps. You've made a good start with your trip to the Forest.

Paul: I can't go on like I have been doing.

Counsellor: What makes you say that?

Paul: Others lost friends and relatives at Hillsborough and I didn't, but they are getting on with their lives.

Counsellor: Are you saying they are all getting on with their lives?

Paul: Well, there was a bloke who lost his daughter at Hillsborough on the TV last week.

Counsellor: Would someone chosen to be on TV be typical?

Paul: Well, no. But my cousin and nephew that I was with are back at work now.

Counsellor: Are they the same as before?

Paul: My cousin is, he never stops talking about Hillsborough. But my nephew will not talk about it to anyone, he's like a bear with a sore head, he used to be very placid and easygoing.

Counsellor: So though they are back at work they sound like they have been affected.

Paul: Now I come to think of it we are probably all scarred.
Counsellor: I guess most people would be affected by such a disaster. How bad it is might depend on how much you have had on your plate previously.
Paul: The ex-wife you mean, she didn't even visit me in hospital or send a card.

Here the counsellor's concern is to counter Paul's implied belief that he must be specially weak to come for counselling. If this were not countered Paul would be likely to default from counselling.

The counsellor challenges Paul's over-generalization that 'Others with worse trauma have coped better.' Note, the counsellor does not directly refute the belief, but encourages Paul to question the validity of it himself, by posing a question. Similarly the counsellor challenges Paul's selective abstraction that because his cousin and nephew have returned to work they have coped much better than he has. The client's hope is maintained by the counsellor locating his increased distress within the framework of the counselling programme and suggesting that it is temporary.

Finally it is acknowledged that pre-trauma disorders such as depression can function as 'fault-lines' (even when as in Paul's case the symptoms had disappeared immediately before the disaster) along which the individual may break down in the wake of a major trauma. Paul's beliefs about his personal weakness surfaced again when the issue of medication was discussed.

Counsellor: Are you taking any medication?
Paul: Well, my GP gave me these. [*Hands the counsellor a container marked Prothiaden.*]
Counsellor: Do you take them in the way prescribed?
Paul: I just take one when I am feeling bad, usually at night.
Counsellor: What stops you taking them as prescribed?
Paul: Well I don't want to get addicted. I want to do the job myself. I did take them like it says for the first week but I got a dry mouth.

There is evidence that antidepressants can be effective in the treatment of PTSD in relieving symptoms of intrusive imagery, but that they do not seem to affect other features of PTSD such as emotional numbing (Frank et al., 1990). Often, however, a patient has not understood or has not been told by his medical practitioner the mode of action of antidepressants; specifically, that they work by building up to an appropriate level and that maximum benefit from the medication is not likely to be achieved in less than three weeks. Frank et al. (1990) recommended that a therapeutic dose of the antidepressant should be taken for a continuous period of eight weeks. Further they indicate that patients who do not respond to one class of antidepressant may respond to another. There are two main classes of antidepressants, tricyclic antidepressants (TCAs) and monoamine oxidase inhibitors (MAOIs). Within the TCAs there are a further two groups, those antidepressants whose mechanism of action seem to resemble amitriptyline and those which resemble imipramine. The taking of antidepressants may be encouraged by furnishing this information. In so doing it may be necessary to assuage the client's fears of becoming addicted by reassurance that serious risk of addiction only applies to tranquillizers, not to antidepressants.

Client compliance with medication is not just a question of understanding their efficacy and *modus operandi*; it also depends on the meaning the client gives to taking drugs, as the following extract shows.

> *Paul:* Now you've explained, I can see that I ought to be taking the tablets properly. But I want to do the job myself.
> *Counsellor:* The tablets are very unlikely to do the whole job for you anyway. But if you've got one problem less on your plate, say a reduction in flashbacks, then you might have some energy to start beginning to overcome some of the things you have been avoiding. The medication could help to get you started.
> *Paul:* Well I suppose if I am not on the tablets for ever, then I can give them a try.
> *Counsellor:* As I mentioned, it may take a couple of weeks for the antidepressants to have an effect. Maybe in the meantime you might control the flashbacks with an elastic band on your wrist.
> *Paul:* An elastic band!
> *Counsellor:* Yes, try each time you get a picture of the horrors of Hillsborough pulling the elastic band and letting it go, saying to yourself 'I will watch the "video" of the disaster properly for twenty minutes before the late evening news. I will give it quality attention then rather than let it constantly meander through my mind.'
> *Paul:* By the time the late evening news comes around I probably won't want to bother.
> *Counsellor:* That's up to you. If you think it is important to watch the video properly you will. If you don't watch the video maybe you are saying it's not that important to watch.
> *Paul:* I will give it a try.

From Box 5.1, it can be seen that one of Paul's trauma beliefs was that he would 'never be able to lead a normal life, the damage is permanent'. In the second interview the counsellor encouraged Paul to view this belief as an hypothesis and not as a fact. To test out the validity of this hypothesis, Paul agreed to try to arrange to go for a drink with a friend at a time when the pub was empty. Paul appreciated that this would be a first step towards a normal life and accordingly this became the homework assignment. Many of the trauma beliefs in Box 5.1 played a major part in Paul's coexisting depression and relationship problems. We meet Paul again in chapter 7 when these difficulties are addressed. Next a more common type of major trauma is considered – physical assault.

Jane and Sean – chronic PTSD following an assault

Jane, a policewoman, and her male colleague Sean had become friendly with the organizers of a pensioners' club which was on their beat. One Christmas, when they had just come off duty, they went to the pensioners' Christmas party to which they had been invited. After an hour or two they left, but as they were walking away they were attacked from behind by youths brandishing baseball bats. Sean was beaten up and knocked unconscious and sustained a fractured skull. Jane was very badly bruised as she tried to stop the attack on Sean. Sean remained unconscious for a few days, did recover physically, but subsequently exhibited PTSD symptoms. Jane's head was badly bruised and at the time of referral, four months after the assault, she still felt she had a numb patch on the top of her head. Since the assault she had become very introverted, scarcely ventured out and experienced regular flashbacks of the assault. In particular she felt compelled to relive the events of that day from beginning to end, not just the assault itself. The details of her case are summarized in Box 5.2.

The following extract is from the fourth counselling session with Jane and the main focus is on attempting to control the intrusive imagery:

> *Counsellor*: At last week's session we left it that you would shout *Stop!* to yourself every time you caught yourself dwelling on the day of the assault.
>
> *Jane:* Well it didn't really work. I was too much into replaying it all before it occurred to me to shout *Stop!*
>
> *Counsellor:* Would it help at all if you put, say, a red dot on your watch, so that it would serve as a reminder to you to interrupt the flow of the video?
>
> *Jane:* I don't think it would work, it just comes on me.
>
> *Counsellor:* Is it not worth trying?
>
> *Jane:* I don't think so.
>
> *Counsellor:* What about trying what I originally suggested, putting an elastic band on your wrist, and pulling it and letting go when you start the replays?
>
> *Jane:* As I said I would be too embarrassed, people would see me with an elastic band on and they would wonder why.
>
> *Counsellor:* Would you be bothered if you saw someone else with an elastic band on?
>
> *Jane:* No.

Box 5.2   *Case summary of Jane*

1 *Major trauma:* Unprovoked physical assault
2 *Date of major trauma:* Christmas 1988
3 *Date of referral:* April 1989
4 *Acute, delayed or chronic PTSD:* Chronic
5 *Pre-trauma personality or psychological disturbance:* None
6 *Family history of anxiety disorder:* Yes/No
7 *Impact of Event Scale (IES):*

Intrusion: 16
Avoidance: 15

8 *Perceived support:*

	Friends	Family
Tangible	Poor	Good
Emotional	Poor	Good

9 *Coping responses:*
   (a) *How is client handling hassles?:* Disengagement
   (b) *How is client handling distressing emotions?:* Self-blame
10 *Medication:* None
11 *Trauma beliefs from Trauma Belief Inventory held to be 'absolutely' or 'mostly' true:*
      I've lost a part of myself.
      I feel responsible for the bad things that happen to me.
      There is something wrong with me.
      I see this world as a bad place to live in.
      I feel like there isn't anything I can do to manage what happens to me.

Counsellor: Well, why should they be bothered?
Jane: I suppose so.
Counsellor: What is it then that stops you using this strategy?
Jane: I know it just wouldn't work, they [the intrusive recollections] are too powerful.

In the above extract the counsellor has tried unsuccessfully to encourage use of simple 'first aid' methods of dealing with intrusive imagery. But Jane does not apparently expect a positive outcome from these endeavours. Rather than badger Jane into further intrusive thought/image coping procedures, for a homework assignment the counsellor inquires further about the meaning of her mental video.

Counsellor: What do you think makes you play the whole day of the assault over in your mind and not just the assault itself?

Jane: There we were. It was Christmas, we were going to a party in our own time, we had a good laugh with the pensioners and then this happens. It shows you just can't really win. There was no point in it. Why?

Counsellor: Maybe it is as if you're thinking 'If I watch the video I will find the answer to why.'

Jane: It seems like it, doesn't it. It's stupid.

Counsellor: How do you mean stupid?

Jane: Well there are yobos, you've just got to accept it and get on with it.

Counsellor: Maybe what you're balking at is that a yobo should affect you personally at Christmas.

Jane: When you put it like that it sounds daft but I have always really liked Christmas.

Counsellor: Maybe it's the energy you get from occasions like Christmas that makes you feel able to cope with the horrors you see as a policewoman, and if they are knocked you run out of steam. Perhaps in the video where you recall being at the party you are trying to remind yourself that life can be good.

Jane: It is accepting the good and the bad side by side.

Counsellor: Yes, avoiding saying that the bad cancels out the good or vice versa, they are both part of living. Maybe it would be possible to, as it were, watch a headline summary of the video rather than the whole thing. Perhaps each time the assault comes to mind you try shouting to yourself 'There's the good and the bad.'

Jane: Yes, I'll try that.

Whilst clients wish to be rid of intrusive imagery because of the distressing memories it invokes and because it impedes engaging in normal activities, as the above extract shows there is also a need to try and make sense of what happened. The attempt to understand the trauma necessitates some focus on it. Jane's initial negative response to controlling the intrusive imagery was in effect saying 'I have important questions to sort out first.' This is in line with Epstein's suggestion (Epstein, 1990) discussed in chapter 2, that the effect of a major trauma is to forcibly raise questions about the dangerousness and meaningfulness of the world. It is important to examine what possible function the intrusive imagery may be playing. In some instances it is more obvious than in others. For example, Sam, a bus driver, knocked down and killed a woman, and subsequently experienced intrusive imagery of the event. In fact the old lady had a sight problem and simply stepped into the path of the bus. Sam was totally exonerated from blame. He prided himself on being a careful driver and it was suggested to him in counselling that his intrusive imagery was based on a belief that 'I must have been able to play it differently' which in turn was based on a more general belief that 'Bad things are avoidable if you take care.' Sam was able to contain the intrusive imagery using the elastic band once he realized that in watching the video he was searching for the impossible.

Returning to the assault on the police officers, Sean had, like Jane, suffered PTSD symptoms from the time of the assault. In his case, however, it was not obvious what the function of his intrusive imagery was. The following extract is taken from the fourth interview with Sean.

Counsellor: How have the videos of the assault been?

Sean: A little bit better using the elastic band, but not much.

Counsellor: What is actually being shown in the video? [*Sean becomes tearful, looks up at the ceiling to control his tears and pauses before proceeding.*]

Sean: I just see baseball bats coming down on me and I am helpless. I am thinking 'This is it, what about my wife and the baby?' Then I just passed out. The memories of it just leave me devastated.

Counsellor: I can see that replaying the video is certainly a way of reminding yourself the world can be really dangerous.

Sean: But I already know that, why do I have to go over it?

Counsellor: I am not sure why, but repeating it doesn't seem to help. Perhaps we can look at another way of containing the imagery and then exposing you to it so it becomes less overpowering.

Sean: How do you mean?

Counsellor: Some people find it helpful to make a fifteen- to twenty-minute audio tape of their assault and their thoughts and feelings surrounding it. It can be very painful to make such a tape but instead of letting thoughts of the assault constantly drift through your mind you can dispel the fog by saying 'I will listen to it all properly on tape later.' If you play the tape daily, then after two to three weeks you will become less bothered by the events and feelings expressed in it.

Sean: I've got to try something.

Counsellor: When you begin listening to the tape it might be as well to have your wife present. You're likely to find it pretty painful at first. You will be tempted to switch off the tape at the most distressing part, but you must not switch it off until you have reached a less distressing point.

The procedure described here follows the general principles of desensitization – that a fear may be overcome by exposure to it and, importantly, by maintaining the exposure until the distress is reduced. Subsequent exposures result in a gradual attenuation of distress. The acceptability of the procedure to the client, however, can be problematic and has to be carefully explored in advance. For a trauma to be properly processed it is necessary to evoke intermediate levels of fear or distress. The production of overwhelming fear here is counterproductive (as is a trauma tape that evokes no distress). Insurance strategies against overwhelming distress have to be developed. In some instances the client may only be prepared to make and listen to the tape in the presence of the counsellor before using it at home.

Where the trauma involves an atrocity committed in combat, it is usually safer for the procedure to be carried out in hospital. Although it is problematic as to whether the perpetrator of an atrocity may properly be said to meet the full *DSM-III-R* criteria for PTSD they can exhibit very similar symptoms to full PTSD (Kruppa, 1991), and for such persons the use of an imaginal exposure tape may also be particularly distressing. Again the procedure is probably safest if performed on an in-patient basis, where the client's reactions, which could be of a suicidal nature, may be carefully monitored. Kruppa (1991) reports successfully treating a patient incarcerated for raping and strangling his victim. Six years after the event he began to experience intrusive flashbacks. The patient's script of the event was recorded on tape and played back through headphones over the course of five one-hour exposure sessions. This programme completely eliminated the patient's flashbacks and the improvement was maintained eighteen months later. It should be stressed that the goal here was to eliminate intrusive imagery and not to assuage anxiety or remorse associated with the original event, as the latter may have a useful deterrent effect.

Some clients can become very distressed at the mere mention of any imaginal exposure procedure. The topic should not be explored in depth until the client has developed some trust and rapport with the counsellor, and has had some success with other strategies for influencing mood. Even then some clients are still resistant to making a tape of their trauma, and this can be the case even with the safeguard that a tape will be used only in the counselling session.

An alternative strategy in these circumstances is to ask the client in the counselling session to begin imagining their trauma when the counsellor says 'Start', for the client to raise a hand at the point when the imagery becomes unbearable, and then to use controlled breathing. The client is told to use the controlled breathing until the imagery becomes more manageable and to raise a hand again when this happens. The counsellor times how long the client endures the image before raising a hand, and also monitors the time taken for the imagery to become manageable. This is then followed by counsellor feedback of the form 'That was good, you managed to stay with the picture for two minutes, and it took you just a minute to begin to regain your balance.' The point for the counsellor to emphasize is that the client *did* stay with the image (albeit for a limited period) and *did* cope after a short period, and so now has access to a coping strategy. The experiment enhances the client's sense of self-efficacy about the desensitization procedure in a way that is more profound than mere persuasion or an encouragement to engage in the procedures. Often clients express surprise that they coped so well but complain of being left with some residual symptoms, for example 'It was OK but it has left me now with a tightening in the throat that takes me ages to get rid of once it starts.' The therapist may then have to distil another coping procedure to be used to follow on from the controlled breathing. Preferably this extra procedure should be one that has already worked for the client in containing or postponing intrusive imagery, for example the elastic band strategy, or a fantasy. One client when troubled by intrusive images dealt with them by using the supplementary technique of imagining herself lying on a raft on a river with the sun beating down, with tall trees on the banks of the river, closing her eyes and floating along, listening only to the rippling of the water and feeling the heat of her body. For homework, the client should be instructed to practise daily, at a prearranged time, the experiment that they successfully completed in the counselling session, if necessary supplementing the controlled breathing with a further coping strategy.

It should be stressed to clients that the first week of using the imaginal procedure is usually the worst, and in many ways the effects are often akin to what a heavy smoker will go through in the first week after stopping. They may experience heightened irritability, increased tension and disturbed sleep. This can lead the client to question why they are bothering with this procedure at all, particularly as they had just begun to feel a little better since the commencement of counselling! It is imperative that the counsellor acknowledge the client's doubts and assist the verbalizing of them, otherwise the client may well default. The counsellor can stress that usually after about fifteen days of the procedure the client becomes more comfortable with the imagery, but, rather like the ex-cigarette smoker, after such a period there will still be some discomfort, though it will be manageable. To ease matters for the client the counsellor might suggest that their spouse be present, particularly in the first week of using the procedure. Again the counsellor might help the client further extend the repertoire of coping strategies for the residual symptoms, for example by teaching the client to distract themselves with computerized pocket games which give feedback on their performance.

The desensitization procedure can be usefully supplemented using biofeedback. The client can then judge whether the coping strategy which might be necessary to keep their fear response to an intermediate level (for example, the breathing routine for Sean, above) is working. In the following extract the counsellor demonstrates biofeedback to Sean.

> *Counsellor:* What I would like to do is an experiment to see how a tape is likely to work with you. In particular what parts of the tape get to you and how your coping strategy works. [*The counsellor wraps the Velcro pads of the biofeedback device to two fingers of one hand and rests Sean's hand on the desk.*] Start imagining the events of that Christmas, follow it right through to the assault and beyond. When it gets bad use the breathing routine. Try it for a couple of minutes, I will tell you when to stop.

After a minute the biofeedback device is emitting a high-pitched note. The counsellor notices Sean put his hand on his stomach and begin the breathing routine. Sean continues this for two minutes. After a further minute the counsellor tells him to stop.

> *Counsellor:* How was that?
> *Sean:* As I began to picture the baseball bats coming down on me this [*points to the biofeedback device*] started screaming. But my doing the breathing exercise brought the noise down.
> *Counsellor:* So you can influence your distress?
> *Sean:* Yes, that's true.
> *Counsellor:* Maybe try using the biofeedback device in conjunction with the audio tape.

Portable biofeedback devices can be bought reasonably cheaply. An in-session demonstration of the technique is a very effective way of ensuring compliance with a homework assignment. If a client has particularly dry skin some of the cheaper feedback devices do not seem effective, so it is important to check out the device in the session. Progress with the desensitization procedure was reviewed at the sixth session with Sean.

> *Counsellor:* How is the audio tape going?
> *Sean:* I have used it every day now for the past two weeks and the pictures don't come as often now and I can handle them much better now.
> *Counsellor:* Are you still using the biofeedback device?
> *Sean:* Not now, it was really useful for the first week it helped me get

to grips with the worst parts. I have found this last week I have not needed it, the breathing exercise alone is good enough. It has just got steadily better.

It typically takes around fifteen days of exposure for a tolerance of the intrusive imagery to be established using these strategies. An alternative to the fifteen-minute audio tape is to have the client use the three-minute loop tapes used for telephone answering machines. The advantage of a loop tape is that the client can have repeated exposure to the most traumatic aspects of the experience within the fifteen-minute exposure period. Initially, some clients may only be able to tolerate a single daily playing of a three-minute tape. The counsellor should ascertain the pace the client can cope with before setting a homework assignment using the tapes.

In some instances clients find the practice of even brief imaginal exposure too debilitating. An alternative is to embed the trauma in a relaxation tape that is played daily. This was the case with the next client, Marina, a student working as a part-time barmaid.

Marina – chronic PTSD following sexual assault

Marina had been pestered for some weeks by a newcomer to the pub she worked in, asking for a date. She had politely refused. One evening as she walked home she was assaulted and raped at knifepoint by this man as she crossed an area of waste land on a short-cut home. She had considerable guilt feelings about having taken the short-cut, exacerbated by an insensitive comment she had heard from a policeman as she was taken to a centre for medical examination to the effect that 'It takes two to tango.'

At her third therapy session Marina verbalized the details of the assault for about three minutes, reaching a level of distress of 10 on a 10-point self-report scale. Using controlled breathing she was able to bring the distress down to 8 in two minutes. This successful practice was recorded, and she was given it as a homework exercise. However, she found that after playing the tape, although her distress lessened before she switched it off, she was too debilitated for the rest of the day and had a recurrence of nightmares. When she arrived for the next session she was very distressed. The counsellor attempted to verbalize her likely misgivings.

> *Counsellor:* That sort of experience could well make you feel like giving up.
> *Marina:* It did.
> *Counsellor:* Perhaps we did too much too soon. We can take a smaller dose first and so the cost to you will be less and the benefit may not

Box 5.3 *Marina's relaxation tape*

Just get yourself nice and comfortable, you will soon find yourself sinking more and more into the chair ... you will find any tensions just flowing out of you, so that your body becomes limp ... you could lift your arms but they are beginning to feel warm and heavy ... you could lift your legs but they are beginning to feel warm and heavy ... tensions are flowing away ... your blood pressure is going down ... your pulse rate is slowing ... your breathing is becoming slower and slower ... you're sinking into relaxation ... you might picture yourself in a country lane on one of your rambles ... it's a summer's day ... the sun has come out after the rain ... as you walk along you can see the bluebells gently blowing back and forth in the light breeze ... you can see a beautiful deep red rose ... there are a few raindrops on the deep red rose glistening in the sunlight ... it's beautiful ... the fragrance of the rose fills your whole being ... you touch the rose and marvel at its velvet texture ... you walk on down the lane ... and on further and further ... you take a rest by a tree and feel your back sink into it as you look up at the puffy white clouds drifting across the sky ... your eyelids slowly begin to shut ... you're sitting comfortably in a seat in a cinema ... you're munching your favourite chocolate ... you can feel the rich smooth taste in your mouth ... in the picture you see a young woman crossing waste ground ... a man comes from behind and pushes her to the ground and begins to rape her ... the picture has got stuck there, it's frozen on the screen ... you munch through more chocolate whilst the picture is fixed ... it's getting boring, they are taking a long time to fix the picture ... you start yawning ... your conscious mind drifts back to that red rose ... you remember its smell and touch and as you do so any tightness anywhere in your body you can let melt away ... you're looking again at the raindrops sparkling in the sunlight ... the bluebells blowing gently in the breeze ... as you relax allow your eyelids to become heavier ... you're going down a series of escalators in a large shop ... you can feel the hard rubber of the moving handrail ... down and down you go ... with each floor you feel more relaxed ... in a few seconds I will begin to count backwards from 5 to 1 ... when I reach 1 you will be able to open your eyes ... you will feel awake, alert, aware, 5 ... 4 ... 3 ... 2 ... 1.

be that much different to what you would have got eventually with the tape.

Marina: What you mean like a lower dosage of drug with fewer side-effects?

Counsellor: That's it.

Marina: How do we do that?

Counsellor: Well we can put the trauma in a relaxation or hypnosis tape so that you can digest it better.

Marina: I don't mind relaxation, but hypnosis!

Counsellor: What gets to you about hypnosis?

Marina: It makes you do stage tricks.

Counsellor: Only if it is directed at stage tricks. A hypodermic syringe can be used to give penicillin and save someone's life, or by a drug addict to inject heroin.

Marina: I see. But what is hypnosis?

Counsellor: Well the truth is we don't really know where relaxation ends and hypnosis begins. In hypnosis it seems you alter how much you are with us. It is rather like daydreaming: whilst you're daydreaming you are not quite here but are attending to something else. In the relaxation/hypnosis tape I will want you to attend to information that takes the sting out of the trauma, as well as the trauma itself.

Marina: Right.

Box 5.3 gives a transcript of the tape constructed for Marina. The dots indicate pauses of around five seconds. Marina was asked to play the tape daily and to record on a scale from 1 (no distress) to 10 (extreme distress) the high point of her distress and also how she felt when the tape had finished. In the first week her high points were typically 9s, with an end-of-tape score around 7. However, by the end of the second week her high points were typically 8s and her end-of-tape scores about 5, which was a level at which she could function. If the trauma scene incorporated in a relaxation/hypnosis tape does not, at least initially, produce severe distress, that is high point scores of 9 or 10, then it is unlikely that salient parts of the trauma are being targeted. In such a case there is a need for more extensive exploration of the trauma in order to identify and integrate into the tape the relevant aspects. A client may also make progress with the relaxation/hypnosis tape that has been constructed, but only relieving some aspects of the intrusive imagery and not others. Those aspects of the imagery that have not diminished ought to be integrated into a new tape. This is essentially a stepwise desensitization procedure to avoid overwhelming the client and risking defaulting.

Gillian – chronic PTSD from witnessing an armed robbery

Gillian was taking her four-year-old granddaughter shopping and first called in at the bank in the High Street for cash. As she rounded the corner where the bank was she literally bumped into two armed robbers coming out of the bank. They wore stockings on their heads and carried shotguns. One of the robbers pointed his gun at Gillian and she stood terrified, looking down the barrel, then they sped off in a waiting car. Gillian screamed hysterically, and then composed herself as her granddaughter began to cry. The police arrived at the scene, and Gillian and her granddaughter were taken to the police station for further questioning. Five months later Gillian was referred to a counsellor by her general practitioner, who was concerned that Gillian had become virtually housebound, terrified to go out. In addition, her harmonious family relationships had deteriorated considerably. She had become uncharacteristically irritable and had taken to sleeping with the light on. She couldn't stand to be in the house by herself. Flashbacks of the event were still a regular occurrence. The case summary for Gillian differed from Jane's in Box 5.2 in just two respects, first the nature of the major trauma – witnessing an armed robbery rather than suffering an assault – and second, Gillian, unlike Jane, had been prescribed medication.

Gillian had been prescribed carbamazepine and this did seem to reduce her intrusive symptoms after two weeks, but she developed a rash, so its use was discontinued. Her general practitioner did not wish to prescribe benzodiazepines both because of the paucity of evidence as to their efficacy with PTSD and because of their potential for addiction. Subsequently Gillian was offered antidepressants but declined them be use she wanted to 'get over the problem myself'. She had always been a very resourceful person.

There is some evidence to support the efficacy of both antidepressants and carbamazepine in the treatment of PTSD but less evidence in favour of benzodiazepines (Lipper, 1990). However there is further evidence from a study of the treatment of depression that those high in learned resourcefulness do better with counselling whilst those low in resourcefulness do better with medication (Simons et al., 1984). For those high in resourcefulness taking medication can be a major challenge to their identity, nullifying any pharmacological gains. The following extract is taken from the third counselling session with Gillian and the main item on the agreed agenda for that session was her avoidance behaviour.

Counsellor: So the hardest thing for you to do would be to go into the bank by yourself is that right?

Gillian: Yes.

Counsellor: What can you do by yourself at the moment?

Gillian: Nothing. I can't even stay in the house by myself.

Counsellor: What would happen if you did?

Gillian: I would just go to pieces.

Counsellor: If you were left for two minutes would you go to pieces?

Gillian: Well, maybe not.

Counsellor: What about for five minutes?

Gillian: I don't know.

Counsellor: What about being alone for ten minutes?

Gillian: I think I would be a nervous wreck by the end of that.

Counsellor: OK, if our starting point was to stay in the house for five minutes each day by yourself, week by week we could build up the time you spend by yourself. Then we could go on to you gradually going greater and greater distances by yourself until eventually you can go to the bank by yourself. What do you think?

Gillian: I will give it a try

Counsellor: What could you plan to do in your five minutes a day alone, this week?

Gillian: I suppose I could put on some favourite music very loudly, then I wouldn't feel as alone.

Counsellor: OK, we could start with that. It might turn out that we should have started with two and a half minutes but we don't really know until we have a try. We can always change the starting point if needs be.

In the above extract the counsellor is clarifying at one extreme what behavioural task would constitute a return to normality and at the other what just might presently be manageable to the client. A major theme of the counselling programme is the negotiation of 'stepping stones' in between the extremes. The counsellor also insures against failure experiences by suggesting that so-called 'failures' simply mean that a smaller-sized step has to be taken. Failure is not to be seen as an attribute of the client.

At the fourth counselling session the counsellor was surprised to learn that Gillian had stepped up by five minutes a day the time she spent alone in the house, so that by the time of the session she was now managing half an hour a day. The counsellor congratulated her but cautioned that it was as important not to go too fast as to avoid going too slow. The former could produce demoralization if she was not careful. For her homework assignment at the end of the fourth session it was agreed that she would attempt a daily walk to her local shop, a distance of 200 metres from her house. Gillian felt she would be happy in the shop because she knew the proprietor. The following is an extract from that part of the session.

Counsellor: What would you do if you felt panicky, say, half-way to the shop?

Gillian: Run like hell!

Counsellor: How would you feel then?

Gillian: Well if I ran home, disappointed, but if I ran to the shop, I would feel at least I had done it.

Counsellor: Sometimes it helps people to hang on in these situations if they focus on something and keep describing it in detail. For example you might try and look at, say, a cigarette pack in the gutter, imagine the feel of the silver cigarette paper, the way in which it would glisten in the sun, the sound of rustling the paper, the smell of the tobacco. Really, anything that could engage all your senses.

Gillian: I think I would just want to get the hell down the road as quickly as possible!

Counsellor: The trouble with that is you deprive yourself of the opportunity to disconfirm your belief that it is dangerous to go at a measured pace down the road. Next time you will run again because you still don't know that nothing catastrophic will happen by going steadily.

Gillian: I see what you mean, so it's important to do it steadily.

Counsellor: That's right.

In the above extract, although the task set is a behavioural one, going to the local shop daily, her ability to do this routinely depends on changing her belief about the dangers of going at a normal pace. In this way the cognitive and behavioural elements are intertwined. The fifth session begins with a review of the homework assignment.

Counsellor: How did you manage going out?

Gillian: Fine, I went to the shops every day.

Counsellor: How did you handle any panic feelings?

Gillian: Some days I just counted flowers in bloom in the gardens I passed and on other days the number of children playing in the street. It was OK except on Saturday when the shop was crowded, I got flustered, but stuck it out, bought a newspaper and returned home.

Counsellor: Do you think crowds are likely to be a problem for you?

Gillian: Not really, I have just got to know what to expect. I can't cope with surprises. I have got to prepare mentally for things.

Meichenbaum's (1985) Self-Instruction Training (SIT) is an excellent way of helping a client prepare for a difficult task. The client derives coping statements from each of four categories, which she then repeats to herself. An example is given in Box 5.4. The counsellor goes on to integrate SIT into Gillian's mental rehearsal in the following extract.

Counsellor: I can see the need to be prepared for things. In fact there is a special way of being prepared called Self-Instruction Training. [*Counsellor describes the first three categories of SIT.*] But you seem

---

Box 5.4 *Gillian's coping statements*

- *Preparing for the stressor:* 'It never turns out as bad as I expected'; 'Just keep cool.'
- *Coping with feelings of being overwhelmed:* 'OK my tension is pretty high at the moment, nine or ten. I will just distract myself for a couple of minutes, and then take another reading.'
- *Coping with success:* 'I will reward myself by buying something nice.'
- *Coping with failure:* 'Some steps are bound to be too big but you can't know until you try, it's not the end of the world.'

---

to be saying that if there is a surprise you will not be able to cope.

Gillian: Yes, that's right.

Counsellor: That must get you tensed up before you go out?

Gillian: It does.

Counsellor: But can you have a solution for everything in advance?

Gillian: I suppose not.

Counsellor: Sounds like you are attempting the impossible, over-preparing rather than preparing.

Gillian: I do just feel so exhausted.

Counsellor: How did you use to handle surprises? For example if you suddenly found that you did not have some essential ingredient for the evening meal and could not obtain it?

Gillian: I would always sort something out somehow.

Counsellor: So you were prepared for and could accept partial solutions to a problem. It wasn't a case of 'It's either the making of a meal I originally wanted or I am a failure.'

Gillian: We would always get by.

Counsellor: It sounds like having the surprise of the armed robbery has made you feel you have to have solutions to all surprises. You are over-generalizing because you think you did not have a solution to seeing the robbers. You seem to have concluded that you don't have solutions to any surprises. Does that make sense?

Gillian: You've hit the nail on the head; deep down I do know I can sort things out. Somehow I should just remind myself of this.

Counsellor: The difficult bit I guess is telling yourself that the robbery was a one-off, an atypical event. It's very unlike the overwhelming majority of situations you would meet.

Box 5.5 *Practice summary – chronic PTSD*

1 The counsellor should emphasize that disengagement from tackling the trauma produces more discomfort in the long run than orienting oneself to resolving the trauma. It is a case of short-term pain bringing long-term gain.

2 The client may experience coming to an appointment as a revictimization because of the need to discuss the trauma. There is a need for the counsellor to acknowledge this explicitly or the client may default.

3 The generation of hope is crucial to engaging the client.

4 The client can to some extent be inoculated against slippage if the whole programme is characterized as 'two steps forward and one step back' and slips are conceptualized as learning experiences.

5 The counsellor will probably need to move flexibly between teaching strategies to manage various PTSD symptoms and examine the meaning of the trauma.

6 Imaginal desensitization using an audio tape should be introduced only after rapport has been established and containment and distraction techniques have proved insufficient. The tape should only be used in a supportive context.

7 Antidepressant medication may be a useful adjunct, and compliance with medication should be encouraged.

6

Counselling for PTSD from Prolonged Duress (PDSD) – Illustrative Cases

In *DSM-III-R*, PTSD is defined as a response to a major trauma. Indeed according to *DSM-III-R* a diagnosis of PTSD cannot be made if such an event has not occurred. But this raises two important questions. First, what makes an event traumatic as opposed to being simply stressful? Second, can an accumulation of stressors produce PTSD-like symptoms? The cases to be described in this chapter suggest an affirmative answer to the second question.

PTSD is a relatively newly defined disorder and there are naturally some 'growing pains' in its clarification and classification. The *DSM-III-R* criteria for PTSD are clearly applicable to major disasters, both natural and man-made, and to extreme invasive trauma such as sexual and physical assault and other violations of individual integrity. Indeed the presumption, supported by the syntax of the definition (criterion B speaks of 'the event', criterion C of 'the trauma'), is of a single, overwhelming experience of great intensity but limited duration. However it has been claimed that a sequence of individually less intense events can also lead to PTSD-like symptoms. Ravin and Boal (1989) cite a number of cases including the example given in Box 6.1 (from Ravin and Boal, 1989: 14).

Ravin and Boal note that the precipitating stressor was only the last in a prolonged series of stressful circumstances and probably not in itself the most taxing. Certainly in this example the stressor is of lower intensity than those usually associated with PTSD, but nevertheless because of the duration of duress the same psychological effects are produced as with a more intense but briefer trauma. It may be that PTSD symptoms are the product of intensity times duration of distress, and that various combinations of the two factors may produce the same result. Low-intensity stressors persisting over a long duration would normally produce stress. But the predominant PTSD symptoms of avoidance behaviour and intrusive imagery may also be found occurring in response to enduring circumstances involving prolonged duress.

Box 6.1 *Ravin and Boal's example of PTSD from prolonged duress*

J.W., a 42 year old shipyard worker, had experienced, and survived for some four years, a series of devastating layoffs engendered by his employer's constantly shrinking business. He had consciously experienced embarrassment when meeting ex-fellow workers in the stores of the local area. With each layoff, J.W. had become progressively more anxious, a process that he attributed to uncertainty about the future and the resultant financial insecurity, should he be one of the unlucky ones.

In the aftermath of the most recent layoff, in which his son-in-law lost his job, J.W. explosively, and uncharacteristically, had words with his foreman over a trivial matter, told him off and walked off the job.

Once off the job, he was adamant in his refusal to return, going out of his way not to pass the yard. He was unable to read the news or watch the television for fear he would hear of additional layoffs. When his son-in-law or daughter visited, he would briefly greet them and then isolate himself. He was preoccupied with the intrusive recollection of scenes in which friends told him that they had been laid off. He was drinking beer at night in a desperate attempt to anaesthetize himself to sleep.

Such situations where PTSD symptoms arise because of prolonged duress we here term PDSD (prolonged duress stress disorder). It is possible that there are more cases of PDSD following everyday (relatively) low intensity traumas of long duration than there are those arising from the dramatic acute stressors which have heretofore been taken to be the hallmark of PTSD. PDSD may be applicable to many battered wives, or to the carer of a relative with a prolonged terminal illness. The first case illustration of cognitive-behavioural counselling for PDSD involves a female police sergeant, Disa.

Disa – PDSD from prolonged duress in the workplace

Counsellor: What seems to be the main problem?
Disa: I just can't take it any more. I've had enough of the job. [*Pause. Disa's tears flow down her cheeks.*]
Counsellor: What in particular gets to you?

> *Disa:* I was in my friend's, it was a month ago, her baby daughter's birthday. I had brought a present but I couldn't give it I just burst into tears when I saw the baby. That was the last straw.

The above is a typical introductory exchange: the client is afraid to put directly into words what is troubling her. The counsellor has to allow the client ample time to explicate the connections and the counsellor facilitates this with a 'Columbo-style' expression of befuddlement.

> *Counsellor:* You mentioned the job and your friend's daughter?
> *Disa:* I am sick of the job. I used to love it. I was off work eight months ago for three months. I had a slight physical injury on the knee, but I was really exhausted. I had had enough. I forced myself back but I just can't take it any more.
> *Counsellor:* Can't take which?
> *Disa:* There's too many memories. I can't get this picture of the baby out of my mind. Another colleague and I ended up rushing a baby and her mother to hospital but the baby was well dead when we arrived. We just sat on the bench outside the hospital for about half an hour. We didn't say much. I just hugged the mother and then we all went inside the hospital.
> *Counsellor:* It's incredibly sad when a baby dies.
> *Disa:* Oh, I have seen it all. Being a woman, I handle the child abuse cases. I have become quite an expert on child sexual abuse.
> *Counsellor:* Had the child you had taken to the hospital been abused?
> *Disa:* No, the mother, who lived virtually next door to the police station came running into the station with the baby. The baby looked ghastly, so we all set off immediately to the hospital. It was all such a waste. [*Long pause.*]
> *Disa:* In this job you are constantly swimming in the sewer of life.
> *Counsellor:* Have there been any good parts to the job in recent months?

Eight months previously Disa had clearly reached the state of being burnt out (see Maslach and Jackson, 1981). After a three-month absence she had returned to work feeling better. However, her working environment had not changed and the cumulative stressors of the following five months triggered the intrusive imagery (of the baby) and avoidance behaviour (not going to work).

> *Disa:* It was nice to be congratulated by my superintendent and the parents of a four-year-old toddler for the way in which I had looked after the little boy, when he lost his parents in the City Centre shopping crowds.
> *Counsellor:* So the job's not all black?
> *Disa:* No, years ago I thoroughly enjoyed it, but nowadays there is too much of the bad.
> *Counsellor:* Is that because you may have chosen to do more of the bad – going on special courses for sexual abuse, for example?

Disa: I think I might have been a fool, I have caused my own problems.

This extract highlights a common case of PDSD where the stressor is work related, the individual blames themselves and is aware that if they had chosen other options at an earlier stage they might not have been experiencing their current difficulties. The counsellor goes on to lessen Disa's self-blame.

Counsellor: Hindsight is a wonderful thing, it is quite easy looking back to say maybe if I had chosen differently all would be well now. But looking at the situation at that time, I doubt you could have foreseen what was likely to happen.

Disa: It must be about two years ago that I began taking a specialist interest in sexual abuse of children. I didn't think much about it at that time. There are so few women police officers anyway, so one of us from our area had to volunteer. The other women officers were not keen and so I thought I might as well volunteer. Then I became 'the expert' and found cases were passed on to me. That was good for the ego to begin with, but sometimes I would get inundated. I felt I was trapped. I couldn't get out of it.

Counsellor: How do you mean you could not get out of it?

Disa: Really I could have diverted the flow. I have always given the job 110 per cent. I wanted to be approved of by the colleagues that I value.

Counsellor: So your addiction to the approval of others got you exhausted?

Disa: I wouldn't have put it that way, but I see what you mean.

In this extract the counsellor is implying that whilst the client is not responsible for the problem (hence the inappropriateness of self-blame) she has a responsibility for the solution, overcoming her addiction. The counsellor goes on to look more closely at the origins of this search for approval.

Counsellor: Do you see seeking approval as a problem for you?

Disa: Well, being a woman in the police you really have to prove yourself to the men. If there was an incident I would always be there quickly and taking control.

Counsellor: What about before you joined the police?

Disa: My older sister was brilliant academically. I was OK but I pushed myself with sport, I suppose to prove to my parents that I was someone to be proud of as well. But I felt I was always in her shadow.

Counsellor: How do you get on with your sister now?

Disa: Fine. We joke how we both felt inferior to each other without realizing it and really our parents were very kind, they would not have thought any the less of either of us.

Although historical material is not a prime consideration in cognitive-behavioural counselling, it illuminates where present dysfunctional beliefs might emanate from. The counsellor then goes on to elaborate on what seems to be one of the core assumptions on which the client is operating.

> *Counsellor:* It sounds as if, in the absence of evidence to the contrary, you assume others are demanding a flawless performance of you.
> *Disa:* I know, it doesn't make sense does it?
> *Counsellor:* Would it be possible to practise saying 'No' to people during the next week?
> *Disa:* There's not much opportunity with being off work. But I could tell my mother-in-law that when we go shopping I haven't the energy to spend hours, which is perfectly true anyway.
> *Counsellor:* The best reason for saying 'No' to people is as you were saying, we all have only a limited jar of energy and therefore have to carefully measure out what energy we give to what. If we pretend we have infinite energy, we become emotionally bankrupt.

It is not sufficient to teach clients simply to say 'No' and thereby prevent the accumulation of hassles, it is also necessary for life to contain uplifts. In the next section the counsellor inquires about the scheduling in of some uplifts.

> *Counsellor:* You mentioned that you used to do a lot of sport at college, do you do any of that now?
> *Disa:* Not for a couple of years. The job just gets too much.
> *Counsellor:* Did you like sport when you did it?
> *Disa:* Yes, I really got a high from it.
> *Counsellor:* Whilst you are off work would it be possible to schedule in some sport?
> *Disa:* Yes, I could go swimming every day. Now I think about it, I kept all my worries at college at bay by exercise. I have always been a worrier, but I used to get it all out of my system.
> *Counsellor:* Maybe one of the things we have to do is to get you used to that old coping mechanism again. I know by itself it does not take away the work problems and the memories, but it's a start to making things different.
> *Disa:* That's fine.

In this sequence the counsellor has tried to emphasize the client's influence on events; previously she had been controlled by intrusive imagery and the need for the approval of other people, producing feelings of helplessness. In the following extract the counsellor looks more directly at strategies for combating the intrusive imagery.

> *Counsellor:* If there was a knock at the door or the phone rang would that stop the pictures you get of the baby?
> *Disa:* It does for a time, but if I have nothing else to do afterwards they come back. I have tried keeping busy but it doesn't work.
> *Counsellor:* It seems that you have used distraction to try and stop

yourself thinking about the baby. But this is really asking too much of distraction. It is rather like saying do not think of pink elephants, most people would, in those circumstances, find it difficult not to think of pink elephants. What is much easier is to use distraction to postpone thinking about something. Perhaps telling yourself you will pay the baby due respect by watching a fifteen minute 'mental video' about him at a certain time of the day. If you get a 'photograph' of the baby coming to mind during the day, regard it as a reminder to watch the video later on. Count how many reminders you get in a day by ticking them off on your hand or on a card. It may be that some days depending on what you do you will get more reminders than others. The important element is not to feed the reminders by getting agitated. Simply note the photograph, tick it off, take a deep breath and as you breathe out repeat 'Rela-a-ax-x-x'. It will take lots of practice, rather like becoming proficient at sport. Some days' performances will inevitably be better than others.

Here the counsellor has constructed a meaning for the intrusive imagery ('a reminder') that is in keeping with the client's reverence for the baby. This makes it possible for the client to accept the intrusive imagery rather than fight it. The act of monitoring the frequency of the 'photograph' introduces an element of detachment, making it easier for her to remain calm. This exercise could also provide data as to whether the frequency of intrusive imagery is related to other circumstances in her day. Again, the brief relaxation exercise should also help her remain calm. However, in PDSD there are, typically, three or four intrusive memories. In the next extract the client raises this problem.

Disa: That sounds fine for the baby but there are other memories as well.

Counsellor: Which ones?

Disa: Four months ago I had to deal with a thirteen-year-old, she had been sexually abused for two years. When it all came to light the child was distraught. Her father who had abused her had told her he would tell her mother about her cigarette smoking if she said anything. To begin with the mother would not believe the child. The child became very disturbed at this. The mother finally came to believe the child but was devastated because she believed that she had had a 'perfect' marriage, then I found the kid had started smearing the walls of her home with excrement. She was taken into care of the local authority and I went to visit her for further statements. She was like a zombie.

Counsellor: In a way it is also like a child death. The child was robbed of her childhood. Would it be possible to try and think of flashbacks of the young teenager as reminders to watch a 'loss of childhood' video? The baby that died could also figure on the same video. Or do you anticipate it would be too overwhelming to have both memories on the one video?

Disa: No, I can see, they belong together.

> *Counsellor:* Are there any other memories which are causing problems?
> *Disa:* There have been a couple of comments from two male colleagues about my work in this area, and I am just so angry about them. Most of my colleagues are fine, but two colleagues are always making sexual innuendoes. The general banter I don't mind, but their ignorant comments about this child probably initiating her own abuse made me see red. I can't forgive them and they are on my shift. I keep on visualizing them saying these things and I just get angrier and smash something.
> *Counsellor:* They sound pretty immature.
> *Disa:* They are certainly that, though I would put it stronger.
> *Counsellor:* Each time you think of them, maybe think of them wearing nappies with excrement coming out.
> *Disa:* You are joking!
> *Counsellor:* No, seriously.
> *Disa:* I will give it a try.

Here the counsellor has used imagery to help transform the client's view of her two colleagues from one of their being deliberately wicked to being extremely immature. By the fifth counselling session the client's intrusive imagery and her anger at her colleagues had subsided but she was still very anxious about returning to work.

> *Disa:* I am feeling a lot better but I don't know whether I can face going back to work again. I went back last year after a couple of months off and look what happened.
> *Counsellor:* But when you went back to work then you were not equipped to play things differently. Now you have developed new skills, how to say 'No', how to plan uplifts, and how to contain intrusive thoughts.
> *Disa:* That's true. But I don't think I could cope with any further failure.
> *Counsellor:* It's difficult to be sure how it would work out if you returned to work. But perhaps it would be possible to amend matters as you went along.

The counsellor is here concerned that the client first attribute her improvement to her new skills, and second that she see maintenance of improvement as dependent on the use of her own skills. The client has dichotomized the return to work: 'Either it's a success or it's a failure.' The counsellor responds by suggesting that it might be more adaptive to think of gradual refinement of coping strategies in the light of experience. Nevertheless, in the following extract the client continues to be worried about her return to work.

> *Disa:* I don't know now whether I want to go back, even if I could manage to stay.

Counsellor: Sometimes it helps to get it down on paper rather than try and sort it out in your head. If you try and do it in your head it gets all tangled up and you feel that your head is going to come off.

Disa: That's it, the more I think about it, the more I become confused.

Counsellor: Try writing down the advantages and disadvantages of leaving the police. Sometimes the balance of advantages and disadvantages look different if you look at the short term and then at the long term.

Disa: I'll do that, but what could I move to that pays as well as the police with my lack of qualifications?

Counsellor: Well write that down as one of the possible disadvantages. When you have written the advantages and disadvantages you will probably see that there are arguments both ways. The most stable decisions tend to be 'on balance' ones in which you give yourself plenty of time to reflect on the pros and cons.

Disa: Hmmm, that's not easy for me, I tend to be impulsive.

Counsellor: Well, you know what they say, 'Decide in haste and regret at your leisure.' Though the trouble about carefully sifting an 'on balance' decision is that you have to be prepared to tolerate some discomfort. Don't get angry with yourself if you see arguments both ways. You don't have a crystal ball so you cannot make in advance a perfect decision.

Disa: I will try that but I am so afraid of it not working out back at work.

In this extract the counsellor has highlighted to the client some of the key components of stable decision making – a degree of conflict over the decision and space to reflect on the pros and cons. To make a stable decision it is also important that the decision maker is assured by others of their continuing positive regard independent of what decision is made. The counsellor is therefore concerned to maintain the unconditional positive regard during the decision-making process. However, as the counsellor goes on to explain, there can be no guarantee that the decision made is the right one.

Counsellor: If the worst did come to the worst, what would that mean?

Disa: I would just have to pack up my job.

Counsellor: What would be the biggest problems that that would cause?

Disa: I would probably have to sell the house and I would miss some good neighbours. I would feel a failure and I would not know what to do with myself. It would be hopeless.

Counsellor: Would it actually be that hopeless? If we could take each of those problems in turn and work out an action plan, you might then feel that even if the worst happened, it would be less than totally catastrophic.

Disa: You mean that if I know I can survive the worst, then anything else is likely to be a bonus?

Counsellor: Yes, that's right.

The counsellor has helped the client de-catastrophize the worst scenario. If the counsellor had not done this the client might well have tried too hard to perform at work because of the anticipated dire consequences of failure. This was particularly likely in this client's case anyway because of her history of perfectionism. The counsellor then went on to illustrate the use of the problem solving procedure (given in Box 3.3, p. 45) for use with each of the problems involved in the worst-case scenario.

The next case further illustrates how some occupational groups are particularly prone to the effects of PDSD.

Jamie – PDSD from prolonged duress in the workplace

Jamie had been a policeman for twenty years, and for the past ten years had been a scenes-of-crime officer. He had been off work three months when he was referred to a counsellor. The following is an extract from the first session.

Jamie: I have seen probably hundreds of dead bodies over the years but I can't take any more.
Counsellor: Have you felt that way suddenly?
Jamie: No, it's been the events of the last eighteen months.
Counsellor: What happened?
Jamie: [*Tears begin to flow.*] Well, working backwards. I was called to a murder, the husband had stabbed his wife's lover what looked like hundreds of times. There was blood everywhere, the walls were splattered. The husband had gone totally berserk. But I knew the husband from years ago, when I was often called out to domestics between him and his wife. He was actually a very nice guy, but his wife would try the patience of a saint. I just felt so sorry for the husband. I cried at the scene, there was this **** body in the bedroom and the husband downstairs like a lamb, head bowed. It just got to me, the scene just plays over and over in my mind. About six months before that I was called to an incident in which a bloke had hanged himself. It turned out to be a policeman I knew, though I didn't know him well. Then about nine months before that I was called to a dismembered body on a railway line near the village my mother lives in. It turned out to be a neighbour of my mum's who had become quite confused the last couple of years.
Counsellor: It seems that the job, over the last eighteen months, had become personalized.
Jamie: Yes, it's stupid. You've got a job to do and you just get on with it.
Counsellor: Up to the last eighteen months you were managing OK?
Jamie: Fine. I have got a good wife who helps me to unwind. We go and watch the local rugby team when they are at home and go to away games when we can. But now I can't be bothered.

Each of the horrors Jamie encountered served to confirm the belief that grave tragedies could befall people of personal significance to him. The barrier he had erected between his personal and professional life was permeated. In the next extract the counsellor helps Jamie overcome excessive self-blame.

Counsellor: How do other scenes-of-crime officers cope with the horrors?

Jamie: They drink a lot and womanize.

Counsellor: Why do you think that is?

Jamie: It's just a tradition in this job.

Counsellor: Why do you think it became a tradition?

Jamie: I have never really thought about that.

Counsellor: To cope with the extraordinary demands of the job I guess you would need to do something extraordinary.

Jamie: I have got on well with colleagues but never been part of the 'scene'. I am very much a family man and that means a lot to me.

Counsellor: Given how you have tried to cope with the pressures, should you see yourself as inferior to your colleagues?

Jamie: Maybe not, but they are not whimpering like me. .

Counsellor: Is having a cry that bad?

Jamie: It's just really that I have never cried.

Counsellor: Maybe it's a question of giving yourself permission to mourn for a time.

The counsellor has emphasized the reasonableness of the client's being distressed given the extraordinary stressors. In addition the counsellor has enhanced the likelihood of the client accepting his distress by implying it is time limited, 'a period of mourning'. A common problem for clients suffering from PDSD is 'Why now, after all this time?' In the next extract the counsellor addresses this question.

Jamie: I still don't understand why after all these years this should happen to me now?

Counsellor: Perhaps the wonder is that you have survived for so long without any emotional or behaviour difficulties.

Jamie: Hmmm.

Counsellor: It seems that difficulties only began when you saw events in the job as relevant to your personal world. What we could do is examine the relevance.

In this extract the counsellor is altering the angle from which the client is taking a photograph of his career. Continuing the camera analogy, the counsellor is suggesting that the client can either focus on the extremely difficult past eighteen months or on the previous years of coping. This alternative perspective can serve to alleviate the client's mood. In the next extract the counsellor looks further at the relevance of the traumas for the client's personal world.

Counsellor: You are getting lots of mental reminders of how horrible your world can be. But maybe the see-saw needs balancing out with reminders of how beautiful your world can be too.

Jamie: I am due to go on holiday with my wife to the Canary Islands in two weeks, maybe I need to get away from it all.

Counsellor: I wouldn't see the holiday as getting away from it but serving as a positive reminder that life can be good. I am not suggesting that you blot out how awful life can be, but if you're going to have negative reminders, use them as triggers for positive reminders.

Jamie: How do you mean?

Counsellor: If we take each of the three 'horrors' and come up with a positive antidote. For example, when you think of the lady from your mother's village killed on the railway line, imagine in detail, say, a pleasant village scene you encountered on holiday. Can you think of one?

Jamie: Yes, I was on holiday in the west of Ireland about five years ago, and I sat and chatted to a village blacksmith about his job. It seemed very peaceful, his way of life was unchanged for centuries.

Counsellor: The secret is to make the positive reminders as vivid as the negative reminders. What I would like you to do, for example, is to recall where exactly you were talking to the blacksmith, what the scenery and smells were like, etc.. Try writing out the positive reminders. For homework I would like you to write descriptions of two further positive reminders which could then serve to counteract the other negative scenes.

The counsellor is giving the client a strategy for avoiding using a single 'mental filter' about life. It is suggested to the client that if he is going to remember extreme negative events he has also to remember extreme positive ones. (This strategy does, of course, presuppose that the client has had some extreme positive experiences in life. Where this is claimed not to be the case the client is likely to be suffering from depression as well as PDSD and strategies for handling this are discussed in chapter 7.)

Again, the importance of homework assignments is stressed; the independent practice by the client of skills taught is a key feature of cognitive-behavioural counselling. The second interview with the client began with a review of the homework assignment.

Counsellor: How did the homework go?

Jamie: Good and bad. Thinking of the village scene in Ireland helped to balance off the picture of the lady from mum's village. Thinking of the joys of my own marriage helped to balance off the scene of the **** body but somehow I couldn't balance out the scene of the colleague who had hanged himself.

Counsellor: That's good, you have had an influence on two out of three. Perhaps we could look in more detail at the one you could not manage.

Jamie: OK.

Counsellor: What do you see when you think of your colleague who committed suicide?

Jamie: I just see his bulging eyes. I felt they were staring at me. I wonder whether he had any regrets after kicking the chair away from under him. It is not an instant death, there must have been time. It just creases me up to think of it all. [*Tears welling up.*]

Counsellor: You say you felt his eyes were staring at you?

Jamie: You can't talk personally to colleagues in the police, at least not easily. You have to carefully check out who you will say what to. I felt he may have been saying, if only I had had the chance to talk.

Counsellor: Would he not have had a chance to talk?

Jamie: Actually the officers in the police station he was based in were not a bad crew at all. The atmosphere in there after the suicide was terrible. There wasn't the usual banter, everything was quiet, it was eerie – it gave me the creeps.

Counsellor: Are you saying he would probably have had more chance to talk in that particular police station rather than others?

Jamie: Yes, I guess he would. I think he had drained his wife with his depression and she had left him six months previously.

Counsellor: Maybe the pill that you are having difficulty swallowing is that not all tragedies are avoidable.

Jamie: At one level I know that, but at another I have difficulty in accepting it.

Counsellor: It might help to think of having two parallel streams of thought, one the rational stream telling you that 'Not all horrors are avoidable' and the second stream saying 'That mustn't be the case.' If you play the first stream of thought on your mental audio tape you will feel a little less disturbed than if you exhaust yourself playing the second tape. To insist that things 'mustn't' happen is rather like banging your head against a brick wall, it does not get you far.

Jamie: But it's not right that such things should happen!

Counsellor: I agree, but you might feel a whole lot better if you changed your 'must' for a 'wish'.

Jamie: What will I do then about the flashbacks to the hanging?

Counsellor: Perhaps when you picture his eyes, see them focused on a dock in a courtroom and the dock is empty, nobody stands accused.

In this extract the counsellor has had to inquire about the content of the residual imagery in order to develop a relevant coping strategy. Conversely, when a coping strategy does not seem to be working it is often because the meaning of the trauma has been incorrectly assessed.

Whilst some occupational groups are more vulnerable than others, the particular style of management in an organization can be a critical stressor for bringing about the prolonged duress under enduring circumstances of PDSD. The following example of Charles illustrates this point.

Charles – PDSD from prolonged duress in the workplace

Charles was a middle manager in a well established insurance company. He had little formal education but had worked his way up the organization from being a clerical assistant when he left school. For two years there had been talk of a merger with a larger insurance company and this had created an unsettling climate within the organization. Charles felt particularly vulnerable because he had always felt himself inferior to colleagues at his level of management because of his lack of formal qualifications. Further, he perceived his lifestyle to be working class rather than middle class, which enhanced his feelings of alienation. Charles felt that his own boss was totally dedicated to his own personal survival to the extent that the latter never said 'No' to his superiors and simply passed all tasks down to him. One of the chief sources of job satisfaction for Charles was the approval of staff working under him; he prided himself on being a fair manager. Over the past eighteen months Charles' boss, Graham, had passed on to Charles tasks with impossible deadlines given the staffing resources available. The rationale given was that he had to impress the likely parent company. Charles had suggested that they would need to work overtime to meet the deadlines. However, Graham would not agree to this because it would figure as a cost to his budget. For twelve months Charles had been plagued by constant negative images of Graham which served to sap his enjoyment of family life and leisure pursuits. He had begun to dread going into work, and started having panic attacks when he came in sight of the building.

On one occasion Charles had approved leave for a colleague to attend the funeral of a close friend and Graham negated it. The colleague was very upset and Charles uncharacteristically stormed into Graham's office and told him what a despicable person he was. Morale amongst Charles' staff began to slump, and there were increasing absences. This in turn created a greater backlog. Charles felt trapped and went off sick. Six weeks later he was referred to a counsellor.

This case serves to illustrate further the point that the precipitants of PDSD are often commonplace, but the symptoms are similar to and no less debilitating than those of PTSD following acute, extreme stressors. It may be, .in fact, that PDSD is a more common condition than PTSD. In this first interview Charles was very worried about what his staff and superiors would think of him.

Charles: I am not fair to my staff being off. The work will just be piling up.

Counsellor: Sounds like the organization is not being fair to you or your staff and you have used the only weapon at your disposal, that is to withdraw your labour.

Charles: I will lose any chance of promotion after all this.

Counsellor: Did you want promotion?

Charles: I thought I did.

Counsellor: What would you have gained with promotion?

Charles: Increased salary, but the difference wouldn't have been that great at my level.

Counsellor: Looking at your superiors over the past year or so, do you think you would have been happier to be one of them?

Charles: No, looking at Graham, he is a miserable ****! But it would have been nice to be looked up to.

Counsellor: Do you look up to senior managers?

Charles: No. Most of them have no idea how to handle people.

Counsellor: What makes you think then that people would have been looking up to you?

Charles: They possibly wouldn't. It's how I treat them that matters.

Counsellor: And you were saying that at this point in time the organization is preventing people like you acting fairly.

Charles: So, if I can't treat them fairly there's not a lot of point in the job.

Counsellor: Are there any positions in the organization which would allow you to treat people fairly?

Charles: There may be on the administration support side but not in sales, but it would involve a demotion. I don't know that I could stand that.

In this extract the counsellor has been concerned to tease out what are the key assumptions upon which Charles operates, and they seem to be, first 'At all costs I have to be fair', and second 'I need the approval of colleagues of my rank and above.' Unfortunately these two beliefs are pulling him in opposite directions. In the next extract the counsellor helps Charles resolve the state of dissonance.

Counsellor: Why must you have the approval of all same-ranking and superior-ranking colleagues?

Charles: I haven't got to have the approval of all of them. Indeed, I am past caring about Graham's opinion. He's just a ****! But there are those whose opinions I do value.

Counsellor: I want you to think of six colleagues at your level and above. Of the six, how many would think less of you if you took a demotion?

Charles: Well they would all talk about it, and there would be a few sniggers.

Counsellor: How long would that last for?

Charles: A week or so. They have got too much to think about themselves with the merger imminent.

Counsellor: Of the six, how many would definitely think less of you?

Charles: Two of them. They live and breathe the organization.

Counsellor: What, they are addicted to it?

Charles: Hmmm.

Counsellor: You sound doubtful.

Charles: It is the use of the word addiction.

Counsellor: Is it not an addiction when something dominates your life and stops you being human?

Charles: I guess so.

Counsellor: Maybe someone should help them give up their addiction, but I guess they don't see they have a problem yet. [*Charles laughs.*]

Counsellor: How many of the six would look at your demotion sympathetically?

Charles: Probably two.

Counsellor: And the other two of the six?

Charles: I am not quite sure where they would stand.

Counsellor: Is it possible that they would not stand anywhere, neither for or against you, neutral?

Charles: Apathetic rather than neutral, I would say.

Counsellor: OK. Could you learn to be at least just reasonably content with the disapproval of two contemporaries?

Charles: I think I could. I wouldn't be taking home briefcases of work and snapping at the children when they interrupted me. If I moved one grade lower to the administration support unit I don't think the difference in salary would be that great. I would like to find out, but I cannot bear to go near work or even to ring them up. I avoid it like the plague.

In this extract the counsellor challenges the accuracy of the client's inference that he would not have the approval of his contemporaries. Once a more accurate inference is made the counsellor moves on to challenge the client's evaluation of the circumstances, that is the notion that he could not tolerate the discomfort of the disapproval of two colleagues. Implicitly the counsellor moves Charles away from his own addiction to the organization, and helps him to discover that there are other sources of satisfaction, such as a more satisfying home life. However, as the next extract from the second interview with Charles shows, he was somewhat overtaken by events.

Counsellor: How have things gone since the last session?

Charles: I pulled and released the elastic band on my wrist every time I thought about Graham and I tried just thinking about him for a few minutes at 9 p.m. It was beginning to work then I had a phone call from, guess who? Graham! I nearly put the phone down on him. I was absolutely staggered, he was asking how I was feeling and saying that when I returned we must have 'a good talk' and to take my time to get better. I felt a great weight lifting from my shoulders, but then I began to wonder, what is he up to.

Counsellor: That doesn't sound like Graham?

Charles: No it's not. He's probably sick of having to do a lot of my work himself and wants me back as soon as possible. But nevertheless he was definitely open to discussion and sounded concerned. My wife just got more angry with me when I said that he might be concerned about me. I don't know what to do about my job.

Counsellor: How likely do you think it is that there would be a relatively permanent change for the better in Graham's behaviour?

Charles: Not likely, but it is possible.

Counsellor: It might be helpful before the next session to write down the options with regard to work and go through the pros and cons of each. Try and decide on a solution and its implementation and you could later revise the solution in the light of experience.

Charles: Yes, that's good. I do tend to think if I come up with a solution I am stuck with it, but solutions are usually changeable.

The counsellor has helped Charles become problem oriented as a step towards overcoming his avoidance behaviour. The client has also moved from his rigid position of thinking he had to generate a perfect, once-and-for-all decision. At the beginning of the following counselling session the client's problem-solving efforts are revised.

Charles: I have decided that I want to return to work with Graham but I am terrified of the prospect.

Counsellor: What frightens you most about a return?

Charles: Arriving to find a backlog of work on my desk. As I make a start on it there is a whole stream of interruptions, not just Graham but others making demands.

Counsellor: So you have decided you want to return to work and now the problem is to sort out the 'how'. Is that right?

Charles: Yes.

Counsellor: Would it help to go in, say, forty minutes early and prioritize the backlog? That way you could avoid meeting people until you were sorted out.

Charles: That's a good idea.

Counsellor: What would be useful is to construct a mental video of how you are going to handle this return to work. Into this video we have already put your arrival at work forty minutes early, and you can picture yourself sorting out the backlog uninterrupted. What else should we put into the video?

Charles: I am going to be pretty nervous putting my suit on to go to work. I will probably be thinking, as I always do when I get up of a morning, of the raging row with Graham months ago.

Counsellor: What could you say to yourself that would counter the apprehension?

Charles: That it is unlikely given the recent telephone conversation with Graham that there would be an immediate conflict, and even if there were I have always got other options.

Counsellor: Right, tell yourself that out loud.

Charles: 'There is unlikely to be conflict, and so what if there is.'

Counsellor: How did it feel to say that?

Charles: Fine sitting here, but it might be a different scenario on the morning of my returning to work.

The client's coping self-statement and behavioural assignment were designed to help him prepare for the stress of the return to work. Indeed preparing for the stressor is the first phase of Meichenbaum's (1985) Self-Instruction Training (SIT). (The other phases of SIT are encountering the stressor, coping with feeling overwhelmed, coping with failure of the endeavour, and coping with success – see Box 4.1, p. 62.) To complete the construction of the client's 'mental video', the counsellor takes him through the succeeding stages of SIT.

Counsellor: You mentioned that you feel panic just at the sight of work?

Charles: Yes, I am sweating before I have even parked my car. My heart is racing and I go light-headed.

Counsellor: Perhaps you could put a favourite music tape on as you drive to work and turn up the volume as you come in sight of it.

Charles: I could give it a try. I am very fond of brass bands so maybe I could blast the fear out of my mind!

Counsellor: Would it be possible to play a tape like that on a personal stereo in work?

Charles: Not during the day, but perhaps I could for a few minutes at lunch time.

Counsellor: It might just help to defuse your tension, stop you feeling overwhelmed. What do you think you could say to yourself or do when the going gets really tough?

Charles: I could take myself off and walk around the building for a few minutes.

Counsellor: What would you be telling yourself when you are walking around?

Charles: I could tell myself to play it cool.

Counsellor: Fine. Maybe congratulate yourself in some way if your efforts are successful. Could you do that?

Charles: Yes, I used to enjoy reading a novel, but haven't read one for a long time. I could buy myself one.

Counsellor: I hate to raise this, but what would your plan for coping be if you became too distressed at work?

Charles: I guess then I would be able to tell myself at least now I know for sure that I have to change my role.

Counsellor: Try rehearsing the whole of the mental video of your return to work a couple of times a day before you actually return to work. This way you become very familiar with your plans and you will not have to think about them too much when you are in the stressful situation, they will have become, hopefully, almost automatic by then.

The counsellor is suggesting that the client will be less stressed in work as his coping strategies become automatic. To accelerate the process of automatized response, the counsellor is suggesting frequent rehearsal of the imagery before first setting foot in the stressful situation. In the event, the client's work situation had not changed at all, he took a demotion, but was very content in his new post and the PDSD symptoms soon dissipated. This example highlights the fact that stress should be regarded as an interactive phenomenon: it is not a property solely of the person or of the environment, but of their interaction. It follows that the counsellor should not be exclusively concerned with intrapsychic changes in the client, but should also focus on what environment might be better suited to the client's needs.

Whilst the contribution of enduring workplace duress to the development of PTSD-like symptoms has been under-researched, the role of extreme and enduring demands present in everyday life has been even less studied. The case of Margaret, who cared at home for her husband for eight months whilst he died, illustrates how a relatively common but protracted duress can evoke PDSD.

Margaret – PDSD from prolonged duress in the home

Margaret was referred for counselling eighteen months after her husband, Johann, had died of a brain tumour. They had been married for eighteen years and had been extremely happy, though disappointed that they had not been able to have children. Don, a bachelor friend of her husband, helped her cope with the grief and they became very close and married six months after Johann's death. To Margaret and Don's great joy she conceived almost immediately and they very much looked forward to the birth. Unfortunately, she had a long and difficult labour and the baby was eventually delivered by Caesarean section. At the time of Margaret's referral the baby was four months old. Margaret was distressed that she did not feel as warm to the baby as she had anticipated, and that she didn't feel as loving to Don as she should. Though she believed both Don and the baby were 'lovely', she found that her mind was dominated by the 'horrors' of the eight months during which Johann was seriously ill and then died.

Intrusive imagery of the events of those eight months was almost constant, and she now avoided medical and surgical contact. For example she would not attend an appointment for a review of the current state of a previously benign cyst in her breast. She had become uncharacteristically angry with people and was easily startled. There were three events during the eight-month period of her husband's illness that figured prominently in the intrusive imagery. One scene was of her husband clinging to her, knowing he hadn't long to live and his eyes seeming to pop out of his head. The second was when she witnessed a conflict between the consultant for the Renal Department, which her husband attended for dialysis, and the consultant of the Neurology Department, both wanting the other to provide a bed for him. In the event Margaret felt Johann was 'shunted' into a disused stock room near the Renal Department. She had cared for him at home as much as possible, and had the assistance of a neighbour who was also a nurse. There were many sleepless nights and much exhaustion as she helped Johann, much against the odds, to learn to walk again after his first operation. The third scene arose from the final stages of his dying. She vividly recalled the struggle to acquire a machine from the hospital to help clear Johann's airways to ease his breathing.

For the eighteen months since Johann's death Margaret had only been able to recall the horrors of his dying; she was unable to focus on the eighteen years of wedded bliss. In the first interview the counsellor explores the function of the intrusive imagery for Margaret.

> *Counsellor:* What would you feel if you didn't have the constant flashbacks to the months of Johann's death?
> *Margaret:* Relieved.
> *Counsellor:* Relieved?
> *Margaret:* Yes, I would be able to get on with my life. I don't know how Don puts up with me.
> *Counsellor:* If Johann was sitting in this chair [*points to another chair*], what do you think he would say about you getting on with your life?
> *Margaret:* He would be all for it. He wasn't a selfish man.
> *Counsellor:* Are you saying that for Johann's sake you should get on with living?
> *Margaret:* Yes, I should.
> *Counsellor:* But isn't this what you have done: you've remarried, had a baby.
> *Margaret:* Well I suppose I have in one way, but not in another.
> *Counsellor:* Could you say that you have made a start as Johann would have wished, but there is still some way to go?
> *Margaret:* That about sums it up.

In this extract the counsellor is checking that the client 'has permission' to let go of the intrusive memories. The counsellor went on to encourage the client to elaborate specifically on the good times in her marriage to her deceased husband. Three high spots in the marriage were detailed. Each time the client recalled one of her 'horror events' she had to try and balance it by recalling one of the 'high spots'. At the fifth interview the counsellor reviews progress with this strategy.

Counsellor: How has balancing out the horrors gone?

Margaret: It seems to stop me dwelling on the 'horrors' but thinking of the pleasant things has got me thinking of what I have lost. So I have been feeling very low.

Counsellor: Have you actually lost something or is it just past?

Margaret: I am not sure what you are saying.

Counsellor: Have you ever had a good friend maybe at school or at work, whom you don't see now but whom you think well of?

Margaret: Yes, Jean, she was my bridesmaid when I first got married. We were really good friends, had been since school. She emigrated to Australia a few months after Johann and I got married.

Counsellor: Do you remember some good times together?

Margaret: Oh yes, lots.

Counsellor: Does it make you sad when you think of those occasions?

Margaret: No, they make me smile.

Counsellor: So, the occasions are past but they are not lost to you.

Margaret: I see what you mean.

Counsellor: Because Jean had gone to Australia you didn't conclude that there could not be other sources of pleasure or achievement, did you?

Margaret: No, there was my marriage to Johann, and I had just got a new job in an estate agent's.

Counsellor: Can you think and behave over Johann the way you did about Jean?

Margaret: I can try, but it gets to me that he's not around.

Counsellor: Were you happy enough if Johann was away on business for a few days?

Margaret: Yes, there was always lots to do.

Counsellor: So Johann's physical presence wasn't necessary for your happiness?

Margaret: Hmmm, no. But I wonder whether I can be as happy with Don.

Counsellor: Is there any particular obstacle to attaining happiness with Don?

Margaret: No, but I just don't feel about him and the baby the way I did about Johann.

Counsellor: You were married to Johann eighteen years, you have only been married to Don eighteen months. You can't expect to feel the same yet.

Margaret: No. I do care about them a lot, but I have just got to tell myself that I don't 'have' to feel about them now the way I did about Johann.

Clients can make it difficult for themselves to make a fresh start after a bereavement if they believe the deceased was and remains the only route to happiness. In their perception of 'love' they exaggerate the differences between one human being and another. However, rather than get into a confrontation with the client about the possibilities of happiness after their partner's death, it is more fruitful for the counsellor to suggest that the client experiment with engaging in life and judge the results by realistic standards. The engagement in life then makes it possible to savour joys that are now past. This savouring of the good makes it possible to balance out the bad. It is important to tackle not only the client's intrusive imagery but also the avoidance behaviour. In the next session, the counsellor raises this issue.

> *Counsellor:* Some weeks ago you mentioned that you couldn't go near a hospital again even though you are due to have a check-up for the cyst in your breast.
>
> *Margaret:* I just freeze at the thought of going to hospital.
>
> *Counsellor:* If you went to hospital what do you think would be the likely sequence of events?
>
> *Margaret:* I think they would have to take me in a straitjacket!
>
> *Counsellor:* What would be the likely outcome of going?
>
> *Margaret:* I know it's only a check-up, it's probably nothing at all.
>
> *Counsellor:* What if it were cancer?
>
> *Margaret:* Well they would have to operate, maybe remove the breast.
>
> *Counsellor:* How would you feel about that?
>
> *Margaret:* Very upset, but if it saved my life it would have to be done.
>
> *Counsellor:* Do you know anyone who has had a breast removed?
>
> *Margaret:* Yes, my Auntie. She's fine now.
>
> *Counsellor:* Before Johann was ill, you would have readily gone for a check-up, is that right?
>
> *Margaret:* Oh, yes.
>
> *Counsellor:* If your Aunt hadn't gone in for her medical care what would have happened?
>
> *Margaret:* I guess she would have died. I would miss her, she's eccentric but fun.
>
> *Counsellor:* Maybe write down the advantages and disadvantages of your attending for a check up and chat to Don about them.
>
> *Margaret:* I will do that; it's not fair to Don and the baby not to go really.
>
> *Counsellor:* Perhaps when you think of hospitals you should think of your Auntie.
>
> *Margaret:* Right.

The client's traumas have resulted in avoidance behaviours that can further damage her. The counsellor helps the client overcome the avoidance behaviour by suggesting that the focus of the behaviour (the hospital) is, in her case, more appropriately associated with life than death.

Penny – PDSD from prolonged childhood sexual abuse

PTSD symptoms may arise as a result of prolonged childhood physical or sexual abuse. It has been estimated (Famularo at al., 1989) that overall perhaps 21 per cent of children who are abused may suffer PTSD. Where there is any sexual maltreatment, however, the incidence rises to 31 per cent, compared to 13 per cent for children suffering physical abuse alone. Often the abuse remains undetected until the child presents as an adult to a counsellor. Prolonged abuse can be particularly difficult for a client to come to terms with, as the case of Penny illustrates.

Penny was sexually abused by her uncle from the ages of nine to sixteen. She had not told her parents about the abuse because the uncle was well thought of by her parents and she feared they would not believe her. He used to babysit for her parents. For some months, she remembered, she tried to fight him off. Then she 'just gave in'. The counselling begins with Penny sobbing bitterly.

> *Penny:* I just gave in.
> *Counsellor:* What other options did you have at that time?
> *Penny:* I could have told my parents.
> *Counsellor:* What stopped you doing that?
> *Penny:* They wouldn't have believed me.
> *Counsellor:* So what other option did you have?
> *Penny:* I thought of telling a teacher at school.
> *Counsellor:* What stopped you?
> *Penny:* They would have probably brought my parents in and it would just be more horrible at home. They were always rowing, only happy when they were going to the pub.
> *Counsellor:* So what option did you have?
> *Penny:* None.
> *Counsellor:* Did you choose to give in or were you forced by circumstances to give in?
> *Penny:* I guess it was the circumstances but I can't believe I let it go on and on.
> *Counsellor:* You used the word 'let'. That suggests you had a choice.
> *Penny:* No, really there was no choice in it.
> *Counsellor:* It sounds like you were the victim.
> *Penny:* But was I the victim? I took part in it. I am worthless. I can't believe it was me.

In the next extract the counsellor introduces the notion of dissociation to help her make sense of the sequence of struggle and capitulation.

> *Counsellor:* How do you mean you can't believe it was you?
> *Penny:* It just didn't feel it was me. It is weird but I was watching me.
> *Counsellor:* We have got a name for that state of affairs – it's called dissociation. It comes about when people have tried every way they know of avoiding a horror, for example being tortured, and nothing works. The conscious mind then has to give up the struggle; if it didn't you would just become totally exhausted. The non-conscious mind then takes over. It copes by effectively saying that it is not really me going through this horror so you become detached from

your own experience. In some ways it is a bit like the experience some people have described of seeing their own body on an operating table and viewing all the medical proceedings from the ceiling – what is called an out-of-body experience. When the non-conscious mind has to take over there is no question of will any more than there is in dreaming or out-of-body experiences.

Penny: I understand what you're saying, I know it makes sense, but I still feel worthless.

Counsellor: What makes you feel worthless?

Penny: I had orgasms so I must have enjoyed it.

Counsellor: The human body is a bit like a computer: if you press certain buttons you get a certain print-out. Did you have any choice on the buttons pressed?

Penny: No.

Counsellor: You might still feel strongly that you are worthless, but you can make a start telling yourself there are no grounds for believing it.

In this extract the counsellor is helping the client cope with emotional reasoning, believing she was guilty because she felt guilty. The counsellor also makes the point that it is repetition of the rational responses that eventually produces a change in feeling state and that it is far from instantaneous.

The thinking that is operating in the client's feeling of worthlessness is that which developed during the years of her abuse. A powerful way of challenging these beliefs is to have the client alternate in playing the role of the child and the adult, the latter using her knowledge to comfort the child. In Penny's case she was asked to spend ten minutes a day sitting 'thirteen-year-old Penny' in a chair opposite her and listening to her thoughts and feelings about the abuse, and then for the adult Penny to offer her more adaptive interpretations of her situation. The adult Penny had to conclude by giving the child Penny (a cushion) a hug to tell her all was now well.

Box 6.2 *Practice summary – PTSD from prolonged duress (PDSD)*

1 PTSD symptoms are at least as likely to arise from events that do not hit the newspaper headlines as from those that do.

2 The counsellor has to be aware that the client will have more difficulty in legitimizing their distress because of the 'everyday' nature of their experience.

3 Severe depression often coexists with PDSD. Excessive blame – 'Why did I let it go on so long?' – is often a part of that depression.

4 Imaginal desensitization using an audio tape is often inappropriate as a strategy, either because it is general rather than specific memories that are evoked or because of the number of discrete specific memories which intrude, and also because of the severity of coexisting depression.

5 The counsellor must be able to emphasize that the trauma memories are but one theme running through the client's life and that equal attention should be devoted to positive thoughts. The scheduling of uplifts should be made a regular target of treatment sessions.

6 Where the workplace has been the trigger for PDSD the counsellor can help the client to use problem-solving procedures to work towards a course of action.

7

Counselling for Concurrent Anxiety and Depression

A pure case of post-traumatic stress disorder is somewhat of a rarity. PTSD often occurs in conjunction with other affective disorders, particularly anxiety and depression. This chapter begins with a description of the major features of anxiety and depression and then provides an elaboration of a cognitive-behavioural response to anxiety and depression occurring concurrently with PTSD.

Features of anxiety and depression

The symptoms that can be a part of anxiety and depression may be categorized under four headings: thoughts, feelings, behaviours and physiological effects. Beck (Beck et al., 1985) has described the thought content of anxiety and depression in terms of the cognitive triad of self, world and future, as depicted in Box 7.1. Looking at Beck's anxiogenic cognitive triad in Box 7.1 it may readily be seen why PTSD has been classified as one of the anxiety disorders on Axis 1 of *DSM-III-R*.

Box 7.1 *Thought content of anxiety and depression in relation to Beck's cognitive triad of self, world and future*

Anxiety	**Depression**
View of self as vulnerable 'Something awful is about to happen.'	*View of self as negative* 'I am a failure.'
View of world as threatening 'You cannot trust anybody.'	*View of world as negative* 'It's just one catastrophe after another.'
View of future as unpredictable 'I have to keep on guard, anything could happen.'	*View of future as negative* 'It's hopeless, there's nothing to look forward to.'

Box 7.2 *Typical feelings, behaviours and reactions associated with anxiety and depression*

	Anxiety	**Depression**
Feelings	Apprehension	Sadness
Behaviours	Avoidance Excessive dependency	Procrastination Indecisiveness Impaired concentration
Reactions	Tension Palpitations	Difficulty getting off to sleep Early morning awakening

---

The feelings, behaviours and physiological reactions associated with anxiety and depression are shown in Box 7.2. Thoughts, feelings, behaviours and physiological reactions can influence each other to maintain anxiety and depression. For example a soldier who was involved in an ambush in which a friend or colleague was killed might start on the pathway to depression with the thought 'I normally patrol that part of the street, that night I didn't, it should have been me, I am just not fit for anything, I am a waste of space.' This negative over-generalization might lead to a change of behaviour, such as not associating with previously valued colleagues. This behaviour leads in turn to a lack of positive reinforcements and consequent negative feelings. In the negative emotional state the soldier will have greater access to other failure experiences, for example he might now graphically recall how disappointed his parents were with his school performance. The memory of this serves to depress his mood further. This in turn increases access to other negative memories and a depressive spiral ensues. In addition, because of his trauma the soldier may have become hyperalert in everyday situations, for example when queuing at a cash dispenser checkpoint his physiological reaction may be that he starts to breathe quickly and deeply. He notices he is becoming light-headed and this may lead to thoughts such as 'I ought to be in total control in this situation, I am not, I just can't stand it.' His distress may be further exacerbated by a belief that he will make a fool of himself. As a consequence he takes flight from the queue and thereby reduces his anxiety. Because taking

Box 7.3   *Indicators of anxiety and depression from Snaith and Zigmond's HAD Scale*

Anxiety	Depression
Feeling tense or wound up	Not enjoying things the way you used to
Getting a sort of frightened feeling as if something awful is about to happen	Being unable to laugh and see the funny side of things
Having worrying thoughts going through your mind	Not feeling cheerful
Inability to sit at ease and feel relaxed	Feeling as if you are slowed down
Getting a sort of frightened feeling like butterflies in the stomach	Losing interest in your appearance
Feeling restless as if you have to be on the move	Not looking forward with enjoyment to things
Getting sudden feelings of panic	Being unable to enjoy a good book or radio or television programme

flight proves rewarding (it reduces his anxiety) he never again has the opportunity to test out his belief that situations such as queues are dangerous. That is, he deprives himself of opportunities to disconfirm his threat-related beliefs and thereby remains anxious.

As this example illustrates, it is possible to suffer the three disorders of PTSD, anxiety and depression simultaneously. The cognitive behavioural approach to each of these disorders is to attempt to change the emotional state of the client via their thoughts, behaviours and physiological state. If strategies designed for anxiety sufferers such as relaxation exercises are applied to depressives they are likely to be of no avail. It is important therefore to be able to distinguish anxiety from depression, especially as both of them often coexist with PTSD, and to do so early in treatment.

The Hospital, Anxiety and Depression Scale (HAD) (Snaith and Zigmond, 1983) separates anxiety and depression symptoms as in Box 7.3. Each symptom is graded on a 4-point scale from 0 to 3 in increasing order of severity. Persons scoring below 8 on either scale are said to be normal, those scoring from 8–10 are deemed borderline, and those scoring above 10 pathological. The HAD is probably the best brief self-report measure for identifying clinical cases of anxiety or depression, though strictly speaking it should be used as a measure of the severity of these disorders once they have been established by diagnostic interview and the possibility of other disorders such as schizophrenia has been excluded. From the lists in Box 7.3 it can be seen that the central characteristic of depression is of life losing its flavour, whereas in anxiety it is a sense of imminent danger.

PTSD and anxiety

Many of the therapeutic strategies developed for the treatment of generalized anxiety disorder (GAD), panic disorder and phobic disorders are applicable to PTSD. This is not surprising, as PTSD differs from the other anxiety disorders largely in the specification of a particular aetiology such as a traumatic event. At the level of symptomatology there is often considerable overlap. The main features of GAD, panic disorders and agoraphobia are now briefly reviewed.

Generalized anxiety disorder
DSM-III-R suggests that the specific manifestations of anxiety vary from individual to individual, but generally there are signs of tension, hyperactivity, apprehensive expectation, vigilance and scanning. Mild depressive symptoms are common. To meet the criteria for GAD the anxiety has to have persisted for at least a month.

Panic disorder
The essential features are recurrent panic attacks that occur unpredictably, though certain situations (for instance driving a car) may become associated with a panic attack. The panic attacks are manifested by the sudden onset of intense apprehension, fear or terror, often associated with feelings of impending doom. The most common symptoms experienced during an attack are palpitations, chest pain or discomfort, choking or smothering sensations, dizziness, vertigo or unsteady feelings, feelings of unreality (depersonalization), hot and cold flushes, sweating, faintness, trembling or shaking, and fear of dying, going crazy or doing something uncontrolled during the attack. Attacks usually last minutes, more rarely hours. The individual often develops degrees of nervousness and apprehension between attacks.

Agoraphobia

Agoraphobia (literally 'fear of the market- or public meeting place') involves a fear of being in places or situations from which escape might be difficult or embarrassing or in which help might not be available in the event of a panic attack. As a result of this fear the person either restricts travel or needs a companion when away from home. Common agoraphobic situations include being outside the home alone, being in a crowd or standing in a line, being on a bridge, and travelling in a bus, train or car. Often the PTSD sufferer shows similar avoidance behaviours. In this case it involves avoiding activities or situations that arouse recollections of the trauma. It may simply be avoiding what is a carbon copy of the original trauma so that following a ferry disaster a victim may in future avoid ferries. More usually the avoidance behaviour has been generalized beyond the original trigger for recollection of the trauma and at its most extreme avoidance may result in a victim being nearly or completely housebound or unable to leave the house unaccompanied. There are obvious similarities between agoraphobia and the phobic avoidance evident in PTSD, and much of the counselling for the latter derives from well validated treatments for the former.

Within the cognitive-behavioural perspective adopted in this text the common theme that runs through anxiety disorders is one of potential danger, threat or harm to the individual.

Loretta – PTSD with concurrent anxiety

Loretta was a thirty-four-year-old single woman, a conscientious civil servant. She lived at home with her seventy-year-old father who was in good health. Her mother had died ten years previously in a car accident. To distract herself from the loss of her mother she buried herself in work. She was well thought of by colleagues and rose rapidly up the hierarchy to become a senior manager by the time she was thirty-one. However, she had become a workaholic. She was constantly tense, worried she would fail to meet deadlines, experienced butterflies in her stomach and was having difficulty in getting off to sleep. At the age of thirty-one Loretta was referred by her general practitioner to a counsellor, suffering from generalized anxiety disorder. Loretta readily accepted the counsellor's rationale for her difficulties, namely that she operated rather like someone trying to drive a car who only ever drove in one gear. For homework the counsellor gave her the task of planning breaks into the day. Loretta went out of work for a half-hour walk each day at lunch time and she tried to schedule in coffee breaks. She also decided to leave work by 5.30 p.m. and not 7 p.m. as was her usual custom. In order to facilitate the scheduling in of breaks, the counsellor needed, in cognitive therapy style, to challenge her silent assumption that 'it's lazy not to always be doing something that achieves a goal'. This involved Loretta reconceptualizing work as a means to an end rather than an end in itself. She came to see work as a means of acquiring a sense of achievement and pleasure, but not as the only means. The counsellor taught her to schedule work activities on the assumption that there would be some unanticipated interruption and accordingly to allow some extra time for task completion. Hitherto Loretta had scheduled work activities on the basis of what was theoretically possible within the time, thereby ensuring frustration.

She also had an exaggerated belief in the importance of activity and did not take time to prioritize work. Loretta rushed about from one unfinished task to another, leaving little opportunity for a sense of accomplishment. She was persuaded to make lists of her tasks, where possible completing one before proceeding to the next. She also had problems with delegating, believing that if she was responsible for the department she had to check everyone's work. This was both time consuming to her and increasingly irritating to her staff. For homework she was asked to check only key pieces of work from her immediate subordinates in order to test out if the results would be as catastrophic as she imagined. In addition she scheduled leisure time to go to concerts and to go jogging. This programme was effective in resolving generalized anxiety disorder in just eight sessions of treatment at weekly intervals.

Though Loretta had improved there was one area of her life that had not been tackled. This was car driving. Because her mother had died in a traffic accident Loretta had avoided learning to drive. She could travel as a passenger in a car but she always 'felt a bit edgy'. Loretta's inability to drive did not, she felt, greatly interfere with her social or working life. She had decided that overcoming a fear of driving was not worth the investment of time and nervous energy. Accordingly it was not targeted as a therapeutic goal.

Uplifted by her general quality of life, in the two years subsequent to the initial counselling Loretta finally took driving lessons, passing her test at the second attempt. She had found the experience of learning to drive 'hairy' but was well pleased with her accomplishment. After a year of successful driving her fear of driving had largely disappeared, though she continued to be slightly edgy if she was a passenger in the car, preferring to be 'in control of events'. Unfortunately when she was parked outside some shops one day sitting in her car waiting for a friend to come out, she looked in her mirror and saw a car coming up from behind at great speed. The vehicle clipped the rear of Loretta's car and she badly wrenched her neck and also damaged her hand as it hit the dashboard under the impact. As well as the physical injuries she subsequently experienced flashbacks in slow motion of the car running into her from behind. This intrusive imagery was associated with feelings of powerlessness. She became phobic about travelling in cars and began to experience panic attacks. These could be triggered by the sight of cars but could also occur seemingly at random. Two months after the accident she contacted the counsellor. By the first counselling session her neck had improved to the point that she no longer had to wear her surgical collar. However her hand still gave her considerable pain and she was very frustrated because this impaired her concentration in studying for the final stages of her Masters in Business Administration degree. Fortunately it was not her writing hand that was damaged.

Hyperventilation (filling the lungs fully and emptying them completely in quick succession) is thought to be an important factor in panic disorder (Clark, 1989). The suggestion is that individuals may overbreathe in this manner when confronted with a feared object. The consequences of overbreathing may include light-headedness, dizziness and palpitations. If these symptoms are interpreted in a catastrophic fashion, as for example 'My heart is pounding, I am going to have a heart attack', this further fuels panic and a vicious circle is set up. After describing the classic symptoms of panic Loretta was given the hyperventilation challenge (p. 62).

It would have been possible to have given Loretta the likely explanation of her panic as soon as she volunteered her symptoms, but giving her the 'hyperventilation challenge' first makes the explanation that much more credible. (This challenge should *not* be used with clients who have any history of pains in the chest, have heart trouble, are diabetic or pregnant.) Loretta was then taught the '3Ss' strategy for panic – that is breathing slowly, smoothly and shallowly. To begin with she was asked to practise breathing in for a slow count of five and out for a slow count of five, counted at two digits per second. She found she could breathe rhythmically at this pace. (In some instances clients may be more comfortable with a shorter period of intake, as brief as two seconds or with a longer period, as much as three seconds. Some practice between counselling sessions may be needed to strike a comfortable pace.) Loretta was instructed to regularize her

---

Box 7.4 *Homework task for Loretta*

1 Monitor panic attacks.
  Keep a diary of:
    time of attack;
    duration of attack;
    where the attack occurred;
    what you were thinking during the attack;
    what you did in response to the attack;
    how severe the panic was, on a 0 to 10 scale where 10
      is very severe.
2 Play pain relief tape[1] at least once daily (side 1 stresses
  the influence of attitudes on level of pain experienced and
  recommends engaging in normal activities as far as is
  humanly possible, side 2 provides a relaxation exercise for
  pain sufferers).

---

[1] Tape *Coping with Pain* available from: Pain Relief Foundation, PRF Pain
Tape, PO Box 1, Wirral, Merseyside L47 7DD, England, at a cost of £5.99
including postage and packing. (Price correct at time of going to press.)

breathing in this way when she noticed the first signs of panic,
which in her case were feelings of light-headedness. In addition she
was requested to continue the regular breathing in the situation in
which the panic occurred until the panic subsided. (Fleeing from
the situation when panicking produces a sense of relief, which
serves as a reward for further avoidance behaviour.)

At the end of the first counselling session the counsellor gave
Loretta the homework tasks set out in Box 7.4. At the second
counselling session a week later the previous week's homework
assignment was reviewed. Loretta had recorded four panic attacks
in the previous week. She was surprised to notice how they varied
in duration and intensity. Her longest had lasted half an hour and
she had given it a severity rating of 10, whilst her shortest had
lasted between five and ten minutes and carried a severity rating of
only 6. Her worst panic occurred in the shopping parade near
where the accident had happened. She had recorded thinking in
this panic 'I am going to faint and make a fool of myself in front
of all these people.' Loretta interpreted the panic as occurring
'because I was near where it [the accident] happened'. The
counsellor offered an alternative explanation: that being in the
vicinity of the accident took her to the brink of panic, but that
what pushed her over the edge was her belief that she was going
to faint and make a fool of herself. Loretta accepted the cognitive

reformulation of the attack. The next step for the counsellor was to challenge the cognitions responsible for the final push into panic. This was done in two stages. First it was explained to Loretta that in clients with panic attacks (with the single exception of those with blood phobias) fainting is extremely rare because panic alters blood pressure in the opposite direction to that needed for fainting. The feelings of light-headedness arose simply because more oxygen was being pumped to the muscles, as if in preparation for a fight, and less to the brain. Second, she was asked why if when other people appear ill in public she does not consider them fools she would think of herself being a fool if she appeared unwell? Loretta could see the inconsistency in her logic and agreed to place cards in strategic places that said 'So what if I don't appear well in public?'

With regard to her least severe panic (rated a 6) she volunteered 'I could stand it if they were all just like that.' The counsellor encouraged her to elaborate on which panics were more tolerable than others. This discrimination between panic attacks was important in preventing the development of a fear of panic attacks *per se*, as such a fear is likely to increase their frequency. This then made it possible to see success in terms not simply of reduction in frequency of attacks but in severity. In the short term it may be that the frequency of attacks shows little or no reduction but the client can take comfort and encouragement from the fact that already the severity of some may have diminished. This helps prevent early demoralization.

Loretta found the pain relief tape helpful in that it encouraged her to engage in activities when of late she had been brooding a great deal. Accordingly she had made more contact with friends. She had also found the relaxation exercise included on the tape helpful with sleep. However, she was worried that she could not concentrate sufficiently for the final stages of her MBA degree.

It emerged that there were two sources of impaired concentration. The first was the physical pain she was experiencing and the second was flashbacks to her own recent accident and dwelling on the accident in which her mother had died ten years previously. For homework she was asked simply to greet the flashbacks of her own accident, rather in the manner a person standing on a railway platform might wave back to some unknown person waving from a train that was passing through the station. The rationale given was that she could if she chose get irritated with the person waving to her and the noise of the passing train or alternatively she could choose simply to greet it calmly as it passed by. The option of saying 'The train should not come' was not a viable one. At the appropriate time she would herself be choosing to board other trains of thought. Because of time constraints in the session, looking at her reawakened thoughts about her mother's death was put on the agenda for the next counselling session.

Loretta arrived at the following counselling session in buoyant mood. She had concluded that it did not matter too much if she postponed the final module of her MBA for a year – 'It would give me a chance to pursue other things.' Loretta was telling the counsellor at great length what these other options might be when the counsellor recalled that the item agreed for today's agenda was her recall of her mother's death. When the counsellor interjected that this had been put on the agenda Loretta began to sob quietly. (This is quite characteristic of anxiety sufferers – the thoughts that are problematic are avoided.)

> *Counsellor:* What went through your mind when I mentioned about your mother?
> *Loretta:* Her pain. [*Pause*]
> *Counsellor:* Her pain?
> *Loretta:* Yes, I know the excruciating pain I went through with my accident; the pain she went through must have been so much worse.
> *Counsellor:* What happened exactly?
> *Loretta:* She was going down the motorway when a lorry going in the opposite direction jack-knifed across the central reservation.
> *Counsellor:* Did she live long?
> *Loretta:* No, she was already dead when the emergency services arrived.
> *Counsellor:* How long was that?
> *Loretta:* Minutes, she was a horrific mess they told me. There was nothing to recognize her as she was. [*Increased sobbing. Pause.*]
> *Counsellor:* It must have been instant.
> *Loretta:* Yes, I suppose it was. At least the pain didn't last.
> *Counsellor:* Her pain was extremely intense but was over in an instant. But maybe your pain over her is less intense but has been prolonged for years.
> *Loretta:* She wasn't just a mum, she was my best friend.
> *Counsellor:* That must have left a terrible gap.
> *Loretta:* It did. I have got lots of good friends in the past couple of years but it's not the same somehow.
> *Counsellor:* Yet, despite that, before this accident you had been at least just reasonably content with life.
> *Loretta:* That's true, life wasn't that bad at all.
> *Counsellor:* Could it be that way again?
> *Loretta:* I guess it could. I just miss my Mum.
> *Counsellor:* Perhaps the missing just gets worse at times of great upset. Then when the upset is past the missing becomes more bearable.

Because anxiety sufferers do not always have access to the thoughts that cause problems, when they are away from the evoking situation (for example in the counselling session) it is useful to carefully observe non-verbal responses to prompts in sessions and to work at uncovering their meaning. In the above extract two themes emerged: the client's concern with her mother's pain, and her own loss. Both themes were then subjected to cognitive restructuring.

By the next counselling session the panics had decreased to one mild one a week and Loretta had become more engaged in normal activities. The intrusive imagery had attenuated considerably, though she was still avoiding travelling by car. It was possible for her to travel to work and meet friends by public transport but she concluded that not driving herself interfered with her life too much and she wanted to overcome it. An anxiety hierarchy was constructed starting with her sitting in her car in her garage with her father for five minutes and progressing in steps up to driving to work. To keep her anxiety manageable she employed a variety of distraction techniques which included singing loudly and playing a cassette tape. Within a further five sessions she was able to drive to work successfully.

PTSD and concurrent depression

Box 7.5   *DSM-III-R criteria for major depressive disorder*

- Depressed mood most of the day nearly every day
- Markedly diminished interest or pleasure in all or almost all activities most of the day nearly every day
- Significant weight loss or weight gain when not dieting (for example more than 5 per cent of body weight in a month)
- Insomnia or hypersomnia
- Psychomotor agitation or retardation
- Fatigue or loss of energy nearly every day
- Feelings of worthlessness or of excessive or inappropriate guilt
- Diminished ability to think or concentrate or indecisiveness every day
- Recurrent thoughts of death (not just fear of dying), recurrent suicidal ideation without a specific plan, or a suicide attempt, or a specific plan for committing suicide

---

Box 7.5 shows the criteria for major depressive disorder elaborated by *DSM-III-R*: the presence of at least five of the symptoms nearly every day for a period of at least two weeks, including one or other of the first two symptoms listed. Depression is a cluster of symptoms – a syndrome – so that not every depressed client will have the same symptoms. For example one client may be suicidal whilst another may not be. *DSM-III-R* permits a diagnosis of major depressive disorder to be made even though the client may be exhibiting some psychotic symptoms. Clients who have had at least two but always less than five symptoms for a continuous period of two years can qualify for the diagnostic category of dysthymia in *DSM-III-R*. Dysthymia represents an 'intermediate' classification between clinical disorder and normality.

Assessing for suicidal risk

It is important to clarify whether a client's suicidal thoughts are active or passive. Many depressed clients have passive suicidal thoughts – 'I would not be bothered if I did not wake up tomorrow morning' or 'I would not mind if some joy-rider knocked me down.' These passive thoughts give less cause for concern than the client who has made specific plans – 'If I did commit suicide I would go into the garage when my wife has left for work, I would attach a tube to the exhaust, lead it into the car and that would be it.' If the client is an impulsive person or has a drink problem this heightens the risk further. There are two self-report measures that are particularly helpful with suicidal clients – Beck's Hopelessness Scale and Linehan's Reasons for Living Inventory. These are now briefly considered in turn.

Beck's Hopelessness Scale This scale (Beck et al., 1974) consists of 21 items with the client responding true or false to statements such as 'I can look forward to more bad times than good times' and 'There's no use in really trying to get something I want because I probably won't get it.' Marking nine or more items as true is taken as indicating a state of severe hopelessness. Beck and his colleagues found that a score of nine or above successfully predicted 94 per cent of suicidal persons from an out-patient population followed over a six-year period.

The Reasons For Living Inventory The RFL (Linehan et al., 1983; Linehan, 1985) has 48 items, such as 'I am too stable to kill myself.' Each statement is rated in terms of its importance as a reason for not committing suicide if the thought were to cross one's mind. The scale has six sub-scales: (i) survival and coping; (ii) responsibility to family; (iii) child-related concerns; (iv) fear of suicide; (v) fear of social disapproval; (vi) moral objections to suicide. Linehan (1985) has suggested that the absence of strong positive reasons to live are most predictive of suicidal behaviour.

The first three sub-scales – survival and coping, responsibility to family and child-related concerns – contain the items most pertinent to the presence or absence of positive reasons for living. As well as being a measure of the likelihood of suicidal behaviour the RFL has important counselling implications. The counsellor can help to keep the client mindful of their espoused reasons for inhibiting suicidal behaviour.

Depression is often present to varying degrees with clients suffering from PTSD. The depression may be mild, at a sub-clinical level, in which case clients might typically score in the borderline zone on the depression sub-scale of the HAD. At this level clients could well meet the criteria for dysthymic disorder as defined in *DSM-III-R*. Dysthymic disorder typically affects 5 per cent of the general population and though it is a mild disorder its course is chronic, often extending over many years, and it causes considerable personal, social and work dysfunction (Burton and Akishal, 1990). At the other end of the severity continuum and more rarely occurring are depressed clients with psychotic features. Suicidal behaviour is not uncommon amongst depressed clients and tends to be associated more with the severe depressions. Approximately 15 per cent of depressives eventually kill themselves. The next case study can serve as a template for the counselling of wide bands of PTSD sufferers with concurrent depression. There then follows a case study of counselling a PTSD sufferer who is exhibiting suicidal behaviour.

Paul – PTSD with concurrent depression

Paul, who was introduced in chapter 1, exhibited PTSD symptoms in the wake of the Hillsborough football stadium disaster in which ninety-five people were killed. Chapters 1 and 5 described his counselling for the specific PTSD symptoms. Here his counselling for a moderate depression is elaborated.

Prior to Hillsborough Paul had been a gregarious character. His main leisure pursuits were going to football matches with his friends and to clubs and pubs. He had enjoyed his job as a bus driver, relishing the banter with passengers. His taste for life took a severe blow two years prior to Hillsborough when his marriage broke up; his wife went off with their two children to another city to live with a man with whom she had been having an affair. Paul had been suicidal at that time but with the support of his friends and his mother he was enjoying life again by the time of Hillsborough.

Following the football disaster he found it impossible to sit in the cab of his bus: he felt trapped. As a consequence he lost his job. He became a recluse, avoiding both friends and crowds. He followed closely the protracted, two-year legal proceedings aimed at determining liability for the disaster. Paul found the periodic disclaimers of responsibility for the disaster very distressing. From time to time he had himself to give information either to solicitors in respect of compensation or to the police. He was very distressed for days afterwards. Paul's life had become largely bereft of any positive activities.

Counselling for Paul's depression began with acknowledgement by the counsellor of the frequency of events in his life that pushed his mood downward. In the early stages of counselling, rather than challenge the meaning Paul gave to the negative events, the counsellor inquired about whether they might be made more manageable if there were 'uplifts' or at least potential uplifts timetabled into his week. To have challenged negative meanings at this point would have risked alienating him. This also follows the general principle of cognitive therapy for depression that counselling strategies are predominantly behavioural at the outset and become increasingly cognitive as therapy progresses. Paul's immediate response to the counsellor's suggestion of the timetabling in of uplifts was that there was no point as he just became irritated with his friends when he met them. He did concede, however, that he needed to become active if he was ever to enjoy life. Accordingly he enrolled in day classes for maths and computing GCSE.

Over the first few counselling sessions the counsellor arrived at a cognitive-interpersonal formulation of Paul's depression. He was in the trap depicted in Figure 7.1. From this it can be seen that Paul's trauma belief has two components, the first a conclusion – 'The people you trust let you down' – which he derives from his experiences, and the second a programme for action based on his conclusion. His programme for relating to other people results in aggressive and avoidance behaviours which are highly likely to be perceived negatively by significant others. Consequently they do not provide the sort of uplifts that had previously helped him cope with the earlier trauma of his marital break-up. This serves to underline his trauma belief that people are not to be trusted. He becomes increasingly isolated, at the periphery of existence and no longer at the centre of a web of mutually satisfying relationships. The continued isolation exacerbates depression. In the depressed state there is greater access to negative memories such as the break up of his marriage and a vicious circle is set up.

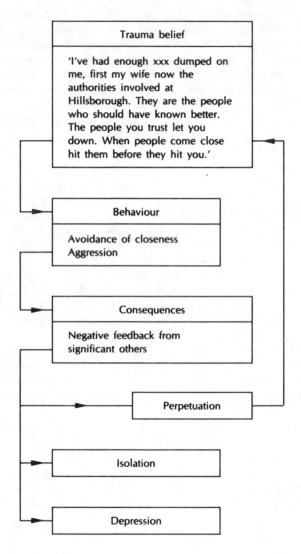

Figure 7.1 *Paul's trap*

Elaborating a pictorial representation of the client's difficulties using the headings of Figure 7.1 – beliefs, behaviour, consequences – helps to highlight for the counsellor a variety of possible points for intervention. When presented to the client it also gives a succinct summary of the factors that serve both to cause and to maintain the difficulties. The client can see the action implications more readily than in a purely verbal exchange with the counsellor.

Paul greeted the representation of his difficulties with a sigh of relief. The counsellor had two choice points in addressing Figure 7.1. The first option was to challenge Paul's negative view of the world and the second was to challenge the utility of his programme for relating to other people. The counsellor chose the latter option to begin with. Paul was asked 'Is it actually working for you to hit others first, does it get you what you want?' He responded to this with something of an aside, which the counsellor took a mental note of to be addressed later – 'I don't know what I want.' The counsellor continued.

> *Counsellor:* Is verbally hitting others when they do or say anything that irritates you making you feel better?
> *Paul:* No.
> *Counsellor:* Why continue to do something that doesn't work?
> *Paul:* They shouldn't be such idiots.
> *Counsellor:* Were they always idiots?
> *Paul:* No.
> *Counsellor:* When did they change?
> *Paul:* They haven't really. Deep down I know it's me. I'm useless.

The counsellor has satisfactorily made the point to Paul that his present programme for relating to others does not work. The obvious next step is for the counsellor to suggest that Paul experiments with a different interpersonal style. Unfortunately, before the counsellor has got there Paul has derailed him with the kind of negative self-image statement that is almost the hallmark of depression. The counsellor persists.

> *Counsellor:* You have mentioned two things in passing that I think it's important for us to discuss in depth, say at our next counselling session. First the idea that you are 'useless' and second the feeling that you do not know what you want out of relationships. For now I would like to concentrate on the practicability of making any interactions you have with others this week easier than they have been of late. Is that OK?
> *Paul:* That's fine by me.
> *Counsellor:* How could you play it differently when you meet people this week?
> *Paul:* I should be the way I used to be.
> *Counsellor:* How will you achieve that?
> *Paul:* I've got to keep my cool, but I don't know how.
> *Counsellor:* Maybe if you can exaggerate the situation and use humour it will make it easier. What you might do when you notice the first signs of anger is to imagine you are putting the other person in front of your own one-man firing squad. As you raise your gun you think 'They don't really deserve it' and you visualize yourself walking up to them and escorting them away from the firing wall.

> *Paul:* [*laughing*] I could give it a try.

This extract illustrates that often the best way to change a negative belief is first to change a behaviour. If as a consequence of non-aggressive behaviour Paul experiences positive feedback this is a powerful argument against his negative view of the world. Because the negative belief is already weakened the counsellor can go on to challenge it further. Thus in a subsequent session the counsellor asked whether Paul was over-generalizing in his negative view of the world, citing the lifelong support of his mother and the helpfulness of his maths and computing teacher at day school. Paul concluded that his view of the world was overly negative and unnecessarily so. As agreed at the previous session, Paul and the counsellor addressed first his negative view of himself and then his 'wants' with regard to relationships at the next session.

> *Counsellor:* What makes you say you are useless?
> *Paul:* The fact that I am here seeing you. Other people went through Hillsborough and haven't ended up like me.
> *Counsellor:* How do you mean 'ended up'?
> *Paul:* Well, unemployed, on the scrap heap.
> *Counsellor:* Does being unemployed mean you are on the scrap heap?
> *Paul:* Lots of people think it does. They just think I am malingering.
> *Counsellor:* Who are 'They'?
> *Paul:* The woman over the road made a snide comment the other day when I met her in the supermarket. 'Enjoying your compensation are we?' she said. I could have butted her after what I've been through.
> *Counsellor:* But is everyone like her?
> *Paul:* No, she's always been a silly xxxx.
> *Counsellor:* Have any good things come out of being unemployed?
> *Paul:* Yes, I am getting the hang of maths now and I never thought I would be up to computers.
> *Counsellor:* Can you really be totally useless?
> *Paul:* No, I'm not. There are some things I am not good at and some I am.
> *Counsellor:* Isn't that the same for everybody?
> *Paul:* It probably is.

The counsellor has again countered Paul's tendency to over-generalize. The issue of over-generalization is also the starting point for addressing the next item on the agenda: Paul's wants, needs and expectations in relationships.

> *Counsellor:* Last time we met we said we would look at how you are playing relationships; if we can turn to them now.
> *Paul:* Fine.
> *Counsellor:* I got the impression that because of your experiences with your ex-wife and how the authorities handled Hillsborough you've virtually concluded 'To hell with human beings.'

Paul: I wouldn't have put it as strong as that.

Counsellor: How would you put it?

Paul: I keep my distance.

Counsellor: What will happen if you get close?

Paul: Nothing really, I suppose.

Counsellor: Are you going to continue to keep your distance?

Paul: Probably.

Counsellor: Does that make you happy?

Paul: No.

Counsellor: I'm confused! So you are saying to yourself 'I am going to keep my distance. I know it doesn't make me happy and I also know that nothing much will happen if I do get close.'

Paul: Hmm. It doesn't make sense, does it?

Counsellor: I can't quite follow it.

Paul: I just feel frightened with people and 'hit' them and then that's the end of the contact.

Counsellor: So if you 'hit' them you get the reward of lessening your anxiety?

Paul: Yes, but I also feel guilty for being snappy with them.

Counsellor: Suppose you could learn to tolerate the discomfort of meeting people, how would life be then?

Paul: I wouldn't feel as guilty.

Counsellor: Is it possible that you could also begin to enjoy some relationships again?

Paul: I might but I don't think I could chance it with a close relationship with a woman.

Counsellor: How do you mean?

Paul: I can see that if I wasn't as ratty with old friends things would be easier but I don't want anything close with a woman. I couldn't stand to go through the break-up of my marriage again.

Counsellor: Perhaps for now you could start with old friends. What would you eventually like to be able to do with some of your old friends?

Paul: Go fishing the way we used to.

Counsellor: OK. When you notice yourself getting anxious with friends imagine yourself when you are enjoying sitting fishing with them. For homework I would also like you to recall your fishing expeditions each time you have a drink. That will make it easier to recall fishing when you are getting anxious in friends' company.

Paul: I will do that.

Depressed clients typically 'want' to do something (in Paul's case avoid company) that is at odds with their 'needs': they are in a dilemma. The needs of a client can be gauged by assessing what have been the major sources of uplift in their life (for Paul this has been friendship). The conflict between wants and needs can often be resolved by examining the client's unrealistic expectations (for Paul the belief that friends are a threat).

The counselling session with Paul ended with a further

Box 7.6 *Homework task for Paul: monitoring shifts in mood*

1 About what time did your mood take a downturn?
2 Briefly recall what you were thinking and/or doing before the downturn.
3 What thoughts or images do you think might have pushed you downhill?
4 What did you think or do when you realized your mood was slipping?
5 Looking back now, is there a better way you could play the same situation if it cropped up again? Please specify.
6 If you come up with a better way, on a scale of 0–100 per cent certain, how sure are you that you would be able to apply the better way in practice?

---

homework assignment, the monitoring of shifts in mood. The format of Box 7.6 was used. We can illustrate the use of this with an instance taken from the client's experiences. In Paul's case the counsellor used the example of his meeting the neighbour in the supermarket, her pejorative comments, his appraisal of those comments and his subsequent despair. The sequence begins with helping the client locate and elaborate on the context in which the distress occurred. This is particularly important for anxious clients, as without such priming they often do not have access to the cognitions that caused distress. The later part of the sequence is concerned with the client enlarging their coping repertoire by deriving implications for action from the negative experiences. Implicit is the notion that the client becomes more problem focused in response to upsets – 'What can I do about this in the future?' – as opposed to the emotion-focused 'Isn't this awful'. Further the emphasis is on the client's responsibility for bringing about enduring change. At question 6 of the sequence the client rates their self-efficacy, the belief in their ability to implement a solution. One of the goals of counselling is to enhance the client's self-efficacy. To do this effectively the counsellor has to go beyond encouragement. Unrealistic encouragement is likely to demotivate the client. The counsellor has to help the client assess whether they are nearer to achieving a goal than they think, or whether there is not some more efficient means of achieving the goal.

John – PTSD with concurrent depression and suicidal behaviour

John, a soldier, had taken a drugs overdose three months after his friend was killed in action. He blamed himself for his friend's death. John had been due to go out on patrol but was showing flu symptoms. He had gone to his superior officer and asked for and was granted relief from his duties for that night; his friend substituted for him. Tragically the friend was killed by a sniper's bullet. John felt very guilty. He told the counsellor 'It should have been me.' He attended his friend's funeral and was very distressed at the graveside to see his friend's mother try to throw herself into the grave with her son. Since the funeral he had been plagued by intrusive imagery of his friend's mother and the belief that he was responsible for her distress. He knew the family well, and was almost like an adopted son. The family did not blame him at all for the death, but nevertheless this served to heighten John's distress – 'How could I hurt such nice people?' His colleagues had been very supportive. The final straw for John came when he rang his mistress in his home country only to learn that she had rung his wife to sort out 'what sort of game he thinks he is playing at, leaving one of us and going back to the other like a ball in a game of tennis'. She told him he was despicable. John put the phone down and went and took an overdose.

> *John:* I could have gone on patrol if I had wanted to.
> *Counsellor:* But your superior could see your flu symptoms.
> *John:* Oh I had the flu all right but I could have got by on patrol. I made them seem worse because I couldn't be bothered with anything. I had been fed up for weeks.
> *Counsellor:* What had made you fed up?
> *John:* I have got a wife and kids and a girlfriend with a child. I can't decide which one to stay with. When I'm with one I get flak about the other one. I can't win. It's hopeless.

As mentioned earlier, a pervasive sense of hopelessness is a major predictor of suicidal behaviour. The counsellor goes on to examine the client's self-blame.

> *Counsellor:* Do you think you are in an impossible situation or are you an impossible person?
> *John:* Both.
> *Counsellor:* What makes you conclude that you are an impossible person?
> *John:* Just look what I have done to my friend and his family, my wife and the kids, the girlfriend and her child. It must be me, I'm the one to blame!
> *Counsellor:* You are certainly saying you are or have been making

mistakes, even big ones. But I don't follow how that makes you an impossible person?

John: They think so.

Counsellor: Do they? What about your friend's mother, brother and sister?

John: They are just nice people.

Counsellor: Sounds like if there is a positive you discount it.

John: Hmmm.

Counsellor: Can your wife and girlfriend really despise you through and through? Would they keep contact if you really were a despicable person?

John: I guess not.

Counsellor: A year ago if you knew a friend was having a bad time in his personal life and also not feeling too well, would you have stood in for him on duty?

John: Yes, that's what friends are for.

Counsellor: Then why was it not OK for your friend to stand in for you?

John: I see what you mean.

In this extract the counsellor was concerned to modify the global extent of the client's self-blame as it is this that tends to be linked to suicidal behaviour rather than regret for specific courses of action. The counsellor then goes on to use the technique of time projection to decrease John's sense of hopelessness.

Counsellor: If you went to visit Gus' family in five weeks' time how would you feel?

John: Awful. It would remind me of what I had done.

Counsellor: And what had you done?

John: Nothing, I suppose.

Counsellor: It's difficult for us all to swallow the fact that very awful things can happen as a result of quite innocent actions of ours.

John: Yes, when I was about ten I had a friend about the same age who was taking his younger brother who was about four to the shops. To get to the shops they had to cross the road. My friend was holding his brother's hand and the little one let go and ran across the road and was killed. I couldn't believe it when I heard.

Counsellor: Could you blame your friend?

John: No he was only a kid himself doing what he did most days.

Counsellor: Perhaps when you say 'What have I done?' pause long enough to answer it. If you leave it hanging in mid-air it will sap your energy. Perhaps you could practise answering the question with 'I haven't done anything with regard to Gus that was deliberate, you can't be responsible for chance.'

John: I will do that.

Counsellor: If you go and see Gus' family in five months how would you feel?

John: Sad for them and me but it will be good to be with them.

Counsellor: Could we look at using this time projection strategy with your relationship with the women in your life?

John: OK.

Counsellor: Suppose it's five years hence and you are back with your wife and children: how would life be?

John: OK, I guess.

Counsellor: But didn't the relationship with the girlfriend arise because the marriage hadn't been working?

John: Only partly. The marriage had been going through a bad patch before I met her, I was sick of being in the married quarter, got irritable with the wife and she gave me back everything I gave her and it escalated. So I went into town looking for some fun and got to know the girlfriend: she is the manageress of a pub, and a single parent. I find I can talk to her more easily than I ever could to my wife and one thing led to another. But the early days of my marriage were OK. I wasn't complaining.

Counsellor: So whichever relationship you choose, in five years' time you would think that you would be at least just reasonably content?

John: I had not thought of it like that before, but you're right. What you are saying is that it's not going to matter that much who I choose.

Counsellor: I don't want to be a cynic but George Bernard Shaw once said 'Love is an exaggeration of the differences between human beings.' Maybe within limits there is some truth in that.

John: [*laughing*]. That's not very romantic!

Counsellor: But if there is a large grain of truth in it, it might take some of the sting out of making a decision. It's not going to be catastrophic for you whichever choice you make.

John: I can see that now. But I can't stand hurting my wife or girlfriend.

Counsellor: Maybe that's why you go backwards and forwards. After the novelty of a few days with one has worn off you go back to the other to relieve her pain, which you do for a few days. Then you think of the pain of the other and the knight in shining armour rides off again.

John: I can't go on like that.

Counsellor: But you will continue like that for as long as you can tell yourself 'I can't stand the guilt of leaving one of my women in pain'! Given the situation you have no option but to leave one in pain. The danger is that if you delay a decision too long they will both dump you, they are each reinforcing the other's negative view of you.

John: So I've got to tell myself I can stand the pain. It's like in the running I do we have a phrase 'no gain without pain'.

The time projection strategy helps to make reasons for living explicit and these reasons can then serve to inhibit suicidal behaviour. In the short term, however, the client often has to face a number of hassles. To help offset these the client can be encouraged to generate uplifts. But for the thought of uplifts to have a significant effect on mood and suicidal behaviour there is evidence (Williams and Dritschel, 1988) that they have to be recalled vividly, as the next extract illustrates.

> *Counsellor:* What could you do that improves your mood?
> *John:* I used to enjoy running but since Gus' death I can't be bothered.
> *Counsellor:* Perhaps try it out in small doses, because you will only get to enjoy it by keeping on trying.
> *John:* I'll just do a couple of miles.
> *Counsellor:* That sounds a lot to start with.
> *John:* Oh, last year I managed to run the London Marathon. It wasn't a good time, but I was pleased with myself that I finished.
> *Counsellor:* Can you make an enjoyable mental video of the marathon? Perhaps recalling what it felt like crossing the finishing line, who greeted you, what they said. Your feelings of excitement at the start. Then play this video in your mind, maybe each time you have a drink. This way we might balance out the negative thoughts you have with some positive ones.

In this exercise the counsellor is focusing on enhancing the specificity of positive memories to reduce the likelihood of suicidal behaviour. Then the counsellor is seeking to improve the client's mood by improving the balance of negative and positive thoughts. There is evidence suggesting that mental health requires a balance of around three positive thoughts to two negative ones as negative cognitions are typically given greater subjective weight or importance (Kanouse and Hanson, 1971; Schwartz and Garamoni, 1986, 1989).

Box 7.7 *Practice summary – concurrent anxiety and depression*

1 The theme running through depression is of life having lost its flavour, whilst the theme in anxiety is one of threat.

2 The counsellor's goal in anxiety is to help the client test out whether there really is the degree of danger in situations that they suppose.

3 Useful strategies for anxiety include relaxation exercises for generalized anxiety disorder, controlled breathing for panic disorder, and graded exposure to feared situations for agoraphobia.

4 The counsellor's primary goal in depression is to help the client question the criteria by which they count themselves worthless or a failure and then to question their negative view of the future. Attention also has to be paid to how the client views and relates to their immediate social world.

5 Where the client is suicidal the counselling task is to help expand on reasons for living, that is, what has kept the client from suicide so far. Time projection is a useful strategy for encouraging the view that it is not absolutely impossible that life could get better.

8

Counselling for Concurrent Irritability

Much of the focus in the treatment of post-traumatic stress disorder has been on the two components intrusive imagery (criterion B in *DSM-III-R*) and avoidance behaviour (criterion C) whilst disordered arousal (criterion D) has been relatively neglected. This chapter seeks to redress the balance, focusing particularly on irritability (criterion D2: see Box 1.4, p. 4). This term permits an important distinction between outward irritability (OI) and inward irritability (II). Outward irritability can have very negative effects on relationships, leading to a diminution of support from significant others which in turn increases the likelihood of depression. Inward irritability may lead to self-mutilating behaviours and suicide.

Experience suggests that most PTSD clients have a problem with outward irritability. There is considerable overlap between the concept of outward irritability as used here and the concept of anger, but the term outward irritability highlights better the interpersonal dimension of the problem. Anger is an almost universal precursor of aggression (though in some instances there may be aggression without anger, for example the 'paid assassin'). Aggression is clearly 'bad news' for the significant others in the PTSD client's life. It also means the client is less likely to achieve their goals. As well as being an often occurring symptom associated with PTSD, outward irritability is a theme running through cluster B of personality disorders in *DSM-III-R*. As indicated in chapter 2, individuals with personality disorders may be more prone to suffer from PTSD following a major trauma. Those personality disorders which are most associated with outward irritability are shown in Box 8.1, together with the pertinent aspect of the disorder defined in *DSM-III-R*.

Whilst it is predominantly the cluster B personality disorders of *DSM-III-R* that have an irritability dimension, the Paranoid Personality (from cluster A) may also show irritability – 'is easily slighted and quick to react with anger or to counter-attack' – and so may those suffering the Passive Aggressive Personality Disorder

Box 8.1 *Personality disorders as defined in DSM-III-R cluster B*

Antisocial Personality Disorder	Evidence of conduct disorder with onset before age 15 and anti-social behaviour since the age of 15
Borderline Personality Disorder	Inappropriate intense anger or lack of control of anger beginning by early adulthood and present in a variety of contexts
Histrionic Personality Disorder	Is self-centred, actions being directed toward obtaining immediate satisfaction, has no tolerance for the frustration of delayed gratification
Narcissistic Personality Disorder	Reacts to criticism with feelings of rage, shame or humiliation (even if not expressed)

from cluster C who 'may become sulky, irritable or argumentative when asked to do something he or she does not want to do', 'may protest without justification that others make unreasonable demands on him or her', and who 'resent useful suggestions from others concerning how he or she would be more productive' (APA, 1987). In the Passive Aggressive Disorder the irritability may be more inward than in the cluster B personality disorders. Overall approximately half of the personality disorders have an irritability aspect. It is not suggested that an individual with a personality disorder is necessarily ill or non-functioning; they may function and remain perfectly well given a conducive environment. However, in the wake of a major trauma the environment is likely to be disturbed, and the maladaptive features of the personality disorder assume prominence, serving to contribute to the genesis and maintenance of PTSD.

Outward irritability may be assessed using the OI items of the Irritability, Depression, Anxiety Questionnaire (Snaith et al., 1978). The IDA contains four outward irritability items.

I lose my temper and shout or snap at others.
I am patient with other people. [Reverse scored]
I feel I might lose control and hit or hurt someone.
People upset me so much that I feel like slamming doors or banging about.

Each item is rated from 0 to 3 on perceived frequency of occurrence, a higher score indicating more pathology. The scores on each OI item are summed to give an OI total score. Clients scoring over 7 (against a scale maximum of 12) are regarded as pathological with regard to OI, those below 5 as normal, and those scoring 5–7 as borderline. As noted above, there is considerable conceptual overlap between outward irritability and anger, and the State-Trait Anger Expression Inventory (STAXI) (Spielberger, 1988) can usefully be employed to measure state anger, trait anger and anger expression. Unfortunately, there is no simple measure of inward irritability, despite the intuitive appeal of the concept. In this chapter it is taken to indicate a variety of emotional responses, from getting angry with oneself at one end of the spectrum to suicidal behaviour at the other end, with a wish to hurt or harm oneself in between.

OI scores are likely to be highly correlated with an individual's perception of the quality of relationships. For example Scott and Stradling (1987) found that outward irritability was a better predictor of mothers' perception of number and frequency of child behaviour problems than either maternal depression or anxiety. It is possible, of course, to assess the quality of a particular relationship directly using instruments such as the Dyadic Adjustment Scale (Spanier, 1976) for couples.

This chapter is devoted to counselling strategies for the various manifestations of irritability occurring in conjunction with PTSD. In keeping with the tenor of the book, the underlying model is cognitive-contextual. Thus it is not simply, say, that a client's belief that 'the whole world ought to be organized to meet my every need' creates a problem of low frustration tolerance, but it is the response of a significant other to that expression of frustration which serves to fuel or dampen the frustration. If the client exceeds the tolerance threshold of the significant other then the latter is likely to respond in a way that is beyond the tolerance threshold of the client, and a vicious circle of escalating conflict and distress ensues. The counselling implication is that where possible such significant others should be involved in the counselling as well as the client.

The counselling approach to concurrent irritability is illustrated here by four case studies. The first concerns a policeman who was badly assaulted by young men out on a stag night. He felt 'out of control' in his subsequent display of outward irritability, but his significant others did not see it as problematic. By contrast the second case involves a general practitioner who was assaulted by youths on her way to make a late night call to a patient living in a largely vacated block of flats awaiting demolition by the Council. Her subsequent outward irritability put very great strains on her marriage and on colleagues at work. The third case is of a woman whose irritability towards her children and towards the other residents of a battered women's refuge was driven by a history of being physically and sexually abused by her husband. In the fourth case inward irritability is the focus. This is the case of a soldier who had been a mercenary in Mozambique. He was haunted by the memory that, partly because of a language problem, he had shot three soldiers, believing them to be government troops when, in fact, they were on his side. On his return to England he began self-mutilating behaviours.

Simon – the 'out of control' policeman

One Saturday evening Simon was called to a bar at the end of a pier. The landlord had called the police because a stag party was getting out of hand and causing annoyance to other customers. Simon and a colleague arrived at the scene, and tried to calm the revellers. Some of them made abusive replies to his request and before he could reply his colleague ordered them all out of the pub. Simon very much felt that it was the wrong thing to do, but felt obliged to back up his colleague. As one of the young men was going through the pub doorway he tripped over the step and alleged to his friends that Simon's colleague had pushed him. At this the stag party turned on the two policeman and assaulted them. Simon was dangled over the railings of the pier and was terrified as he knew the currents around the end of the pier were lethal. The men left Simon and his colleague on the pier, badly beaten up. Subsequently Simon experienced intrusive flashbacks of being held over the end of the pier staring at the sea. He was very annoyed with his colleague because he believed the situation had been avoidable. Simon was a believer in quietly and calmly talking his way through difficult situations and believed that the sight of his uniform and gentle persuasion were his protection. The trauma shattered this belief. Simon's wife and two children were very important to him and he had a very happy home life. He was distraught to find that he had become irritable with his wife and two teenage children. However, they were very understanding and able to let his irritability wash over them. To Simon's dismay he found that in his role as organizer of the police Snooker League he was also becoming very irritable. Fortunately he was well thought of and liked by colleagues in the league and they were not reacting to his provocations. Simon expressed his concerns to the counsellor.

> *Simon:* I am just totally out of control.
> *Counsellor:* How do you mean totally?
> *Simon:* Well I'm horrible to everyone.
> *Counsellor:* What, all the time?
> *Simon:* Well no.
> *Counsellor:* How much of the time?
> *Simon:* Too much of the time.
> *Counsellor:* So sometimes you are very irritable with people and sometimes you're not and you want to reduce how often you are 'horrible' to people. Have I got that right?
> *Simon:* That's right.

Here the counsellor has helped redefine the problem in a way that implicitly conveys the message that the client does, in fact, already exhibit a degree of control in his interactions, but at the moment it is unfortunately not as much as the client would wish. The counsellor is challenging Simon's dichotomous thinking, which was of the form 'Either I am in control or I am not.' The counsellor goes on to suggest a self-monitoring exercise.

> *Counsellor:* What makes you sometimes go over the top with friends and family and then sometimes not?
> *Simon:* It must just be how I am feeling at the time.
> *Counsellor:* I would like to try and get behind the feelings that take you over the top. It could be very useful to try and record what you were doing or thinking before you go over the top.
> *Simon:* I'll do that. It's probably when I'm tired that I am at my worst. I am still not sleeping that well.
> *Counsellor:* Perhaps try out this sleep audio cassette tape on your personal stereo to help you get off to sleep.

The counsellor is setting the client out on a fine-grained analysis of the factors that trigger or inhibit his outward irritability. The client was also afraid that his irritability was going to interfere with his ever returning to and functioning at work. In the next extract the counsellor encourages the client to see this fear as a hypothesis to be tested and not as a fact.

> *Counsellor:* Would you put a bet on with a friend that you would over-react with a member of the public, when you are back at work? Say, for £50?

Simon: No, I don't think so.

Counsellor: Then how certain can you be that you will over-react – 0 per cent, 25 per cent, 50 per cent, 75 per cent, 100 per cent?

Simon: Maybe 25 per cent.

Counsellor: Looking at your track record of handling difficult situations, I think the risk is probably less than that. But neither of us really knows, we have not got a crystal ball, we wouldn't know until you tried going back for a period.

Simon: I can see that, but the consequences would be so dire if I go over the top. I could lose my job and could even end up in jail.

Counsellor: But how real is the 'if' likely to be?

Simon: I agree it's unlikely but I am still anxious about it.

Counsellor: Perhaps you could go through the problem-solving routine to see how you could reduce the risk.

Diane – the 'short fuse' general practitioner

Diane was assaulted *en route* to visit a patient in a partly vacated block of flats. It seemed likely to her, in retrospect, that the youths were drug abusers and after her medical bag. But because Diane clung ferociously to the bag they had viciously assaulted her. By the time she came to see the counsellor she had largely recovered from her physical injuries. She had returned to doing clinics and surgeries in the Health Centre, though the other partners had taken over home visits. Diane was troubled by intrusive memories of the assault, but they were beginning to diminish in intensity. The event that propelled her into seeing the counsellor occurred during morning surgery. Diane was seeing a patient who had cancer. The patient was pressing for specificity in the prognosis. Just as she said 'It's not looking good, at all' there was a knock at her door. Diane shouted for the person to come in: it was a receptionist delivering notes that had been mislaid earlier that morning. At this the patient became distraught, yelled at Diane 'Nobody has got any time for me' and stormed out of the Health Centre. Diane went into the Health Centre kitchen and started smashing the crockery. The noise could be heard in the waiting room and the senior partner went to calm her down. Unfortunately, matters were compounded by Diane's husband, a cardiac surgeon.

Diane: When my husband, Charles, found out from the senior partner, instead of being sympathetic to me he was furious. Charles lectured me on behaving professionally, told me there is no room for emotional outbursts in our work. I told him that if I had become just a bloody plumber like him then there wouldn't be any need for emotion. He became bitterly sarcastic and said 'Enter the saviour of the world', and I hit him.

Counsellor: Are you usually as irritable with Charles?

Diane: It was going downhill before the assault, but the relationship's got much worse since.

Counsellor: What was making it head downhill before the assault?

Diane: I think we were both so busy in what we were doing that when we got home we were both like coiled springs.

Counsellor: Where do you see the relationship heading?

Diane: We can't go on the way we have been, there's no point.

Counsellor: Is there any point in trying out some strategies to improve the relationship?

Diane: For the first couple of years of marriage we were fine, so if we could get back to that.

This illustrates the interpersonal dimension to outward irritability. It is not simply that a client may have a low tolerance of frustration, but that a significant other exceeds their tolerance threshold. Before recommending marital therapy to help with the client's irritability, the counsellor is establishing its likely success. In this case it is a question of regaining lost ground rather than teaching new skills of relating and the outcome is, therefore, that much more likely to be successful.

Counsellor: Would Charles be willing to come for marital therapy?

Diane: I think he would agree we have got to change things, but I can't see him coming to counselling. He'd probably see it as a weakness.

Counsellor: Maybe we should try and conduct marital therapy via yourself and see how far we can get.

Diane: OK.

Counsellor: What did you used to do in the early days of marriage that you don't do now?

Diane: If we could both get off for a day at the weekends, we would go walking in the hills of North Wales. We both used to really enjoy that.

Counsellor: Could that be a start in planning some uplifts into your life?

Diane: Yes, but that's not going to be enough.

Counsellor: Perhaps you could plan two or three pleasant surprises for each other before the next session.

Diane: I will have to think through how I get that over to Charles. I'll probably have to say something gross like if you want a return on this marriage you will have to invest in it.

The first stages of marital therapy tend to be behavioural rather than cognitive. A behavioural exercise such as the one specified above offers the prospect of an immediate success experience. Such an experience is much needed to enhance motivation and engage the client. The return on cognitive interventions tends to be less immediate and is potentially more threatening. Nevertheless cognitive changes are needed for enduring gains. At a later session the counsellor focuses on the cognitive dimensions.

Counsellor: You and Charles seem quite different people. You choose to work in a run-down city area, you get assaulted, your car is often vandalized, you have long consultations with your patients. Your surgery is still going on when others have finished. You get very upset if a patient is not happy with you, and you feel guilty if you take any personal time. Meanwhile Charles is pushing on and on up the hierarchy in the teaching hospital and primarily wants to achieve. It is almost as if you say, 'If I have got everyone's approval then I must be OK' and Charles says 'If I achieve, I am OK.'

Diane: I can see that climbing the greasy pole which is what Charles does is stupid. Many of those at the top are twits.

Counsellor: Is there anyone at the top who is not a twit?

Diane: One or two.

Counsellor: So it is theoretically possible to be at the top and be human?

Diane: It's possible.

Counsellor: So you can be achieving and human?

Diane: I guess so.

Counsellor: So you don't disagree with what Charles is doing in principle?

Diane: No.

Counsellor: Does he disagree with what you're doing in principle?

Diane: It certainly feels like it.

Counsellor: Try and be Charles for a minute and I'll be you and you answer as Charles would.

The role reversal helped the client to better get in touch with her husband's underlying attitude towards her work. The client concluded that Charles did not disagree with the values underpinning her work, but did disagree about the means of expressing those values. His sarcasm, she thought, reflected his frustration at her refusal to adopt a more appropriate expression of her values. Establishing that spouses do not have conflicts about goals but simply about the means to achieve them itself engenders hope.

Counsellor: In the last session you concluded that there is a basic respect for each other's values in the marriage.

Diane: Yes, there is. Since the last session we have done some talking. We have planned to go walking next weekend as we are both off work for two days. But I still can't see me changing things at work much.

Counsellor: What stops you changing them?

Diane: Guilt. I wouldn't feel so bad if I wasn't so involved. But there is also a bit of me that since the assault says what's the point any more.

Counsellor: So you seem to have two modes of thought at the moment: the first is as if you are saying to yourself 'If I am to do anything worthwhile for patients I have got to slave-drive myself' and the second is 'What's the point? What I do is only a drop of water in the ocean' and you flip from one mode to the other.

Diane: I also feel betrayed. I have given everything to this job, if I am honest I have even given my marriage for it, and look how I end up, badly beaten up. I am terrified it could be worse next time. I don't know whether I will ever be able to visit alone at night.

Counsellor: Who do you feel betrayed by?

Diane: No one really, it's just the world.

Counsellor: It almost sounds as if your bottom line is 'If I care enough the world should appreciate it.'

Diane: That sounds extreme, but it should, shouldn't it?

Counsellor: I think we all like our care returned, but how useful is it to go on insisting that it should?

Diane: It just gets one wilder and wilder.

Counsellor: If then it isn't useful to continue to use 'shoulds' about people's responses to your caring, perhaps it might be useful to explore another style of caring.

Diane: How do you mean?

Counsellor: Perhaps we could draw a line. At this end of the continuum we might put 'I have got to slave-drive myself' and at the other end 'There's no point, they (the world) just dirty on you anyway.' Adopting either extreme position causes you distress. Could you for homework write a script for yourself that avoids the extremes and would enable you to function better? It would contain the sort of things you could say or do in those difficult situations you encounter, such as interruptions during a surgery. In addition I would like you to timetable into your work some uplifts.

Diane: Right.

Here a major trauma, the assault, had shaken the client's core belief in the perfectibility of the world if only she cared enough. Partly because of the negative interactions with her husband, she was in danger of answering the question forcibly raised by the trauma with a dysfunctional trauma belief. The counsellor uses the notion of a continuum to shift the client away from dichotomous thinking. Further, the onus is placed on the client to come up with a new script for living that is consistent with her values. Homework assignments are particularly important with the PTSD client with concurrent irritability as they can easily use the sessions to dump all their irritations on the counsellor. It follows that it is important to follow up non-compliance with a homework assignment as it may be driven by a dysfunctional belief such as 'Given what I've gone through, I shouldn't have to put effort into things.'

At the next counselling session the client produced a list of activities that she could delegate, and came up with the image of travelling further with her car (that is, herself) if she drove it at an optimum 50 m.p.h. rather than speeding at 75 m.p.h. The counsellor suggested she put pictures of cars in strategic places to remind her of her coping plan. There were, however, still niggles between the client and her husband. The counsellor suggested that

---

Box 8.2 *Communication guidelines*

In stating a problem, always begin with something positive.
Be specific.
Express your feelings.
Admit to your role in the problem.
Be brief when defining problems.
Discuss only one problem at a time.
Summarize what your partner has said and check with them you have correctly understood them before making your reply.
Don't jump to conclusions, avoid mind reading, talk only about what you can see.
Be neutral rather than negative.
Focus on solutions.
Behavioural change should include give and take and compromise.
Any changes agreed should be very specific.

---

they spend no more than twenty minutes a day using the guidelines of Box 8.2. Each day they would take it in turn to choose a problem to discuss in 'prime communication time'. To start with they would choose the less emotionally loaded problems. Each partner had the right to point out violations of the guidelines during 'prime time'. If a problem was unresolved at the end of the twenty minutes it was put on ice. The client's response to the suggested use of the guidelines was typical of many clients.

Diane: They seem very artificial.
Counsellor: They are, but if the natural way of communication is not working then it may be worthwhile to experiment with something else.
Diane: We'll give it a try, but I am worried that by the time we get round to discussing a problem, I have been stewing on it so long, I am in such a bad mood that Charles is going to have to send me to the sin bin as soon as we start on the guidelines.
Counsellor: You could try to defuse the situation to some extent by keeping a 'How I Felt' diary. [Box 8.3 gives an example.] If you felt comfortable enough you could share your diary with Charles.

Box 8.3 *Example from Diane's 'How I Felt' diary*

When you	– came home from work and started working again immediately after tea
I felt	– lonely, left out, sad
Because I was thinking	– your work is more important to you than me, I didn't count
Is there a more realistic and possibly less distressing way of thinking or behaving in this situation?	– It's just that we've both got a lot on at the moment. We do have plans to be away together at the weekend.

Rose – a battered spouse

Rose had been living in a battered women's hostel for ten weeks, when she was referred to a counsellor by the officer in charge. She had been in the hostel a number of times in the ten years of her stormy marriage. This time, however, the officer in charge was concerned at the change in Rose. She was uncharacteristically angry, both with the other residents of the hostel and with her own children aged four and six. Rose had been physically and sexually abused by her husband, Vin, on numerous occasions in their marriage. Usually Vin's assaults were drink related, and as she felt 'he wasn't that bad when he was sober' she had in the past returned to him after a few weeks in the hostel. However, his last assault occurred when she found evidence that he had been unfaithful and she had challenged him about it. She was raped and later that day left the marital home with her children 'for good'. Rose had experienced PTSD symptomatology for years and it had become particularly intense whenever there was the beginnings of an argument with Vin. Arguments, even mild ones, served as cues for intrusive imagery. She would retreat from Vin. This would serve to heighten Vin's frustration and aggression after the argument. She also avoided him sexually. The fear of men had generalized such that she would avoid sitting next to a man on a bus if possible, and if sitting on the same seat was unavoidable would perch herself on the edge.

Counselling for Rose was conducted in two stages. In the first, Rose was referred to the group parent survival programme (described fully in Scott, 1989a) which included a wide cross-section of parents, some of whom were self-referrals. The effect of this on Rose was that she felt, as she put it, 'still part of the human race', and it gave her a respite from the stigmatization of a battered women's refuge. In the group she rediscovered her child management strategies such as Grandma's law 'When you have done X then you can do/have Y', catching the children being good (positive reinforcement) and time out (2–5 minutes) from positive reinforcement for the children's most serious misbehaviours.

As a consequence she became less outwardly irritable with her children and the perceived number of child behaviour problems reduced. She gained some sense of control over her disordered arousal. She had also established sufficient rapport with the group leader to risk addressing her rapes. Few (less than 10 per cent) rape victims volunteer themselves directly to professionals, and often it is some less personally threatening outreach that engages them and that can be a stepping stone to a focus on their trauma.

Rose was then taken through a ten session programme derived from Lang's (1977) three-component model, focusing on her physiological, behavioural and cognitive responses to the trauma. For each channel she was taught two coping strategies. In the physiological channel her first coping strategy was progressive muscular relaxation. Unfortunately, in the refuge Rose did not have access to a tape recorder and so she was asked to tense a muscle group for ten seconds, then relax it for five seconds, 'feeling the tension flow out like the tides of the sea', and to work through each muscle group in turn. It was agreed that probably the best time for her to practise this exercise was after the children had gone to sleep.

For Rose the first signs of her becoming tense were a tightening of the muscles in the throat and a difficulty in swallowing. It was suggested that when this occurred she should tip her head back and imagine looking at a puffy white cloud in the sky with a seagull flying by until she felt a slight reduction in the tension. Rose, however, had difficulty in implementing this cue controlled relaxation response. The situations in which she expressed a tightening of the throat muscles were those that demanded an assertive response which she felt unable to volunteer. Rose feared that if she used the cue controlled relaxation response this might provoke aggression in others.

This required work in the cognitive channel. The therapist suggested that she was over-generalizing about people's responses on the basis of her husband's behaviour. Whilst Rose agreed that this was probably the case, she nevertheless felt very anxious about trying it. In the spirit of collaborative empiricism the therapist suggested that it was impossible to know what assertive responses would generally produce without trying them. It was agreed that Rose would practise an assertive response with the lady who was supposed to help her on the cleaning rota at the hostel on Tuesday and Saturday.

Rose and the therapist role-played with Rose making a direct request of the lady to begin the cleaning, involving eye contact, a firm voice and a very specific call to action, for example: 'Could you give me a hand with the dishes now.' If Rose received a negative response she was to practise the cue-controlled relaxation and follow this by a matter-of-fact repetition of her original request with no further elaboration. Though the scenes were satisfactorily role-played in the session, Rose was still very anxious. Rose, it seemed, had never stood up to adults and did not believe she had a right to. She personalized matters; her bottom line was 'If something has gone wrong it is my fault.' This led to a discussion of how much of the break-up of her marriage was due to her and how much to her husband. Implicitly this moved Rose away from the dichotomous thinking of 'Either I am to blame or he is to blame' and she concluded that 90 per cent of the break up was due to her husband's behaviour and 10 per cent due to her response to that behaviour. This cleared the way for Rose to believe that she had a right to be assertive. However, further work was necessary to demonstrate that there could be a positive outcome as a result of assertive behaviour. This was achieved by pointing out the positive benefits already accrued from being assertive with the children (using the strategies taught in the parent training programme) and that therefore there was no reason in principle why there might not be beneficial consequences from assertive behaviours with adults. The two major cognitive changes for Rose were that she had a right to be assertive and that it could be beneficial to exercise this right. Although Lang's three channels are separately conceptualized, they have reciprocal interactions and the therapeutic task is to move deftly to and fro between them. In the behaviour channel Rose learned how to make an assertive response and how to plan uplifts into her life, starting with attending an aerobics class (which would in turn affect her physiological channel).

Irfon – a personality-disordered mercenary

Irfon had been a mercenary for ten years, since leaving the British Army after ten years' service. Whilst serving with guerrilla forces in Mozambique he killed three of his own side as a result of a muddle over the language – Portuguese – of which he spoke little.

He had led soldiers into a village and when he encountered three men holding guns he assumed that they were the enemy. Irfon had not understood that another group of guerrillas was to enter the village from the opposite direction, thereby trapping government forces. As it happened, the few government soldiers there had already left the village. Irfon was referred to the counsellor by a psychiatrist because of his self-injurious behaviour. This behaviour had begun three months previously when he had returned from Africa. The referral letter from the psychiatrist suggested that not only was Irfon suffering from PTSD but that this disorder was superimposed upon an Anti-social or Narcissistic Personality Disorder as defined in *DSM-III-R* cluster B.

In his schooldays Irfon frequently played truant and was often involved in fights. He was, however, quite a star sportsman and shone in his local youth club and on adventure weekends. At eighteen he joined the Army where again he had lots of conflict with authority figures but came to be regarded as unquestionably heroic and very creative in his solutions to problems. The view of his superiors was that he was a law unto himself, valued, but with a great capacity for alienating people. After ten years in the Army his conflicts with colleagues and superiors reached such a pitch that he left before he was thrown out. Subsequently he served as a mercenary in many different locations. The counsellor's first encounter with Irfon served to underline the fact that this would be a most difficult case to handle.

> *Counsellor:* Hi, what do you see as the main problem?
> *Irfon:* Haven't you got my notes?
> *Counsellor:* Not the whole file yet, just the referral letter.
> *Irfon:* Well that's no good. I don't want to go through the whole thing again.

At this point the counsellor is beginning to feel irritable and has an automatic thought of the form 'If you don't want my help, sod off!' Personality-disordered clients do tend to evoke intense feelings in the counsellor. These feelings serve to mirror the impact of the client on other people, and as such they convey useful information. It is important, therefore, that the counsellor closely attend to negative feelings towards the client. Precisely because the personality-disordered client does engender negative feelings in others they are likely to go on the offensive and this serves to sabotage the development of the client/counsellor relationship. Not surprisingly, some personality-disordered clients are difficult to engage in counselling. The counsellor has to work extra hard at establishing a collaborative alliance whilst formulating a map to explain the client's distress.

Counsellor: Perhaps we could look at what has been bothering you most this week.

Irfon: It's not being able to lift things with this wrist.

Counsellor: What happened?

Irfon: I slashed it.

Counsellor: Were you trying to kill yourself?

Irfon: Hell, no!

Counsellor: What were you trying to do?

Irfon: I wasn't doing anything, I just wanted to cut myself.

Counsellor: What were you thinking about or doing just before you injured yourself?

Irfon: Thinking about the balls-up in Mozambique.

Counsellor: What gets to you about that?

Irfon: They should have given us proper language training and the accident wouldn't have happened. But they were a bunch of incompetents. Then afterwards they just wanted to get rid of me.

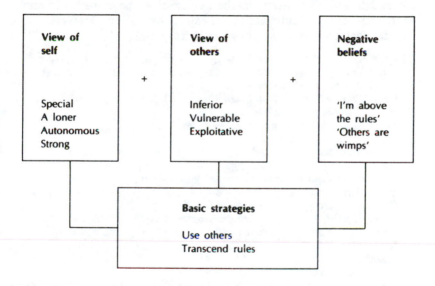

Figure 8.1 *Formulation of Irfon's case: Anti-social and Narcissistic Personality Disorder*

Beck and Freeman (1990) have suggested the following four headings as being useful in formulating cases of personality disorder: view of self, view of others, negative beliefs and basic strategies. Irfon's case is formulated in Figure 8.1 using these headings and drawing on the information conveyed in the last extract. The trauma in Mozambique represented a forceable challenge to Irfon's view of himself and of others as represented in Figure 8.1. His task was to reconcile the evidence of his fallibility manifested in Mozambique with his core beliefs about himself and his programme for relating to other people. (It should be noted that his Anti-social/Narcissistic Personality Disorder had been reasonably adaptive up to the Mozambique catastrophe.) He attempted to reconcile the data with his self schema by exaggerating the negative influence of 'incompetent others' in events. However, the counsellor concluded that from time to time Irfon became aware of a credibility gap and the self-injurious behaviour possibly served as a distraction. But with a personality-disordered client it is important that the counsellor takes time to clarify why it is that the client is not functioning at the present time. It would have been facile, for example, to conclude that Irfon must be consumed with guilt for his behaviour in Mozambique and that he wanted to punish himself. In the next session the counsellor seeks clarification and confirmation of his formulation. However, in typical fashion the client attempts to take over.

> *Irfon:* Do you want to see my wrist? [*He whips off his bandage before the counsellor can reply.*] It looks awful doesn't it? The one at the top is new, I did it this week.
> *Counsellor:* What would happen if you didn't injure yourself?
> *Irfon:* I wouldn't get a kick.
> *Counsellor:* Are there no other ways you could get kicks?
> *Irfon:* Of course there is!
> *Counsellor:* So what would happen if you didn't injure yourself?
> *Irfon:* I wouldn't feel anything.
> *Counsellor:* Injuring yourself makes you able to feel?
> *Irfon:* That's right.
> *Counsellor:* Do you fancy a tea or coffee?
> *Irfon:* Coffee, thanks. [*Counsellor makes a coffee for Irfon.*]
> *Counsellor:* You did want tea rather than coffee, didn't you?
> *Irfon:* No.
> *Counsellor:* Coffee, OK?
> *Irfon:* Fine, thanks.
> *Counsellor:* I am confused. You have just preferred one thing over another and the preference you're experiencing is 'OK' yet you have been feeling without injuring yourself.
> *Irfon:* Hmmm.
> *Counsellor:* Maybe it is not as awful as your having no feeling, but less than you would want. Do you need a dramatic situation to experience feelings?

Here the counsellor is tackling the psychic numbing or vacuum of feelings that is often characteristic of PTSD and self-injurious behaviour. Because the counsellor is dealing with a personality disorder he deliberately slows the pace of cognitive challenge and encourages the client to evaluate his experience. With a personality-disordered client the counsellor has to spend more time than usual on seemingly off-task but relationship-enhancing strategies, talking about a topic of interest to the client. Consequently work with the personality-disordered client is likely to be long term, perhaps twenty-five or more sessions. Further, because the cluster B personality-disordered clients are so difficult to continue to engage in counselling, the counsellor may simply have to weather the client's tirades about various people or events.

The following extract further illustrates use of the client's experience to bring about change.

> *Counsellor:* How did your week go, Irfon?
>
> *Irfon:* I am !***! furious. I waited for half an hour to see a slip of a girl in the Social Security, she was asking me a lot of stupid questions. Because I couldn't be certain of what my address will be, she told me to go away until I knew where I was living. You see I have been living with my uncle, but I have to get out, I need the space.
>
> *Counsellor:* What are you going to do?
>
> *Irfon:* I don't know, I need the money.
>
> *Counsellor:* Would it be possible to, say, ring the manager of the Social Security and maybe arrange a time and discuss it?
>
> *Irfon:* I'd probably give him what for!
>
> *Counsellor:* Would that get what you want?
>
> *Irfon:* No.
>
> *Counsellor:* Why play something in a way that doesn't get you what you want?
>
> *Irfon:* Habit.
>
> *Counsellor:* To get you what you want is it worth the effort of trying to change the habit?
>
> *Irfon:* I've got to do something. I am desperate for money.
>
> *Counsellor:* OK. I will ring the manager of the Social Security and arrange an appointment for you if you agree to rehearse with me ways of avoiding blowing it when you have the appointment. Is that a deal?
>
> *Irfon:* OK.

The counsellor is identifying with the goals of the client but suggesting a more efficient means of achieving them. Clients with Anti-social or Narcissistic Personality Disorders often lack the ability to empathize, and role reversal is a useful strategy for facilitating the development of empathy. The counsellor asks the client to take the part of the Social Security employee while the counsellor takes the part of the claimant.

> *Counsellor:* What the hell have you been doing? I have been waiting half an hour.
>
> *Irfon:* What!
>
> *Counsellor:* Right, let's stop the role play. How did my saying that make you feel?

Irfon: I wanted to punch your face.
Counsellor: Did you feel like listening to my request for help?
Irfon: No.
Counsellor: Does that sort of greeting help you get what you want?
Irfon: I suppose not.
Counsellor: How would you begin at this next appointment?
Irfon: I don't know.
Counsellor: Could you begin by admitting your role in the problem, for
    example, 'Last time I was here I might have confused the girl with
    the position about my address'?
Irfon: That would be creeping!
Counsellor: What's the alternative?
Irfon: I don't creep.
Counsellor: You can get what you want, by what you call creeping.
Irfon: Maybe it is not actually creeping to say that.
Counsellor: Keeping the irritability manageable to get what you want
    may feel unnatural at first, but it pays dividends in the end.
Irfon: I'll buy it.

The counsellor is here essentially enabling the client to modulate
his disordered arousal by teaching him to remain goal focused. A
variety of further positive communication skills were taught and
exchanged for the negative ones. A range of negative and positive
communication habits are given in Box 8.4.

Box 8.4 *Negative and positive communication habits*

Negative habits	*Positive habits*
Accusing, blaming	Using 'I' statements
Putting down, shaming	Criticizing the behaviour not the person
Interrupting	Gesturing when you need to talk, or waiting patiently
Lecturing, preaching	Making brief, clear statements
Talking sarcastically	Talking in a neutral tone
Failing to make eye contact	Looking when you talk
Mind reading	Reflecting, paraphrasing
Getting off target	Talking about one thing at a time
Commanding, ordering	Asking nicely but assertively
Dredging up the past	You can't change the past so stick to the present
Hogging the conversation	Taking turns and talking briefly
Intellectualizing	Speaking in simple language
Not listening	Using reflective listening

Box 8.5 *Practice summary – concurrent irritability*

1 Irritability is a theme running through PTSD and cluster B personality disorders.

2 Irritability poses problems for relationships when one person exceeds the tolerance threshold of another.

3 Clients can be taught simple coping strategies to use at the first sign of irritation, for example calling to mind a set of traffic lights or employing a distraction technique such as switching to another 'channel'.

4 Where irritability is sabotaging relationships the client and their significant others can be taught to employ communication guidelines in regularly scheduled, twenty-minute, quality communication times. Alternatively or additionally, the client might complete a 'How I Felt' diary detailing triggering behaviours from significant others, response to that behaviour by the client, and potentially less distressing alternative responses.

5 With cluster B personality-disordered clients, questioning the utility rather than the justifiability of their expressions of irritation is often more efficacious.

9

Counselling for PTSD – Service Delivery

Service provision

There are two reasons why providing counselling services for post-traumatic stress disorder is more problematic than for many other disorders. The first reason is that by their very nature major disasters catch emergency services unawares. They may have a contingency plan, but it will probably need revision in the light of the actual details of the disaster. Precisely because all major disasters catch emergency services to some extent unprepared, the concentration of effort in the immediate aftermath has to be of a very high intensity. The consequence is that the normal services of mental health personnel are inevitably impeded. Realistically there has to be a limit to the length of time mental health professionals are allowed by their employers to disrupt their normal services. Typically, mental health professionals are given a high profile in the first three months after the disaster and their involvement progressively decreases thereafter over the following fifteen months or so. This model of service delivery has the advantage that crisis counselling (a framework for which is given in Appendix D) is readily available in the immediate aftermath of the tragedy. It also has the advantage that some mental health personnel are still available on the first anniversary of the trauma to help disaster victims at that often poignant time. The disadvantage of the crisis model is that services born as a result of major crisis rarely move beyond crisis counselling. There is a clear need for provision of systematic, therapeutic counselling for those clients presenting with PTSD symptomatology many months – or even years – after the disaster.

The second reason is that PTSD is a disorder associated with the dramatic and with disasters and so counsellors do not expect to find the disorder manifested in clients presenting in quotidian contexts. For example the most obvious symptoms of a relative of a prisoner may be depression and anxiety. Indeed it is these symptoms that she will readily volunteer. Unless the counsellor specifically makes inquiries about, say, whether they suffer intrusive imagery concerning their loved one's arrest and disposal, this information will not ordinarily be furnished. The situation is similar to that which obtains with a significant minority of depressed women – unless the counsellor specifically inquires about whether they were sexually abused as a child this information is unlikely to be forthcoming. Regrettably, such a question ought to be a part of the counsellor's standard interview schedule. There is a need for counsellors to be attuned to the possibility of both dramatic and non-dramatic pathways to PTSD. Were counsellors accustomed to identifying and treating PTSD arising in an everyday context then the provision of systematic help in the wake of a disaster would be more likely to be secured.

Duration of provision

In the general psychotherapy literature a duration or 'dose' effect for psychotherapeutic treatments has been demonstrated (Howard et al., 1986). Across a large number of studies of different client groups the number of treatment sessions a patient received was associated with the amount of client improvement. Approximately 50 per cent of clients were evaluated as 'markedly improved' by the eighth session and 75 per cent markedly improved by the twenty-sixth session. But additional counselling sessions beyond that point made a very small (less than 7 per cent) difference to the percentage of clients who subsequently improved, showing diminishing returns on the investment of the counsellor's time. Outcome studies of counselling for PTSD still remain to be conducted but it would be surprising were the results to differ substantially from those for adult psychotherapy in general. Thus between eight and twenty-six counselling sessions constitutes the band of sessions within which a client is likely to improve if they are going to improve at all. One might anticipate that for PTSD clients without a personal or family history of emotional disorder the number of counselling sessions required will be nearer to eight, whereas for those with such a history the number of sessions needed will be nearer twenty-six.

Relapse prevention

Though clients may have markedly improved in their counselling sessions, relapses in the year afterwards are a distinct possibility. In a study with depressed patients who responded to cognitive therapy, Blackburn et al. (1986) found that 23 per cent had relapsed in the two years following counselling. Strategies for relapse prevention need to be an integral part of all counselling programmes. Clients with PTSD usually come to mental health services looking for a 'cure' for their problems. They may bring to counselling a simple model of being either 'ill' or 'well', and they have an expectation that the professional can move them from the former to the latter state. One of the counsellor's first tasks is to convey that counselling is about 'helping them to cope better' rather than 'curing' them. If the counsellor does not convey a realistic expectation clients may prematurely default from counselling.

Whilst the effect of counselling on PTSD clients is often to reduce avoidance behaviour, intrusive imagery and disordered arousal to levels that they find manageable, they do nevertheless typically report, albeit to varying degrees, that they are 'not the same person'. As a consequence, the client should be counselled that there will be an enduring, residual vulnerability to PTSD, that they will have been 'scarred' by the experience. Whether the symptoms are subsequently triggered will depend on whether environmental stimuli are perceived as approximating to the original trauma. However, the client can be taught how to stop slips into PTSD-like symptoms from developing into the full blown disorder. The following explanation was given to a policeman, Iain, as he neared the end of his regular counselling sessions.

> *Iain:* Since going back, I have just been on light duties. I was on the station desk and I was trying to sort out the problems of an old lady who said she had locked herself out of her house, but she seemed confused. It was taking some sorting out. There was a group of youths in the queue behind her, they became impatient and started swearing. I told them to stop because the old lady was getting more agitated. They gave me even more verbal abuse, so I threw them out and told them to come back when they had some manners. I was shaking, but I did it.
>
> *Counsellor:* That's good, you've handled your first potentially dangerous situation well. Realistically there is going to be a danger a situation like that might trigger off some of the PTSD symptoms.
>
> *Iain:* I am going to have to watch myself.
>
> *Counsellor:* That's true. Some times you will handle situations better than other times. The important thing is not to blame yourself when you have a slip. Concentrate instead on learning from mistakes, then the gaps between slips get gradually longer and longer. You are better off saying that there are going to be slips than suffering the grave disappointment that arises from believing that you are 'cured'. It's rather like overcoming a cigarette addiction: provided that you learn from each slip it is just a question of time before you succeed. Indeed most people manage to give up cigarettes at the fourth or fifth attempt.

If a client comes to think of himself as 'cured' of PTSD because of counselling, the effects of any subsequent PTSD symptoms are likely to be perceived as catastrophic – 'I'm right back to square one' – whereas if the client is forewarned of such an eventuality they can more easily take it in their stride.

Because of the possibility of relapse following counselling for PTSD, not only should the counsellor offer an open door policy but it is also useful to provide the client with two or three booster sessions in the year afterwards. This helps the client gently disengage from the counsellor and provides the counsellor with the opportunity to underline material and strategies previously taught. There is evidence, for example, from a study reported by Lochman (1988) in which delinquent adolescents were taught anger control strategies, that those given anger control training plus booster sessions subsequently fared much better than those with the anger control training alone. As disordered arousal is a major feature of PTSD this study may be of particular significance.

Relapse prevention: substance abuse and PTSD
With clients whose PTSD is complicated by substance abuse the issue of relapse prevention assumes a heightened prominence. Substance abuse often represents a PTSD client's attempt to relieve their own symptomatology. They are more likely to be referred to a counsellor because of the substance abuse than because of the underlying PTSD, and it is not possible to make progress on the PTSD until the substance abuse becomes manageable. At the same time the counsellor has to remain conscious of the function of the substance abuse. Not surprisingly, motivation is a major issue for PTSD clients with substance abuse problems. On the one hand if they seek to overcome their addiction they risk being overwhelmed by the PTSD symptoms. If, on the other hand, they continue their addiction they suffer the negative consequences common to all abusers: of impaired relationships, failing health, and so on. The counsellor has to convey that he or she understands that the client is caught in a dilemma. George Kelly (1955) elaborated the principle that 'People will only move in a direction that makes life more meaningful', and the key to engaging the PTSD client in tackling substance abuse is helping in the construction of a meaningful drug-free life. Somewhat paradoxically, this is often best achieved by playing devil's advocate with the client and getting them to elaborate the case for giving up or reducing substance abuse.

Unfortunately clients with addiction problems tend to move in a direction that is opposite to that the counsellor is suggesting! Thus if the counsellor makes a straightforward case for the client giving up their addiction, the client typically responds with passive aggression, nods politely, but does not actually implement any of the homework assignments recommended by the counsellor and frequently defaults from counselling. Not surprisingly there is reportedly a high turnover of counsellors in the addiction field.

Kuma – PTSD from childhood sexual abuse, with adult alcohol abuse

Kuma had been sexually abused by her father from the age of ten through to thirteen, until he left the marital home after Kuma's mother discovered what had been happening. Kuma felt blamed by her mother for her father's departure and grew up with a debilitating sense of guilt. Kuma was saddened by her father's departure, he was the only family member ever to have shown her any warmth, yet she felt she should have told her mother what was going on at the start. However, Kuma felt that she would not have been believed and would have been punished. Her mother constantly reminded Kuma how pretty and academically able her younger sister was. From the age of seventeen Kuma embarked on a series of unsatisfactory relationships. The pattern was always the same: she would prematurely have sexual relations with a partner, take this as a sign of commitment and either move in with him or he with her. She persisted in relationships long after friends had told her there was no mileage in them, in the belief that 'If I love him enough then he will love me.' Kuma was troubled by intrusive imagery of the day of her father's departure and was very irritable with her men as well as with her mother and sister. She had a number of sexual problems including being put off sex if her partner had a hairy chest because this reminded her of her father, and wanting to stay in control by touching her partner, but not vice versa. Kuma blamed her perceived sexual ineptness rather than the unsuitability of her partners for the dissolution of her relationships. After a decade of unsatisfactory relationships she was living by herself in a bedsitter and had taken to drink to console herself. She was referred to the counsellor by her GP.

> *Counsellor:* What do you see as your major problem?
> *Kuma:* Booze.
> *Counsellor:* How's that a problem?
> *Kuma:* It's a wonder I got here today. I miss appointments at the housing. I forget about bills. I'm a mess.
> *Counsellor:* Are you a mess or are you in a mess?
> *Kuma:* I am one 'xxxx'!
> *Counsellor:* What makes you a 'xxxx'?

Kuma: Have you got three weeks for me to tell you?
Counsellor: Maybe you could make a start today, and we could carry on the discussion in a couple of days.
Kuma: Right.

During the remainder of the session, Kuma explained how drink and her aggressive behaviour led to the break up of her last relationship and how the drinking had become worse since the previous session. It should be noted that she did not volunteer that she had been abused as a teenager. Instead Kuma portrayed herself as a randy, worthless whore.

It was not until the counsellor asked directly about sexual abuse that she burst into tears and the whole background emerged. Kuma and the counsellor agreed to defer discussion of the drink problem until the next counselling session in four days' time. This was an implicit acknowledgement that there was more to consider than just the substance abuse alone. At the next session the drink problem was addressed.

Counsellor: What would you be left with if you gave up the drink?
Kuma: Money to pay the bills.
Counsellor: So if you paid the bills what would that leave you with?
Kuma: A roof over my head.
Counsellor: Does having a roof over your head make that much difference?
Kuma: It could, at least it's mine, it's something I have got.
Counsellor: To do what with?
Kuma: Well I could get it looking nice, instead of like a pigsty. I like plants and cats, they don't give you trouble.
Counsellor: So if you altered your drinking habits you would have money for bills. You could keep your bedsit. You could have plants and maybe a cat. Is that really enough to be bothered altering your drinking?
Kuma: Well I could bring friends as well.
Counsellor: What would you be left with when friends go home?
Kuma: That's the pits. I start thinking of all the things that happen to me. I can't stand it. I reach for the bottle.
Counsellor: Can I just summarize what I think you have said and you can tell me whether I have got it right. The disadvantage of giving up drink is that you will be left watching a horror movie of all your hurt: the sexual abuse, your father's exit from your life, the broken relationships, the sadness and anger about your relationship with your mother and sister. On the other hand the advantages of altering your drinking habits are that you could keep the sort of bedsit you want, and have friends around. Is that right?
Kuma: Yes, but the bedsit would be a haven.

If the counsellor understates the advantages of the client reducing the addictive behaviour the client tends to verbalize additional

Box 9.1 *Janis and Mann's conditions for stable decision making*

1 Decision maker is in a state of dissonance, that is they perceive advantages and disadvantages to whatever course of action they choose.
2 They have ample space to reflect on their decision.
3 They are assured by others that they will still be valued regardless of which particular decision they make.

Box 9.2 *Prochaska and Di Clemente's five stages of addiction quitting*

Pre-contemplation
Contemplation
Action
Maintenance
Relapse

reasons for overcoming the addictive behaviour. There is evidence that people become more committed to positions that they verbalize, so the strategy of understating the advantages of overcoming the addiction serves to enhance the client's motivation. The work of Janis and Mann (1977) suggests that people make the most stable decisions when the conditions of Box 9.1 are fulfilled.

These considerations have considerable implications for the counsellor involved with a substance abuse client. The first requirement means that the counsellor has to convey to the client that they can see that the addictive behaviour made sense to the client by elaborating on the disadvantages of giving up the addiction. The second consideration introduces a time dimension into the counselling. Prochaska and Di Clemente (1982) have suggested that substance abusers may be at one of the five stages in their thinking about their addiction shown in Box 9.2. The first stage they term pre-contemplative. The client in this stage often arrives to see a counsellor at the behest of others. The pre-contemplation complaint is usually that others are 'nagging' them to do something about the substance consumption, but they themselves do not actually see it as a problem. If the counsellor attempts to alter an addictive lifestyle when the client is in this stage the client usually defaults. In Kuma's case she was in Prochaska and Di Clemente's second stage, contemplation, which involves a perception of both the advantages and disadvantages of giving up the addiction. For clients in the contemplative stage it is particularly important that Janis and Mann's second requirement for stable decisions be met, that the person is allowed ample space to reflect. It would be premature, if the client was in this stage, to introduce strategies to modify the addictive behaviour, here for example recommending that Kuma did not drink until the evening. Such homework assignments would only be appropriate in the next – action – stage. The action stage involves a decision which is often arrived at somewhat idiosyncratically. In Kuma's case, after weighing the pros and cons of altering her addictive behaviour she had gone on a visit to her sister. She discovered her sister playing happily in the garden with her three-year-old daughter. Kuma reported in counselling that that was when she decided to stop drinking: she wanted to give a daughter of hers a life she had never had. When this decision was made, she began the act of quitting by postponing drinking until the evening.

For clients in the pre-contemplative and contemplative phases the counsellor's task is primarily one of engagement. In some instances the counsellor can do no more than be available for the client, working on enhancing the client's self-esteem. This may be done in the context, say, of meeting the client at a drug clinic when they call to pick up a prescription for an opiate substitute. Some drug clinics make it a requirement that when an addict calls to pick up a script they must stay for a period in a milieu with other addicts and drug workers (see Van Bilsen, 1986). This usually takes place in a room in the clinic furnished like a sitting room with coffee and refreshments available. Teaching clients how to withdraw and manage relapse would usually be done in regular weekly counselling sessions (Scott, 1989b, gives a detailed exposition). Precisely because relapse is such a major issue in the addictions it is important to plan for follow-up sessions as well as having an open-door policy if the client needs emergency help. The service delivery needs in the period after regular counselling are the same for PTSD and for substance abuse. Both PTSD clients and substance abusers, and particularly those with the dual diagnosis, can benefit from the involvement of a non-addicted relative or friend in the counselling. This person can function as a 'quasi-counsellor' in the community and can help ensure that what is taught in the counselling session generalizes to the client's world. The quasi-counsellor is a more available source of support than the counsellor and can transmit the latter's central messages about learning from mistakes, preventing slips becoming full-blown relapses, and so on.

Often the quasi-counsellor can act as an intermediary with the client's family in a situation where relationships are likely to be strained.

Group counselling

Significant others may serve to either modify or maintain dysfunctional trauma beliefs, so affecting the course of the client's PTSD. A client's dysfunctional trauma beliefs are not maintained in a vacuum, and not only may they be open to modification by counsellors, friends and family but they may also be challenged by fellow victims. Groups for clients who have been exposed to major trauma is an attractive option when mental health professionals have ever lengthening waiting lists. From the client's perspective the group may serve to normalize the trauma experience and reduce the sense of isolation and alienation that is common. Clients can share their coping methods and can be encouraged to put on their own agenda a problem voiced by another group member that hitherto they had felt too frightened to face. Resick et al. (1988) compared the effectiveness of three types of brief therapy in group format with sexual assault victims: stress inoculation training, assertiveness training, and supportive psychotherapy. There were six group sessions lasting two hours each. In the stress inoculation training group members were taught a number of cognitive-behavioural strategies including guided self-talk, thought stoppage and relaxation training. The assertiveness training group rehearsed assertive responses and practised challenging non-assertive thought patterns. In the supportive psychotherapy group the co-leaders (a female and a male) simply facilitated discussion topics selected by the group members. All three groups showed pre- to post-treatment change. These treatment effects were still apparent at a three-month follow-up but were not maintained at six months after treatment. Perhaps this highlights the need for booster sessions after regular counselling. In the adult psychotherapy literature the general finding has been that group therapy is not as efficacious as individual therapy. However Scott and Stradling (1990) reported two studies comparing the efficacy of individual and group cognitive therapy in the treatment of depression and found the two modalities equally effective. The authors attributed this parity to the fact that members of the 'group' condition were given up to three individual counselling sessions alongside group attendance. The group modality still resulted in a considerable time saving but the members' idiosyncratic needs were nevertheless sufficiently catered for. Provision of initial individual sessions was also found to make the idea of joining a group much more palatable to clients.

Assertion groups for women who have been abused can be a useful adjunct to individual counselling. Jehu (1989) reports that many women who were sexually abused in childhood have problems with assertion and intimacy as adults. The group programme conducted by Jehu and colleagues consisted of ten two-hour sessions held weekly, with approximately five clients. There were two group leaders – a male and a female. A brief summary of the programme is given in Box 9.3. Jehu also conducted a follow-up session six weeks later. Group members reported that they all found the group moderately or very helpful. Interestingly, the participants thought it of value to have a male co-leader in order to get a male perspective and to counteract over-generalization with respect to males.

PTSD and children: symptoms and assessment

Children may exhibit PTSD-like symptoms not only as a consequence of the sort of disaster trauma that may affect adults, but also as a result of physical or sexual abuse. Whatever the trigger, the symptoms may be clustered under the following headings:

fear and easy startle;
repetition and re-enactment of trauma;
sleep disturbance and signs of guilt and depression;
disengagement;
explosive, aggressive behaviour.

Eliciting symptoms from children can be a difficult endeavour. In the wake of a major disaster teachers are often fearful lest a mental health professional 'stirs up' a traumatized child by asking questions. Parents too may not want to mention the trauma to the child, perhaps because they find their child's trauma too painful or possibly because they were exposed to the same trauma. As a consequence the child may be thrown back on to their own limited and underdeveloped repertoire of coping skills.

Just as with adult PTSD a wide-ranging assessment is needed. Yule and Udwin (1991) in their study of child survivors of the *Jupiter* sinking report that they found Horowitz et al.'s (1979) Impact of Event Scale suitable for children. To measure depression they used the Birleson Depression Inventory (Birleson, 1981) and for anxiety the Revised Children's Manifest Anxiety Scale (R-CMAS) (Reynolds and Richmond, 1978). The three instruments were administered to twenty-four survivors ten days after the

Box 9.3 *Summary of Jehu's ten-session Assertion Training Programme*

Session 1:   Mini-lecture on the differences between assertiveness, passivity and aggression. Homework assignment – describing in writing or drawing your real self and ideal self.

Session 2:   Sharing experiences since the last session. Discussion of real selves and ideal selves. The role of irrational beliefs in the maintenance of negative self-image. Targeting a situation in which the person would like to be more assertive, and the identification of emotions that might possibly sabotage the endeavour. Disputing the negative thoughts that lay behind the dysfunctional emotion.

Session 3:   Review of previous week. Challenging beliefs that sabotage interpersonal rights such as 'Don't ever inconvenience other people', 'Don't ever refuse to help a friend', 'Don't ever feel mad', 'Don't ever make someone else feel bad'. Fantasizing about what life would be like if the person accepted that they had certain rights – for instance the right to say 'No', the right to express their feelings – and contrasting this with imagining what life would be like if they did not accept these rights.

Session 4:   Review of week. Mini-lecture on the ownership of messages – using 'I' statements in the expression of thoughts, beliefs and feelings as opposed to 'You' statements. Rehearsal of direct communication using the first person rather than the third.

Session 5:   Review of how newly found assertion skills are working out in practice. Coping with the negative response of significant others to the practice of skills. Weighing up the advantages and disadvantages of an assertive response. Refusing requests – beginning the response with the word 'No', speaking in a firm voice, keeping the answer short and clear.

Session 6: Review of week. Managing conflict in interpersonal relationship using the DESC procedure.
D = describe the problem to the other person;
E = express in a positive way the feelings experienced as a result of the other's behaviour;
S = specify the changes desired in the behaviour of the other;
C = identify the consequences which will be delivered if the other person changes their behaviour as well as if they refuse to do so.
For homework write a DESC script based on a target complaint.

Session 7: Rehearsal of DESC script. Homework: think of a situation involving personal rights in intimate relationships.

Session 8: Finding a balance between rights and the risk of rejection. The normality of difficulties experienced in intimate relationships by previously abused women.

Session 9: Sexuality in intimate relationships. Avoidance of sexual pleasure because it represents a loss of control and/or leads to guilt. Sexual pleasure as representing a revictimization. Dissociation from the sexual encounter as a means of maintaining a sense of control. The importance of separating the past from the present to achieve any satisfaction in sexual relationships and the recognition of the element of choice in this.

Session 10: Social gathering with food and beverages.

sinking and again five months later. The IES scores remained statistically unchanged and at the same level as those of child survivors of another disaster – the *Herald of Free Enterprise* sinking – all of whom had been diagnosed as suffering from PTSD. The children's anxiety levels, which had been normal ten days after the sinking, were significantly increased by the five-month assessment. At the initial assessment the children's depression scores had been significantly greater than for a normal sample and by the five-month assessment the depression had significantly deepened. Yule and Udwin's (1991) study is a salutary reminder that children's PTSD symptoms are no more likely to be transitory than those of adults. Further, though the most disturbed children in their study joined a support group in which they would share their experiences, despite this they showed no overall improvement. It remains to be ascertained whether a more structured approach tailored to each child's needs would produce clinically significant improvement.

PTSD and children: childhood trauma and adult disorder

The significance of PTSD in the development of severe disorders for which people are eventually hospitalized is only just beginning to be appreciated. A study by Craine et al. (1988) of 105 hospitalized female psychiatric patients found 51 per cent of them to have been sexually abused in childhood or adolescence. Interestingly, in the majority of cases hospital staff were unaware that the patients had histories of sexual abuse and only 20 per cent of the abused patients believed that they had been adequately treated for sexual abuse. Sixty-nine per cent of the abused patients met the diagnostic criteria for PTSD but none had received that diagnosis. It seems likely that there is a link between major childhood trauma, developmentally appropriate symptoms of PTSD in childhood, and psychological morbidity in adult life. For instance a child in care following abuse might be found to hoard food in their room, thereby minimizing contact with others, and may be seen as manifesting PTSD-related avoidance behaviour. It has been estimated that perhaps 21 per cent of children who are abused suffer from PTSD (Famularo et al., 1989). Further, Young (1990) has suggested that early maladaptive schemas (EMS) lead to the development of personality disorders. These EMS may themselves be the product of unresolved childhood PTSD. The model outlined in Figure 9.1 suggests a role for childhood PTSD in the aetiology of personality disorders.

The model suggests that unresolved PTSD symptomatology reciprocally interacts with early maladaptive schemas. Thus, for example, the abused child has been found to be much more aggressive with peers (presumably a manifestation of disordered arousal in PTSD) which may lead to negative feedback from them. As a consequence, the abused child's schema that they must somehow be unworthy to have suffered such a fate is confirmed. This in turn may enhance the avoidance behaviour evident in PTSD. Young's early maladaptive schemas are summarized in Box 9.4.

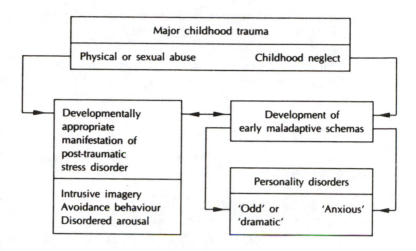

Figure 9.1   *Childhood post-traumatic stress disorder, early maladaptive schemas and personality disorders*

The EMS are implicated in the whole range of personality disorders – anti-social, avoidant, etc. – though Young does not specify which schemas lead to which personality disorder. Cognitive-behavioural counselling for personality disorders is a relatively new field and as yet there are no controlled trials to attest its worth, though recommendations for practice have been published (Beck and Freeman, 1990). The linkage shown in Figure 9.1 between major childhood trauma, childhood PTSD and personality disorder makes it easier to understand why it is that adults with a pre-existing personality disorder are more likely to succumb to PTSD in the event of a major trauma: essentially they have been there before and are being 'revictimized'. Figure 9.1 makes the suggestion that child abuse will be associated more with the development of the 'odd' and 'dramatic' personality disorders (*DSM-III-R*, clusters A and B) while childhood neglect will be associated with the development of the 'anxious' disorders of cluster C.

Layden (1991) describes a case example of counselling a client where the goal was to modify early maladaptive schemas. Her client was a forty-four-year-old woman who had been suicidal for a number of years. In one interview the client mentioned in passing that she had been abused as a child, but showed no emotional distress and summarily dismissed what she had just said with the

Box 9.4 *Young's early maladaptive schemas*

Autonomy

1 *Dependence*. The belief that one is unable to function on one's own and needs the constant support of others
2 *Subjugation or lack of individuation*. The voluntary or involuntary sacrifice of one's own needs to satisfy other's needs with an accompanying failure to recognize one's own needs
3 *Vulnerability to harm or illness*. The fear that disaster is about to strike at any time (natural, criminal, medical or financial)
4 *Fear of losing self-control*. The fear that one will involuntarily lose control of one's own behaviour, impulses, emotions, mind, body, etc.

Connectedness

5 *Emotional deprivation*. The expectation that one's needs for nurturance, empathy, affection and caring will never be adequately met by others
6 *Abandonment or loss*. Fear that one will imminently lose significant others and be emotionally isolated for ever
7 *Mistrust*. The expectation that others will wilfully hurt, abuse, cheat, lie, manipulate, or take advantage
8 *Social isolation or alienation*. The feeling that one is isolated from the rest of the world, different from other people, or not a part of any group or community

Worthiness

9 *Defectiveness or unlovability*. The feeling that one is inwardly defective and flawed or that one is fundamentally unlovable to significant others if exposed
10 *Social undesirability*. The belief that one is outwardly undesirable to others (for example ugly, sexually undesirable, low in status, poor in conversational skills, dull and boring)
11 *Incompetence or failure*. The belief that one cannot perform competently in areas of achievement (school or career), daily responsibilities to oneself or others, or decision making
12 *Guilt or punishment*. The belief that one is morally or ethically bad or irresponsible and deserving of harsh criticism or punishment

13 *Shame or embarrassment.* Recurrent feelings of shame or self-consciousness experienced because one believes that one's inadequacies are totally unacceptable to others and are exposed

Limits and Standards
14 *Unrelenting standards.* The relentless striving to meet extremely high expectations of oneself, at the expense of happiness, pleasure, health, sense of accomplishment or satisfying relationships
15 *Entitlement or insufficient limits.* Insistence that one be able to do, say, or have whatever one wants immediately. Disregard for: what others consider reasonable, what is actually feasible, the time or patience usually required or the cost to others; or difficulty with self-discipline

phrase 'I'm done with that now.' However, when the counsellor pressed her for more details of the abuse she became more emotional. Indeed it transpired that for the past five years she had experienced flashbacks to the childhood abuse. The flashbacks were triggered by her husband physically abusing her daughter, and by herself being raped by a stranger. Until those recent experiences she had been unable to remember the childhood abuse. There had been two critical incidents in the childhood abuse: the first was sexual abuse by her father and his friend, the second was getting lost in a forest, being found by her father and abused. When she described these incidents she was in great distress and spent fifteen minutes repeating 'I'm defective', 'I enjoyed it', 'I'm disgusting'. She had never previously had the opportunity to say what she thought and felt. Layden encouraged her to take an adult perspective on the thoughts she had during the abuse as a child. Nevertheless the client persisted in some self-denigratory beliefs. The counsellor then asked the client to imagine her young self seated on the empty chair next to her. The client had to talk to 'the child' and help the child get a different perspective on the matter. The client was then asked whether the child would now go off with a safe adult. Unfortunately the answer was still 'No'. The next step was to ask the client to ask 'the child' what she wanted. The child replied that she wanted 'to tie him to a tree and get the animals to eat him'. The counsellor asked the client/child to imagine that as having happened. Finally the child said she would leave with a safe adult. The final stage of the therapy involved a time projection task, asking the client what she would like to do. The client replied she would like to walk on the beach with someone she really liked. A 'trust hierarchy' was then created: the first step was walking along the beach with the counsellor, the second step walking with a previous counsellor, and finally walking the beach with a friend.

In tackling EMS Layden made considerable use of imagery, not just relying on rational discussion, and this may be the key to managing some very disturbed clients. The counselling approach with many hospitalized psychiatric patients may have to be multi-layered. At the outer layer will be the disorder for which they were admitted, which would typically be a severe depression or anxiety (PTSD rarely figures as a reason for admission). Attempts to deal directly with these Axis 1 disorders in *DSM-III-R* are likely to meet with limited success because of a coexisting Axis 2 personality disorder. As they are addressed the EMS on which they are based will become more apparent and at the next level the trauma on which they were based will become more evident. How many layers one has to peel back in order to get the client to a functioning state will need to established empirically for each client. Pragmatically it seems sensible to start at the outer layer and see how working at that level effects change before moving on to the next level. This process is likely to be less threatening to the client than, say, a direct attack on their EMS or a desensitization procedure for the original childhood trauma.

When counselling fails

The counselling strategies described in this book are no panacea. Undoubtedly the counsellor will encounter clients for whom the techniques described here are insufficient. There is clearly a need to know with some precision the characteristics of the non-responding client population and whether they would be better served by some alternative counselling regime. From a counsellor's point of view it is not very helpful to know that, generally, older and less verbal clients do less well than younger and more intelligent ones. What a counsellor needs to know are differential predictors, that is what form of counselling is likely to benefit a client of given type and circumstances. Unfortunately the outcome studies that would enable the identification of such differential predictors for PTSD have not yet been conducted. For a significant minority of clients their PTSD will continue to be chronic despite counselling. This raises the question of what, if any, form of service delivery there should be for this population. There is a danger that work with the long-term chronic disorder is relegated to the margins. The financial context in which a counselling service is located will be an important determinant of the help proffered.

An employer funding an employee's counselling because the trauma occurred in a work context is likely to do so only for a limited period. If the employee is not rendered symptom-free they are likely to be medically retired. The employee may still feel they need the counselling service but be without the funds to pay for it, whilst the counsellor may feel they have exhausted the repertoire of coping skills they have to teach the client. In this situation the counsellor may feel trapped and 'a failure'. This can be made more manageable if the counsellor can operate on two models, the first a 'return to pre-trauma functioning' model and the second 'a diabetic analogue model'. The initial goal of counselling operating over the first eight or so sessions should be the 'pre-trauma functioning model'. However if there is little improvement in PTSD in the first eight to twenty-six sessions then it is more appropriate for the counsellor to adopt a 'diabetic analogue model'. This second model recognizes that a 'cure' is not always a realistic goal but that nevertheless clients can be taught to cope with a handicapping condition. In the medical field, diabetes is an appropriate example of this state of affairs. The diabetes sufferer functions reasonably well most of the time, but has to take certain precautions such as regular meals, and may even need brief periods of hospitalization to stabilize sugar levels. The regular taking of insulin, whilst not a cure for the diabetic, enhances functioning. Just as the insulin has to be continuously ingested so too may the chronic PTSD sufferer need regular 'doses' of support.

At the same time, the counsellor involved in supporting chronic PTSD clients has to be alert to new developments in the field. For example, Shapiro (1989) has recently described an eye movement desensitization procedure for PTSD and an uncontrolled trial of its efficacy. Essentially the procedure involves the client visualizing their trauma while the counsellor moves a finger rhythmically and rapidly across the visual field, twice per second at 30–35 centimetres from the client's face, repeating the movement twelve to twenty-four times. Clients rate their subjective units of disturbance (SUDS) on a 0 to 10 scale at the beginning and end of the procedure. During the procedure the client is asked to verbalize any changes in the trauma image. After each set the client is asked to blank out their image before the procedure is repeated. Shapiro recommends that sets be repeated in a counselling session until the SUDS level reduces to zero or one, which may require from three to fifteen sets. Clients are released from the session only when their

SUDS level has become manageable enough for them to travel home. Clients report often feeling tired and light-headed after this procedure. Shapiro recommends that it should not be used in the presence of any eye disease and should be terminated if the client reports pain in the eye during the procedure or if there is no gradual reduction in SUDS from set to set; continuing regardless in the latter situation may result in psychotic breakdown. Clients should be properly briefed before commencing eye movement desensitization: one suggested strategy is to describe it in terms of 'helping you digest the trauma which in the past has been too difficult to swallow'.

Recently Muss (1991a, 1991b) has claimed success with a number of PTSD cases using a 'rewind' technique. Essentially the client is asked to view their trauma as if they were watching it unfold on a screen in a cinema. The 'film' begins by depicting the peaceful prelude before the trauma happened, before moving on to the details of the trauma. Typically Muss has the client watch for a minute, up to the most disturbing aspect of the traumatic episode, and then mentally rewind the film so that the events are seen again in reverse order (though with the client still feeling as well as seeing). Thus a client suffering PTSD from a traffic accident, for example, would on the rewind see their vehicle disentangling itself from the vehicle it had crashed into, then assuming its quotidian shape and moving backwards along the road to the point where the client had been peacefully riding along in their automobile. The rewind stops at this point, having been accomplished in about 15–20 seconds. Muss claims that when a client subsequently suffers intrusive imagery the rewind will rapidly and automatically come into play, taking the client from the trauma image to the peaceful image. He notes that when the trauma image has been replaced in this way another, different, trauma image may arise to take its place and the rewind technique must then be applied to the new image, but Muss believes that there are rarely more than three or four such trauma images to be rendered painless. He claims that good results may be obtained with two weeks' practice at the technique.

Counsellor survival

The heading of the previous section was 'When counselling fails', suggesting a somewhat artificial distinction between counselling and the counsellor. If the counsellor has, as he or she should, been carefully monitoring the impact of their endeavours on the client, on occasion the inescapable conclusion will be that no change has occurred. This should necessarily lead to the counsellor questioning their practice. The parameters of that questioning have, however, to be well defined if the counsellor is not to suffer burnout (Maslach and Jackson, 1981). The counselling of clients with PTSD exposes the counsellor to two sets of problems. First absorbing the enormity of the client's trauma which is often, by definition, outside the normal range of human experience, and second maintaining a critical and creative stance about their own practice.

Counsellors can help themselves with the first problem by balancing out the trauma, by celebrating some aspect of life. Quite what an individual may celebrate will be an idiosyncratic affair. Perhaps the enthusiasm, exuberance and smile of a young child, or the beauty of a scene, or the remarkable resilience of the human spirit in the face of adversity. This 'celebration' involves a turning away from the trauma in order to put it into perspective. From the juxtaposition of the trauma and the celebration the counsellor has to make a synthesis. This invariably involves profound philosophical and religious questions and a spiritual quest in the widest sense of that term. Maybe sanity requires a belief that somehow 'good' outweighs 'bad' but quite why one should believe that is, as they say, a topic for another book.

The second problem, of maintaining a sufficiently critical stance about one's own practice, is also a question of balance. At one extreme the counsellor could be blithely indifferent to the effects of his or her practice on the clients and at the other extreme so hypercritical that they begin to dread their encounters with them. The counsellor has to guard against personalization – assuming that a client's lack of progress is necessarily and solely attributable to the counselling received. Discussion of a case with colleagues can lead to a more realistic appraisal of the obstacles to progress it presents. It should be remembered that the responsiveness of a PTSD client to counselling will probably depend not only on the quality of the counselling but also on the intensity of the trauma (did they think their life was under threat? were they near the epicentre of the trauma?), the duration of the trauma, and the client's pre-trauma emotional history and resourcefulness. The counsellor also has to be mindful that no one counselling approach to PTSD has yet demonstrated clear superiority over another – sufficient research has not been reported. The remarkable thing of course is that, given what they've been through, so many clients find the motivation and resources to recover from their experiences and rejoin the human race. We wish them, and you, many celebrations.

References

American Psychiatric Association (1980) *Diagnostic and Statistical Manual of Mental Disorders*, 3rd edition. Washington, DC: American Psychiatric Association.

American Psychiatric Association (1987) *Diagnostic and Statistical Manual of Mental Disorders*, 3rd edition (revised). Washington, DC: American Psychiatric Association.

Bandura, A. (1977) *Social Learning Theory*. Englewood Cliffs, NJ: Prentice-Hall.

Beck, A.T. and Freeman, A.G. (1990) *Cognitive Therapy of Personality Disorders*. New York: Guildford Press.

Beck, A.T., Weissman, A., Lester D. and Trexler, L. (1974) 'The measurement of pessimism. The Hopelessness Scale', *Journal of Consulting and Clinical Psychology*, 42: 861–5.

Beck, A.T., Emery G.A. and Greenberg R.L. (1985) *Anxiety Disorders and Phobias: A Cognitive Perspective*. New York: Basic Books.

Best, C. (1991) 'Stress inoculation and the management of rape induced PTSD', paper delivered at the University of London, Institute of Psychiatry Conference on PTSD – Clinical and Research Perspectives, 23–4 April.

Birleson, P. (1981) 'The validity of depressive disorder in childhood and the development of a self-rating scale: a research report', *Journal of Child Psychology and Psychiatry*, 22: 73–8.

Blackburn, I.M. and Davidson, K. (1989) *Cognitive Therapy for Depression and Anxiety*. Oxford: Blackwell.

Blackburn, I.M., Eunson, K.M. and Bishop, S. (1986) 'A two year naturalistic follow-up of depressed patients treated with cognitive therapy, pharmacotherapy and a combination of both', *Journal of Affective Disorders*, 10: 67–75.

Blaney, P.H. (1986) 'Affect and memory: a review', *Psychological Bulletin*, 99: 229–46.

Brown G.W. and Harris T.O. (1978) *The Social Origins of Depression: A Study of Psychiatric Disorder in Women*. London: Tavistock.

Burton, S.W. and Akishal, H.S. (1990) *Dysthymic Disorder*. New York: Gaskell.

Clark, D.M. (1989) 'Anxiety states: panic and generalised anxiety', in K. Hawton, P.M. Salkovskis, J. Kirk and D.M. Clark (eds), *Cognitive Therapy for Psychiatric Problems: A Practical Guide*. Oxford: Oxford University Press.

Cobb, S. and Lindemann, E. (1943) 'Neuropsychiatric observations during the Coconut Grove fire', *Annals of Surgery*, 117: 814–24.

Covi, L., Lipman, R.S., Derogatis, L.R., Smith, J.E and Pattison, J.H. (1974) 'Drugs and psychotherapy in neurotic depression', *American Journal of Psychiatry*, 131: 191–8.

Craine, L.S., Henson, C.E., Colliver, J.A. and MacLean, D.G. (1988) 'Prevalence of a history of sexual abuse among female psychiatric patients in a state hospital system', *Hospital and Community Psychiatry*, 39: 300–4.

Dansky, B., Roth, S. and Kronenberger, W.G. (1990) 'The Trauma Constellation Identification Scale: a measure of the psychological impact of a stressful life event', *Journal of Traumatic Stress*, 3: 557–72.

Davidson, J., Swartz M. and Storck, M., (1985) 'A diagnostic and family study of post-traumatic stress disorder', *American Journal of Psychiatry*, 142: 90–3.

Duckworth, D.H. (1987) 'Post-traumatic stress disorder', *Stress Medicine*, 3: 175–83.

Epstein, S. (1990) 'The self concept, the traumatic neuroses and the structure of personality' in D.Ozer, J.M. Healy and R.A.J. Stewart (eds), *Perspectives on Personality, Volume 3*. Greenwich, CT: JAI Press.

Famularo, R., Kinscher, F.F. and Fenton, T. (1989) 'Post-traumatic stress disorder among maltreated children presenting to a juvenile court', *American Journal of Forensic Psychiatry*, 10: 33–9.

Foa, E.B. and Kozak, M.J. (1986) 'Emotional processing and fear: exposure to corrective information', *Psychological Bulletin*, 99: 20–35.

Foa, E.B., Rothbaum, B.O., Riggs, D.S. and Murdock, T.B. (1991) 'Treatment of post-traumatic stress disorder in rape victims: a comparison between cognitive-behavioral procedures and counselling', *Journal of Consulting and Clinical Psychology*, 59: 715–23.

Frank, J.B., Koster, T.R., Giller, E.L. and Ian, E. (1990) 'Antidepressants in the treatment of post-traumatic stress disorder', in M.E. Wolf and A.D. Mosnaim (eds), *Post-traumatic Stress Disorder: Etiology, Phenomenology and Treatment*. Washington, DC: American Psychiatric Press.

Friedman, M.J. (1990) 'Interrelationships between biological mechanisms and pharmacotherapy of post-traumatic stress disorder', in M.E. Wolf and A.D. Mosnaim (eds), *Post-traumatic Stress Disorder: Etiology, Phenomenology and Treatment*. Washington, DC: American Psychiatric Press.

Gleser, G. C., Green, B. L. and Winget, C. (1981) *Prolonged Psychological Effects of Disaster: A Study of Buffalo Creek*. New York: Academic Press.

Hammarberg, M. (1992) 'PENN Inventory for post-traumatic stress disorder: psychometric properties', *Psychological Assessment: A Journal of Consulting and Clinical Psychology*, 4: 67–76.

Heather, N. (1989) 'Brief intervention strategies', in R.K. Hester and W.R. Miller (eds), *Handbook of Alcoholism Treatment Approaches. Effective Alternatives*. New York: Pergamon Press.

Helzer, J.E., Robins, L.N. and McEvoy, L. (1987) 'Post-traumatic stress disorder in the general population: findings of the Epidemiological Catchment Area Survey', *New England Journal of Medicine*, 317: 1630–4.

Hooley, J.M., Orley, J. and Teasdale, J.D. (1986) 'Levels of expressed emotion and relapse in depressed patients', *British Journal of Psychiatry*, 148: 642–7.

Horowitz, M.J. (1986) *Stress Response Syndromes*, 2nd edn. New York: Aronson.

Horowitz, M.J., Wilner, N. and Alvarez, W. (1979) 'Impact of Event Scale: A measure of subjective distress', *Psychosomatic Medicine*, 41: 209–18.

Howard, K.I., Kopta, S.M., Krause, M.S. and Orlinsky, D.E. (1986) 'The dose-effect relationship in psychotherapy', *American Psychologist*, 41: 159–64.

Janis, J.L. and Mann, L. (1977) *Decision Making*. New York: Free Press.

Jehu, D. (1989) *Beyond Sexual Abuse: Therapy with Women Who Were Childhood Victims*. Chichester: John Wiley.

Kanouse, D.E. and Hanson, L.R. Jr (1971) 'Negativity in evaluations', in E.E. Jones, D.E. Kanouse, H.H. Kelley, R.E. Nisbett, S. Valins and B. Weiner (eds), *Attribution: Perceiving the Causes of Behavior*. Morristown, NJ: General Learning Press.

Keane, T.M., Zimering, R.T. and Caddell, J.M.. (1985) 'A behavioural formulation of post-traumatic stress disorder in Vietnam veterans', *Behavior Therapy*, 16: 9-12.

Keane, T.M., Fairbank, J.A., Caddell, J.M. and Zimering, R.T. (1989) 'Implosive (flooding) therapy reduces symptoms of post-traumatic stress disorder in Vietnam combat veterans', *Behavior Therapy*, 20: 245-60.

Kelly, G.A. (1955) *The Psychology of Personal Constructs*. New York: Norton.

Kilpatrick, D.G., Saunders, B.E. Amick-McCullan, A., Best, C.L., Vernon, L.J. and Resnick, H.S. (1989) 'Victim and crime factors associated with the development of crime-related post-traumatic stress disorder', *Behavior Therapy*, 20: 199-214.

Klerman, G.L., Dimascio, A., Weissman, M.M., Prusoff, B.A and Paykel, E.S. (1974) 'Treatment of depression by drugs and psychotherapy', *American Journal of Psychiatry*, 131: 186-91.

Kruppa, I. (1991) 'Perpetrators suffer trauma too', *The Psychologist*, 4: 401-3.

Lang, P.J. (1977) 'Imagery in therapy: an information processing analysis of fear', *Behavior Therapy*, 8: 862-86.

Layden, M. (1991) 'Imagery', paper presented at the British Association for Behavioural Psychotherapy annual conference, Oxford.

Lazarus, A.A. (1966) *Psychological Stress and the Coping Process*. New York: McGraw-Hill.

Leopold, R.L. and Dillon, H. (1963) 'Psychoanatomy of a disaster: a long-term study of post-traumatic neurosis in survivors of a marine explosion', *American Journal of Psychiatry*, 119: 913-21.

Linehan, M.M. (1985) 'The Reasons for Living Inventory', in P. Keller and L. Pitt (eds), *Innovations in Clinical Practice: A Source Book*. Sarasota, FL: Professional Resource Exchange. pp. 321-30.

Linehan, M.M., Goodstein, J.L., Neilsen, S.L. and Chiles, J.A. (1983) 'Reasons for staying alive when you are thinking of killing yourself: The Reasons for Living Inventory', *Journal of Consulting and Clinical Psychology*, 51: 276-86.

Lipper, S. (1990) 'Carbamazepine in the treatment of post-traumatic stress disorder. Implications for the kindling hypothesis', in M.E. Wolf and A.D. Mosnaim (eds), *Post-traumatic Stress Disorder. Etiology, Phenomenology and Treatment*. Washington, DC: American Psychiatric Press.

Lochman, J.E. (1988) 'Long-term efficacy of cognitive-behavioural interventions with aggressive boys', paper presented at the World Congress on Behaviour Therapy, Edinburgh.

Maslach, C. and Jackson, S.E. (1981) 'The measurement of experienced burnout', *Journal of Occupational Behavior*, 2: 99-113.

McFarlane, A.C. (1988) 'The phenomenology of post-traumatic stress disorders following a natural disaster', *Journal of Nervous and Mental Disorders*, 176: 22-9.

McFarlane, A.C. (1991) 'Traumatic reactions in adults. A longitudinal perspective', paper presented at the Post-traumatic Stress Disorder Clinical Research Perspectives conference, Institute of Psychiatry, University of London, 23-4 April.

Meichenbaum, D. (1977) *Cognitive-Behavior Modification. An Integrative Approach*. New York: Plenum.

Meichenbaum, D. (1985) *Stress Inoculation Training*. New York: Pergamon Press.

Muss, D.C. (1991a) *The Trauma Trap*. New York: Doubleday.

Muss, D.C. (1991b) 'A new technique for treating post-traumatic stress disorder', *British Journal of Clinical Psychology*, 30: 91–2.

Oberfield, R.A. (1984) 'Terminal illness: towards an understanding of its nature', *Perspectives in Biology and Medicine*. 28: 140–55.

Parker, G. (1977) 'Cyclone Tracy and Darwin evacuees: on the restoration of the species', *British Journal of Psychiatry*, 130: 548–55.

Patrick, V. and Patrick, W.K. (1981) 'Cyclone 78 in Sri Lanka: the mental health trail', *British Journal of Psychiatry*, 138: 210–16.

Pearlin, L.I., Menaghan, E.G., Lieberman, M.A. and Mullan, J.T. (1981) 'The stress process', *Journal of Health and Social Behavior*, 22: 337–56.

Prochaska, J.O. and Di Clemente, C.C. (1982) 'Transtheoretical therapy: toward a more integrative model of change', *Psychotherapy: Theory, Research and Practice*, 19: 276–88.

Ravin, J. and Boal, C.K. (1989) 'Post-traumatic stress disorder in the work setting: psychic injury, medical diagnosis, treatment and litigation', *American Journal of Forensic Psychiatry*, 10: 5–23.

Resick, P.A., Jordan, C.G., Girelli, S.A., Hutter, C.K. and Marhoefer-Dvorak, S. (1988) 'A comparative study of behavioural group therapy for sexual assault victims', *Behavior Therapy*, 19: 385–401.

Reynolds, C.R. and Richmond, B.O., (1978) 'What I think and feel: a revised measure of children's manifest anxiety', *Journal of Abnormal Child Psychology*, 6: 271–80.

Saunders, B.E., Arata, C.M. and Kilpatrick, D.G. (1990) 'Development of a crime-related post-traumatic stress disorder scale for women within the Symptom Checklist-90 – Revised', *Journal of Traumatic Stress*, 3: 439–48.

Schwartz, R.M. and Garamoni, G.L. (1986) 'A structural model of positive and negative states of mind: asymmetry in the internal dialogue' in P.C. Kendall (ed.), *Advances in Cognitive-Behavioral Research and Therapy, Volume 5*. New York: Academic Press.

Schwartz, R.M. and Garamoni, G.L. (1989) 'Cognitive balance and psychopathology: evaluation of an information processing model of positive and negative states of mind', *Clinical Psychology Review*, 9: 271–94.

Scott, M.J. (1989a) *A Cognitive Behavioural Approach to Clients' Problems*. London: Tavistock/Routledge.

Scott, M.J. (1989b) 'Relapse prevention training' in G. Bennett (ed.), *Treating Drug Abusers*. London: Tavistock/Routledge.

Scott, M.J. and Stradling, S.G. (1987) 'Evaluation of a group programme for parents of problem children', *Behavioural Psychotherapy*, 15: 224–39.

Scott, M.J. and Stradling, S.G. (1990) 'Group cognitive therapy for depression produces clinically significant reliable change in community-based settings', *Behavioural Psychotherapy*, 18: 1–i9.

Shapiro, F. (1989) 'Efficacy of the eye movement desensitization procedure in the treatment of traumatic memories', *Journal of Traumatic Stress*, 2: 199–223.

Shore, J.H., Tatum, E.L. and Vollmer, W.M. (1986) 'Psychiatric reactions to disaster: the Mount St Helens experience', *American Journal of Psychiatry*, 143: 590–5.

Simons, A.D., Garfield, S.L. and Murphy, G.E. (1984) 'The process of change in cognitive therapy and pharmacotherapy for depression: changes in mood and cognition', *Archives of General Psychiatry*, 41, 45–51.

Snaith, R.P. and Zigmond, A.S. (1983) 'The Hospital Anxiety and Depression Scale', *Acta Psychiatrica Scandinavia*, 67, 361–70.

Snaith, R.P., Constantopoulos, A.A., Jardine, M.Y. and McGuffin, P. (1978) 'A clinical scale for the self-assessment of irritability (IDA)', *British Journal of Psychiatry*, 132: 164–71.

Sorenson, S.B. and Golding, J.M. (1990) 'Depressive sequelae of recent criminal victimisation', *Journal of Traumatic Stress*, 3: 337–50.

Spanier, G.B. (1976) 'Measuring dyadic adjustment: new scales for assessing the quality of marriage and similar dyads', *Journal of Marriage and the Family*, 38, 15–28.

Spielberger, C.D. (1988) *State-Trait Anger Expression Inventory*. Odessa, FL: Psychological Assessment Resources.

Spitzer, R.L. and Williams, J.B.W. (1985) *Structured Clinical Interview for DSM-III-R: Patient Version*. New York: Biometrics Research Department, New York State Psychiatric Institute.

Titchener, J.L. and Kapp, F.T. (1976) 'Family and character change at Buffalo Creek', *American Journal of Psychiatry*, 133: 295–9.

Trautman, E.C. (1964) 'Fear and panic in Nazi concentration camps: a biosocial evaluation of the chronic anxiety syndrome', *International Journal of Social Psychiatry*, 10: 134–41.

Trimble, M. (1985) 'Post-traumatic stress disorder: history of a concept', in C. Figley (ed.), *Trauma and Its Wake*. New York: Brunner Mazel.

Van Bilsen, H.P. (1986) 'Heroin addiction and motivational milieu therapy', *International Journal of the Addictions*, 21: 707–13.

Williams, J.M.G. and Dritschel, B.H. (1988) 'Emotional disturbance and the specificity of autobiographical memory', *Cognition and Emotion*, 2: 221–34.

Worden, J.W. (1983) *Grief Counselling and Grief Therapy*. London: Tavistock.

Young, J.E. (1990) *Cognitive Therapy for Personality Disorders: A Schema-focused Approach*. Sarasota, FL: Professional Resource Exchange.

Yule, W. and Udwin, O. (1991) 'Screening child survivors for post-traumatic stress disorders: experiences from the "Jupiter" sinking', *British Journal of Clinical Psychology*, 30: 131–8.

Appendix A

Horowitz's Impact of Event Scale

Below is a list of comments made by people after stressful life events. Please check each item indicating how frequently these comments were true for you during the past seven days. If they did not occur during that time, please mark the 'not at all' column.

	Not at all (0)	Rarely experienced (1)	Sometimes experienced (2)	Often experienced (3)
1 I thought about it when I didn't mean to.				
2 I avoided letting myself get upset when I thought about it or was reminded of it.				
3 I tried to remove it from memory.				
4 I had trouble falling asleep or staying asleep.				
5 I had waves of strong feelings about it.				
6 I had dreams about it.				
7 I stayed away from reminders of it.				
8 I felt as if it hadn't happened or it wasn't real.				
9 I tried not to talk about it.				
10 Pictures about it popped into my mind.				
11 Other things kept making me think about it.				
12 I was aware that I still had a lot of feelings about it, but I didn't deal with them.				
13 I tried not to think about it.				
14 Any reminder brought back feelings about it.				
15 My feelings about it were kind of numb.				

Note: Intrusion subset = 1, 4, 5, 6, 10, 11, 14;
and avoidance subset = 2, 3, 7, 8, 9, 12, 13, 15.

Appendix B

Hammarberg's PENN Inventory

Name _____ Date _____

On this questionnaire are groups of statements. Please read each group of statements carefully. Then pick out the one statement in each group which best describes the way you have been feeling during the PAST WEEK, INCLUDING TODAY! Circle the number beside the statement you picked. *Be sure to read all the statements in each group before making your choice.*

1. 0 I don't feel much different from most other people my age.
   1 I feel somewhat different from most other people my age.
   2 I feel so different from most other people my age that I choose pretty carefully who I'll be with and when.
   3 I feel so totally alien to most other people my age that I stay away from all of them at all costs.

2. 0 I care as much about the consequences of what I'm doing as most other people.
   1 I care less about the consequences of what I'm doing than most other people.
   2 I care much less about the consequences of what I'm doing than most other people.
   3 Often I think, 'Let the consequences be damned!' because I don't care about them at all.

3. 0 When I want to do something for enjoyment I can find someone to join me if I want to.
   1 I'm able to do something for enjoyment even when I can't find someone to join me.
   2 I lose interest in doing things for enjoyment when there's no one to join me.
   3 I have no interest in doing anything for enjoyment when there's no one to join me.

4. 0 I rarely feel jumpy or uptight.

1 I sometimes feel jumpy and uptight.
2 I often feel jumpy or uptight.
3 I feel jumpy or uptight all the time.

5 0 I know someone nearby who really understands me.
   1 I'm not sure there's anyone nearby who really understands me.
   2 I'm worried because no one nearby really seems to
      understand me.
   3 I'm extremely disturbed that no one nearby understands
      me at all.

6 0 I'm not afraid to show my anger because it's no worse or
      better than anyone else's.
   1 I'm sometimes afraid to show my anger because it goes
      up quicker than other people's.
   2 I'm often afraid to show my anger because it might turn
      to violence.
   3 I'm so afraid of becoming violent that I never allow
      myself to show any anger at all.

7 0 I don't have any past traumas to feel overly anxious
      about.
   1 When something reminds me of my past traumas I feel
      anxious but can tolerate it.
   2 When something reminds me of my past traumas I feel
      very anxious but can use special ways to tolerate it.
   3 When something reminds me of my past traumas I feel so
      anxious I can hardly stand it and have no ways to
      tolerate it.

8 0 I have not re-experienced a flashback to a trauma event
      'as if I were there again'.
   1 I have re-experienced a flashback to a trauma event 'as if
      I were there again' for a few minutes or less.
   2 My re-experiencing of a flashback to a trauma event
      sometimes lasts the better part of an hour.
   3 My re-experiencing of a flashback to a trauma event
      often lasts for an hour or more.

9 0 I am less easily distracted than ever.
   1 I am as easily distracted as ever.
   2 I am more easily distracted than ever.
   3 I feel distracted all the time.

10 0 My spiritual life provides more meaning than it used to.
   1 My spiritual life provides about as much meaning as it
      used to.

2   My spiritual life provides less meaning than it used to.
3   I don't care about my spiritual life.

11   0   I can concentrate better than ever.
1   I can concentrate about as well as ever.
2   I can't concentrate as well as I used to.
3   I can't concentrate at all.

12   0   I've told a friend or family member about the important parts of my most traumatic experiences.
1   I've had to be careful in choosing the parts of my traumatic experiences to tell friends or family members.
2   Some parts of my traumatic experiences are so hard to understand that I've said almost nothing about them to anyone.
3   No one could possibly understand the traumatic experiences I've had to live with.

13   0   I generally don't have nightmares.
1   My nightmares are less troubling than they were.
2   My nightmares are just as troubling as they were.
3   My nightmares are more troubling than they were.

14   0   I don't feel confused about my life.
1   I feel less confused about my life than I used to.
2   I feel just as confused about my life as I used to.
3   I feel more confused about my life than I used to.

15   0   I know myself better than I used to.
1   I know myself about as well as I used to.
2   I don't know myself as well as I used to.
3   I feel like I don't know who I am at all.

16   0   I know more ways to control or reduce my anger than most people.
1   I know about as many ways to control or reduce my anger as most people.
2   I know fewer ways to control or reduce my anger than most people.
3   I know of no ways to control or reduce my anger.

17   0   I have not experienced a major trauma in my life.
1   I have experienced one or more traumas of limited intensity.
2   I have experienced very intense and upsetting traumas.

3   The traumas I have experienced were so intense that memories of them intrude on my mind without warning.

18   0   I've been able to shape things toward attaining many of my goals.
1   I've been able to shape things toward attaining some of my goals.
2   My goals aren't clear.
3   I don't know how to shape things toward my goals.

19   0   I am able to focus my mind and concentrate on the task at hand regardless of unwanted thoughts.
1   When unwanted thoughts intrude on my mind I'm able to recognize them briefly and then refocus my mind on the task at hand.
2   I'm having a hard time coping with unwanted thoughts and don't know how to refocus my mind on the task at hand.
3   I'll never be able to cope with unwanted thoughts.

20   0   I am achieving most of the things I want.
1   I am achieving many of the things I want.
2   I am achieving some of the things I want.
3   I am achieving few of the things I want.

21   0   I sleep as well as usual.
1   I don't sleep as well as usual.
2   I wake up more frequently or earlier than usual and have difficulty getting back to sleep.
3   I often have nightmares or wake up several hours earlier than usual and cannot get back to sleep.

22   0   I don't have trouble remembering things I should know.
1   I have less trouble than I used to remembering things I should know.
2   I have about the same trouble as I used to remembering things I should know.
3   I have more trouble than I used to remembering things I should know.

23   0   My goals are clearer than they were.
1   My goals are as clear as they were.
2   My goals are not as clear as they were.
3   I don't know what my goals are.

24   0   I'm usually able to let bad memories fade from my mind.

1 Sometimes a bad memory comes back to me, but I can modify it, replace it, or set it aside.
2 When bad memories intrude on my mind I can't seem to get them out.
3 I worry that I'm going crazy because bad memories keep intruding on my mind.

25 0 Usually I feel understood by others.
1 Sometimes I don't feel understood by others.
2 Most of the time I don't feel understood by others.
3 No one understands me at all.

26 0 I have not lost anything or anyone dear to me.
1 I have grieved for those I've lost and can now go on.
2 I haven't finished grieving for those I've lost.
3 The pain of my loss is so great that I can't grieve and · don't know how to get started.

Appendix C
Trauma Belief Inventory

For each belief statement tick the column that best indicates the answer that applies to you. The scale is as follows:

0 = Absolutely untrue
1 = Mostly untrue
2 = Partly true, partly untrue
3 = Mostly true
4 = Absolutely true

Please answer according to what you believe yourself, not what you think you should believe.

	0	1	2	3	4
I am worthless and bad					
No one can be trusted					
It doesn't matter what happens to me in my life					
It is dangerous to get close to anyone because they always hurt or exploit you					
I will never be able to lead a normal life, the damage is permanent					
Only bad, worthless people would be interested in me					
I am inferior to other people because of what I have been through					
I've lost a part of myself					

	0	1	2	3	4
I feel responsible for the bad things that happen to me					
There is something wrong with me					
Other people can never understand how I feel					
I see this world as a bad place to live in					
I feel like there isn't anything I can do to manage what happens to me					
I have missed out on an important part of my life					
Nothing in the world is any good					
I don't think that justice exists in this world					
I don't like myself					
I feel isolated from others					
I believe that I over-reacted to what happened to me					
I always end up taking care of others without getting anything in return					

Appendix D
Guidelines for Crisis Counselling

Crisis counselling is somewhat different to the systematic cognitive-behavioural counselling for PTSD which is the major concern of this book. A crisis counsellor often only has one session with a client and is typically functioning in an emergency capacity. The role is more one of orientating than of treating, mapping out for the client the sort of difficulties that might be encountered and the directions from which means to resolve the problems might be found. The goal of crisis counselling is to help the client to get their bearings. To orientate the client it is necessary that the counsellor rapidly establishes rapport. This may involve listening repeatedly to the same tale without expressing criticism of the client. The crisis counsellor will often have to help the client answer a number of pressing questions:

'What is or has been happening to me?'
'What is going to become of me?'
'What if I don't get better?'
'Am I safe?'

In addition the counsellor has to provide guidance as to how the client might help themselves and how this might be facilitated by significant others, for example friends or solicitors. The crisis counselling should be low key as the client has had enough drama to cope with. An information leaflet can be constructed which answers these four questions and gives the necessary advice. This is a useful way of implicitly reminding the client that they are not alone with their difficulties and that there is life after trauma. Having said that, it would be difficult to write a separate leaflet for each conceivable natural disaster or type of trauma and an 'all-purpose' leaflet will inevitably be couched in generalities. The crisis counsellor's task is to try to tailor the sort of information in the leaflet to the needs of the particular client. The adaptation to individual needs is described using the four questions as a framework.

'What is or has been happening to me?'

The crisis counsellor should not assume that the client labels the trauma in the way one might anticipate from the 'facts' of the matter. Thus for example the client who has been raped might choose to label her experience as being 'sexually assaulted' or 'molested'. Use of the milder term by the client may serve as temporary protection from the enormity of what has been experienced, allowing for a gradual assimilation. From a crisis counselling point of view there is no merit in insisting that the correct label is used from the outset. However other professionals such as the police and solicitors, of necessity, need factual details and have to apply the realistic label. In such circumstances the crisis counsellor can help as a useful intermediary or buffer between the client and the legal system.

Any PTSD symptoms the client reports can be described initially by the crisis counsellor as 'a normal response to an abnormal situation'. In some cases however the client's distress will be enhanced because the trauma has reawakened memories of earlier trauma. These clients are especially at risk, and steps should be taken if possible to more carefully monitor their progress and ensure that therapeutic counselling is available if symptoms persist.

'What is going to become of me?'

It is reasonable and probably helpful for the crisis counsellor to be realistically hopeful about the outcome for clients presenting in crisis in the immediate aftermath of a trauma. The majority of those experiencing the trauma will have recovered within three months. However, the counsellor has to be careful not to overstate the case, as a significant minority, as much as 40 per cent, do not. Which group the client will fall into will depend on pre-trauma history, support network and coping style (see chapter 2). Again, in instances where these are negative some provision for ongoing monitoring and possible treatment should be made.

'What if I don't get better?'

The crisis counsellor can make two responses to this question. The first is that it is early days and the client is crossing bridges before arriving at them. Second that if they do not recover in the next two to three months there is specialist help available. Where and how the specialist help is available should be specified.

'Am I safe?'

This is a particularly important question for clients whose experiences may repeat themselves, for example a battered wife might need a great deal of reassurance that she is secure in her hostel accommodation and that her husband would be unlikely to have knowledge of or access to the hostel.

The crisis counsellor should give general advice to the client about engaging in normal activities albeit in small doses for the time being; then pacing their return to normality, which needs approaching like a marathon rather than a sprint. It is useful in this connection to make the point that initially they may feel distant from important others in their lives perhaps because the others 'haven't been through the trauma', but if they keep in contact, even at reduced levels, some of the joys of the previous relationship will return.

In the immediate aftermath of a major trauma a client may believe themselves to be functioning perfectly well. Nevertheless, the counsellor should make the client aware of the sorts of problem that can occur later so that they have a potential framework for understanding their experiences. If possible the crisis counsellor should go beyond the client's self-report and elicit the views of those close to him or her as to changes in irritability, startle responses and hypervigilance. This information may contradict the client and the client can be asked what they make of the contradiction.

In crisis the client is too overwhelmed by events to begin systematic counselling and needs space to try out their own coping responses. But the orientating framework can serve to enhance those coping responses and provide an emergency procedure should the natural coping mechanisms fail (and simply knowing that a facility is available is often perceived as a source of support even if the client makes no call on the facility). It should be remembered that most PTSD clients actually present for systematic help many months after the 'crisis'. PTSD clients rarely begin systematic work at the time of crisis.

Index

abuse of children, 165
  see also childhood sexual abuse
acute PTSD, 47–64
addiction *see* substance abuse
addiction quitting, stages of, 158–9
aggression, 133
agoraphobia, 114
Akishal, H.S., 122
alcohol abuse, 9, 156–60
American Psychiatric Association, 1, 2
amnesia, psychogenic, 36, 50
anger, 133, 135
antidepressants, 81
Antisocial Personality Disorder, 9, 23, 134, 149
anxiety, 24, 33, 110–20, 132, 161
armed robbery, 81–4
assault, 53–9, 71–3, 74, 77–8
  sexual, 21, 59–60, 78–80
assertive behaviour, 145
assertiveness training, 160, 161, 162–3
assessment process, 13
audio tapes
  pain relief, 117
  use in desensitization process, 37–9, 75, 78–80, 85, 109
automatic thoughts, 20
avoidance behaviour, 5–6, 8, 41–2, 67, 106, 114, 164

balancing out, 40–1, 132
Bandura, A., 31

Beck, A.T., 23–4, 31, 110, 121, 147, 165
behavioural counselling, 31, 32
Belief Inventory, 25
beliefs
  restructuring of *see* cognitive restructuring
  trauma, 20, 25, 42–4
Best, C., 6
biofeedback, 77
Birleson Depression Inventory, 161
black–white thinking *see* dichotomous thinking
Blackburn, I.M., 33, 153
blame, self-, 54, 129–30
Boal, C.K., 86
booster sessions, 155
Borderline Personality Disorder, 134
brainstorming, 45, 46
breathing
  controlled, 62–3, 116
  '3Ss' strategy, 116
  see also hyperventilation
Brown, G.W., 26
Burton, S.W., 122

childhood neglect, 165
childhood sexual abuse, 106–8, 156–7, 164
childhood trauma and adult disorder, 164–8
children
  physical abuse of, 165
  and PTSD, 161, 163–4

Children's Manifest Anxiety Scale, 161
chronic PTSD, 65–85, 168–70
Clark, D.M., 116
Cobb, S., 2
cognitive-behavioural conceptualization of PTSD, 18–29
cognitive-contextual model of individual functioning, 19, 20–1
cognitive restructuring, 39, 42–4
cognitive triad of self, 110
communication guidelines, 142, 151
communication habits, 150
components of PTSD, 5–8
containment, 37
contemplation stage of addiction quitting, 159
controlled breathing, 62–3, 116
coping responses, 6–8, 24–5, 26, 28
Covi, L., 36
Craine, L.S., 164
crime
    victims of, 21
    see also armed robbery; assault
crime-related (CR)-PTSD Scale, 8
crisis counselling, 152, 185–7
criteria for PTSD, 1–5
cumulative nature of traumas, 21

Dansky, B., 25
Davidson, J., 9, 24
Davidson, K., 33
decision-making, 93, 158
depression, 6, 9, 25, 26, 44, 109, 120–32, 161
    dysfunctional attitudes characteristic of, 23–4
    features of, 110–13
Depression Inventory, 161
desensitization, 37–9, 41–2, 74–80, 109

see also eye movement desensitization
Di Clemente, C.C., 158–9
diabetic analogue model, 169
Diagnostic and Statistical Manual of Mental Disorders see DSM-III-R
diaries, 'How I Felt', 142, 143, 151
dichotomous thinking, 55
Dillon, H., 2
disaster (case studies), 13–17, 27–9, 50–2, 65–71
disordered arousal, 6
dissociation, 107–8
distraction techniques, 60
'downward arrow' technique, 44
Dritschel, B.H., 131
drug abuse *see* substance abuse
drug therapy *see* medication
DSM-III-R, 1, 2, 4, 23, 86, 133
    criteria for generalized anxiety disorder, 113
    criteria for major depressive disorder, 120–1
Duckworth, D.H., 5
duration of counselling provision, 153
Dyadic Adjustment Scale, 135
Dysfunctional Attitude Scale, 24
dysfunctional attitudes, 23–4
dysthymia, 121, 122

early maladaptive schemas (EMS), 164–5, 166–7, 168
environmental appraisal, cognitive biases in, 42, 43
Epictetus, 18–19
Epstein, S., 22, 23, 27, 73
evaluative questioning, 44
experimental tests, 32
exposure
    imaginal, 34, 75–7
    level of, 22–3, 27
eye movement desensitization, 169–70

failure of counselling, 168–70
family
    as quasi-counsellors, 159–60
    support from, 25–6
family history, 24
Famularo, R., 106, 164
Foa, E.B., 34, 38
Frank, J.B., 69
Freeman, A.G., 23, 147, 165
Friedman, M.J., 9
friends as quasi-counsellors,
    159–60

Garamoni, G.L., 132
generalized anxiety disorder, 113
Gleser, G.C., 24
Golding, J.M., 21
group counselling, 160–1

Hammarberg's PENN Inventory,
    8–9, 178–82
Hanson, L.R., 132
Harris, T.O., 26
Heather, N., 33
Helzer, J.E., 1, 23
Hillsborough disaster (case
    studies), 13–17, 27–9, 50–2,
    65–71
historical material, 60, 89–90
Histrionic Personality Disorder,
    134
home, prolonged duress in, 103–6
homework assignments, 32, 35–6,
    141
Hooley, J.M., 25
Hopelessness Scale, 121, 122
Horowitz's Impact of Event Scale,
    8, 161, 177
Hospital, Anxiety and Depression
    Scale (HAD), 112–13, 122
Howard, K.I., 153
hyperventilation, 116
hyperventilation challenge, 62, 116
hypnosis tapes, 80

imagery, intrusive, 5–6, 36–41

imaginal exposure, 34, 75–7
Impact of Event Scale (IES), 8,
    161, 177
indecent assault *see* sexual assault
inferential questioning, 43–4
inquiry domains, 10–12, 13
interpersonal relationships, 26
interview formats, 13
intrusive imagery, 5–6, 36–41,
    71–4, 90–2, 103–4
irritability, 133–51
    inward, 133, 135, 145–50
    outward, 133, 134–5, 136–45
Irritability, Depression, Anxiety
    Questionnaire (IDA), 134–5

Jackson, S.E., 88, 171
Janis, J.L., 158
Jehu, D., 25, 161

Kanouse, D.E., 132
Kapp, F.T., 2
Keane, T.M., 13, 33
Kilpatrick, D.G., 21
Klerman, G.L., 36
Kozak, M.J., 38
Kruppa, I., 75
Kubler-Ross stage model, 48

Lang, P.J., 144
Layden, M., 165, 168
Lazarus, A.A., 24
Leopold, R.L., 2
Lindemann, E., 2
Linehan, M.M., 121
Lipper, S., 81
Lochman, J.E., 155

McFarlane, A.C., 5, 6, 21, 24, 25
Mann, L., 158
marital therapy, 139–40
Maslach, C., 88, 171
medication, 69–70, 81
Meichenbaum, D., 31, 39, 61, 83,
    102
mental video, 37

Muss, D.C., 170

Narcissistic Personality Disorder,
134, 149
neglect, childhood, 165

Oberfield, R.A., 48
outward irritability, 133, 134–5,
136–45
overbreathing *see* hyperventilation

pain relief tape, 117
panic attacks, 118
panic disorder, 113
Paranoid Personality Disorder, 23,
133
Parker, G., 21
Passive Aggressive Personality
Disorder, 133–4
Patrick, V. and Patrick, W.K., 21
Pearlin, L.I., 22
PENN Inventory, 8–9, 178–82
personality disorders, pre-existing,
9, 23, 27, 133–4, 145–50, 165
pre-contemplation stage of
addiction quitting, 158, 159
pre-trauma functioning model, 169
predictors of trauma response, 6,
22–6
presentation of PTSD, 9
probabilities, notion of, 55
problem-solving procedures, 45–6
Prochaska, J.O., 158–9
prolonged duress stress disorder,
86–108
prolonged exposure, 34
psychodynamic counselling, 31, 32
psychogenic amnesia, 36, 50
psychological disorders, pre-
existing, 23
psychotherapy, supportive, 160

quasi-counsellors, 159–60
questions
evaluative, 44
inferential, 43–4

rape victims, 21
rating scales, 8–9
Ravin, J., 86
Reasons For Living Inventory,
121–2
re-experiencing of event, 8
relapse, 25
relapse prevention, 153–6, 159–60
relationships
interpersonal, 26
quality of, 135
relaxation, 144
relaxation tapes, 78–80
Resick, P.A., 160
resourcefulness, 81
responses to trauma, variability of,
21
Revised Children's Manifest
Anxiety Scale (R-CMAS), 161
rewind technique, 170
Reynolds, C.R., 161
Richmond, B.O., 161
role reversal, 44–5, 149–50

Saunders, B.E., 8
schemata, 20
see also early maladaptive
schemas
Schwartz, R.M., 132
Scott, M.J., 18, 135, 159, 160
Scott Trauma Belief Inventory, 20,
25, 183–4
self-blame, 54, 129–30
self-efficacy, 128
Self-Instruction Training, 39, 61,
83, 102
service delivery, 152–71
sexual abuse *see* childhood sexual
abuse
sexual assault, 21, 59–60, 78–80
Shapiro, F., 169
Shore, J.H., 22
Simons, A.D., 81
Snaith, R.P., 112, 134
Sorenson, S.B., 21
Spanier, G.B., 135

Spielberger, C.D., 135
Spitzer, R.L., 13
stage model (Kubler-Ross), 48
State–Trait Anger Expression
  Inventory, 135
Stradling, S.G., 135, 160
stress, amount of, 22–3
stress inoculation training, 34, 160
structured clinical interview
  (SCID), 13
subjective units of discomfort
  (SUDS), 41–2, 169–70
substance abuse, 9, 155–60
suicidal behaviour, 129–32
suicidal risk, assessing for, 121–2
support, 25–6, 28
supportive counselling, 34
supportive psychotherapy, 160
symptoms of PTSD, 2–5

task orientation, 44–6
three-component model, 144, 145
time projection strategy, 130–1,
  132, 167–8
Titchener, J.L., 2
Trauma Belief Inventory, 20, 25,
  183–4

trauma beliefs, 20, 25, 42–4
Trauma Constellation
  Identification Scale, 25
trauma tapes, 37–9, 75, 78, 85,
  109
Trautman, E.C., 2
Trimble, M., 1

Udwin, O., 161, 164
uplifts, generation of, 131–2

Van Bilsen, H.P., 159
vulnerability factors *see*
  predictors

waiting list control, 34
Williams, J.B.W., 13
Williams, J.M.G., 131
Worden, J.W., 48
workplace duress, 87–103
writing about trauma, 39

Young, J.E., 164, 165, 166–7
Yule, W., 161, 163–4

Zigmond, A.S., 112